COMMITTED WORSHIP

A Sacramental Theology for Converting Christians

Volume I:
Adult Conversion and Initiation

Donald L. Gelpi, S.J.

A Michael Glazier Book
THE LITURGICAL PRESS
Collegeville, Minnesota

A Michael Glazier Book published by The Liturgical Press

Cover design by David Manahan, O.S.B.
Cover: Chrismon, SS. Gervase and Protase, Civaux, France

1   2   3   4   5   6   7   8   9

Library of Congress Cataloging-in-Publication Data

Gelpi, Donald L., 1934–
    Committed worship : a sacramental theology for converting
Christians / Donald L. Gelpi.
        p.   cm.
    "A Michael Glazier book."
    Includes bibliographical references.
    Contents: v. 1. Adult conversion and initiation — v. 2. The
sacraments of ongoing conversion.
    ISBN 0-8146-5825-3 (v. 1). — ISBN 0-8146-5826-1 (v. 2)
    1. Sacraments—Catholic Church. 2. Conversion. 3. Catholic
Church. Ordo initiationis Christianae adultorum. 4. Initiation
rites—Religious aspects—Catholic Church. 5. Catechumens.
6. Catholic Church—Membership.   I. Title.
BX2203.G45   1993
264'.0208—dc20
                                                        92-40430
                                                        CIP

Contents

The Sacraments Again

In 1976 I published *Charism and Sacrament: A Theology of Christian Conversion*. Having written one book on the sacraments, I feel a certain constraint to explain to the reader why I have chosen to write a second one.

Charismatic and Sacramental Experience

Charism and Sacrament attempted to address a pressing pastoral need in the American Church of the seventies. I wrote the book in the heyday of the Catholic charismatic renewal. Personal and pastoral involvement in that movement convinced me that we needed a sacramental theology that articulated the intimate relationship between charismatic and sacramental prayer.

Charismatic prayer need not occur in a sacramental context, but when it does it has the power to transform sacramental prayer in dramatic ways. I saw that happen in a student prayer group at Loyola University in New Orleans in the early seventies. Fr. Harold Cohen, S. J., the director of student ministry, headed the pastoral team that led the group. I participated in the prayer and did some teaching during our Friday night meetings.

Fr. Cohen saw to it that the group did not fall into the trap of choosing between charismatic and sacramental prayer. Our prayer meetings always ended with the Eucharist; and in the period after Communion the community reverted to a period of spontaneous, charismatic prayer. The other sacraments also shaped the piety of our prayer group. As a consequence, its members experienced a dramatic transformation of their sacramental worship.

Suddenly all the rites of the Church came alive in new ways. We experienced the Eucharist as Eucharist, as a profound act of joyful praise and thanksgiving to God. The rites of initiation made new sense as well. People saw clearly that in baptism the Breath of God[1] comes to us to conform us to Jesus, to teach us to put on his mind. They also saw the truth enunciated in the Council of Florence that confirmation functions as the pentecost of each Christian (DS 1319). Having experienced the charismatic action of the Holy Breath in vivid and dramatic ways, they recognized spontaneously that lifelong, charismatic openness to God's Breath makes sense of the rite of confirmation. They saw that one could live in faith, hope, and love without possessing expectant faith in the divine Breath's charismatic inspirations, for they themselves had done so for years. People spontaneously associated the first grace with baptism and the second with confirmation. We did not need to explain the new theology of the rite of anointing, that it seeks to heal and not to prepare one for death. The healings which we experienced in charismatic prayer prepared us to expect healing in the sacramental rite of anointing. The healing of memories made sense of the revised rite of reconciliation. People also recognized quite spontaneously that the charismatic call to marriage and to ordained ministry helps endow both vocations with their sacramentality.

While the people in our prayer group saw a clear connection between charismatic and sacramental worship, I knew perfectly well that many other people involved in charismatic prayer did not. As a consequence, they could begin to believe that one had finally to choose between the two. I wrote *Charism and Sacrament* in the hope of protecting people from making that false and destructive religious option.

RCIA: The New Sacramental Challenge

The charismatic renewal continues as a significant movement in contemporary spirituality; but most of the theological questions raised by this movement have, in my opinion, received the attention they deserve. A different pastoral development in the life of the

---

1. Throughout this book I refer to the third person of the Trinity as the Holy Breath rather than the Holy Spirit. I do so because I have come to believe that one can describe the dynamic structure of human experience without invoking the categories of "matter" and of "spirit." Since the account of experience I have developed seeks to avoid any kind of dualism, including matter-spirit dualism, I avoid using the term spirit altogether. Moreover, the term "breath" expresses more accurately than the term "spirit" the intent of the Hebrew word *ruah*.

Church of the eighties clamors for the attention of sacramental theologians: namely, the restoration of the catechumenate. This book seeks, then, to articulate a theology that speaks to the pastoral needs of those involved in the Rite of Christian Initiation of Adults, commonly referred to as the RCIA.

The issues addressed in this study, however, engage the Church as a whole, not just catechumens and the people who instruct them. It should take little reflection to see that a sound sacramental catechesis for adult catechumens addresses the pastoral and theological needs of every adult Christian. Moreover, as I shall attempt to show in the following pages, the restored catechumenate poses a serious challenge to the Church as a whole. Its restoration raises questions about the degree of conversion in most of our parishes. As a result, the kinds of pastoral and theological issues faced by those who lead the RCIA also confront the rest of the clergy and laity.

Finally, as I shall attempt to show, the sacraments of the Church either seal an initial adult conversion or deepen the process of ongoing conversion. Since ongoing conversion spans a lifetime, even the baptized need an account of the sacraments that explores the connection between the official rites of the Church and the processes of initial and ongoing conversion. In other words, while this study targets the RCIA, it addresses every adult Christian who wants to understand the purpose and moral demands of formal sacramental prayer.

I am grateful to Fr. Timothy Kidney and to Fr. Russell Roide, S.J., who kindly took me in at the St. Ann Stanford Newman Center during the sabbatical year in which I wrote the first draft of this study. During that year, I lent some assistance to Nancy Greenfield, the member of the Catholic chaplaincy team at Stanford who directed their RCIA program. I realized as the year advanced, that the restored catechumenate, which emerged originally from the experience of the African Church and was conceived as a way of preparing non-Christians for baptism, needed considerable adaptation to the needs of converts in the United States.

Inculturating the RCIA

Catechumens in this country ordinarily convert to Catholicism from some form of Protestantism. That fact in part motivated the selection of the issues with which this book deals. At the time of the Reformation Catholics and Protestants split primarily over three sets of issues: the relationship between nature and grace, the number and purpose of the sacraments, and the nature of Church order. As a consequence, any contemporary convert to Catholicism from Protestantism has the right and need to know where Catholic teaching stands on these important questions.

The development of both Catholic and Protestant theology since the Reformation has combined with ecumenical dialogue in order to resolve most of the significant disagreements about nature and grace. One finds, of course, within Catholicism a number of different explanations of how the two relate, contrasting explanations that all fall within the spectrum of Catholic orthodoxy. The first section of this book adopts an approach to the question that speaks directly to the experience and needs of converts. It probes the relationship between nature and grace in the course of reflecting on the forms and dynamics of Christian conversion. In the process it attempts to give new, experiential meaning to a number of traditional theological concepts, like justification, sanctification, gratuitous grace, the theological virtues, the seven gifts of the Holy Breath, and the Pauline charisms.

Ecumenical debate has produced some consensus in the area of sacramental theology, but considerable disagreement about the sacraments continues to divide the Churches. A Protestant converting to Catholicism needs therefore to understand the role and function of the sacraments within Catholic worship. I found in the pastoral work I did at Stanford University that adult Christians appreciate knowing the basic biblical foundations for sacramental worship, the way sacramental worship evolved, and the unresolved theological questions that still surround these rituals. In addition to dealing with such issues from the past, the sacramental chapters in this study draw on the theology of conversion developed in its first part in order to argue that all seven rituals of the Catholic Church function as "converting ordinances."

Protestants converting to Catholicism also need to understand how Catholics view the Church. Needless to say, Catholic ecclesiology has evolved considerably since the Reformation. Vatican II provides the latest and most authoritative Catholic statement on the subject. Anyone who has studied the council's decrees reflectively knows that one can use the sacraments as a context for summarizing most of their teachings about the Church. The sacramental chapters which follow attempt to do precisely that.

In other words, by approaching the sacraments through a theology of conversion that deals with basic questions about the relationship between nature and grace and by incorporating into that same sacramental theology the ecclesial insights of Vatican II, I have attempted to address (what seem to me at least) the major theological questions which most North American converts to Catholicism need to face. In the process I have tried to lay more systematic theological foundations for the RCIA in this country than the literature on the restored catechumenate currently contains.

I recognize, of course, that those who conduct the RCIA might well desire to include in their instruction to catechumens a discussion of other theological issues than the relationship between nature and grace, the Church, and the number and purpose of the sacraments. Accordingly, in chapter IV I suggest ways of relating the idea of conversion and sacramentality to the Trinity. Those who wish to pursue these ideas in greater detail will find them in *The Divine Mother: A Trinitarian Theology of the Holy Spirit* and in *God Breathes: The Spirit in the World*. Both books suggest ways of relating a foundational theology of the Trinity to Christology. I am at present engaged in research for a book on the foundations of Christology. Until it is published those interested in expanding the theological foundations of the catechumenate to include Trinitarian and Christological considerations will find some help in the above-mentioned volumes.

The Foundational Approach

Besides a concern with the changing pastoral needs of the North American Church other motives have led me to write this second excursion into sacramental theology. When I joined the faculty of the Jesuit School of Theology in Berkeley in 1973 I set myself the task of trying to write a systematic, inculturated, foundational theology. I use the term "foundational theology" as Bernard Lonergan has defined it. By foundational theology Lonergan means a systematic theology of conversion that probes the religious experiences that authenticate doctrinal statements. My study of *Method in Theology* convinced me that Lonergan's understanding of theological method, his theory of functional specialties, and his redefinition of foundational theology (formerly called fundamental theology) provided practical tools for developing an inculturated North American theology in the tradition of Orestes Brownson, John A. Ryan, and John Courtney Murray. An inculturated foundational theology would draw on the particular culture in which the Church roots itself for its dominant categories and images at the same time that it would use the gospel to challenge anything sinful in that culture. That we need such a theology in the Catholic Church I have no doubt. Catholics in the United States tend to import their speculative theology from Europe, or more recently from Latin America, rather than to address in a systematic way the challenges posed by the North American cultural tradition.

Philosophical Foundations

In *Charism and Sacrament* I began to lay the philosophical foundations for an inculturated theology of conversion. In doing so I tried to draw broadly on the North American philosophical tradition. The more I studied that tradition, the more clearly I saw that linguistic analysis, which I regarded as largely a British import, had changed philosophy in this country from critical reflection on life-transforming issues into a polite and largely boring academic conversation about words. I also recognized that, as a consequence of Whitehead's influence on North American Protestant theology, the American classical philosophical tradition still survived but as philosophical theology rather than as pure philosophy. Process theology, now in its third generation, has in fact carried forward the discussion of the kinds of experiential issues raised by Jonathan Edwards, by the Transcendentalists, by the Pragmatists, and by American Idealism.

As a consequence, in the first chapter of *Charism and Sacrament* I proposed a construct of experience that attempted to correct some of the more obvious inadequacies in Whitehead's and Hartshorne's dipolar construct of experience. Whitehead, I saw, had made the mistake of adopting without sufficient critical reflection William James's notion of drops of experience. In the process he had also acquiesced in James's attempt to construct experience out of percepts and concepts. Hartshorne had built creatively on the philosophical foundations laid by Whitehead and had inspired the third generation of process theologians in this country; but he had failed to critique Whitehead on this important point.

My own study of C. S. Peirce and of Josiah Royce had, however, convinced me that Royce's criticism of James's theory of knowledge in *The Sources of Religious Insight* applied to Whitehead and to Hartshorne as well. Royce wrote *The Sources* after reaching his Peircian insight. Peirce had taught him that if one reduces experience to the dipolar interrelation of percepts and concepts, then all human knowing transpires between one's ears, with the result that one's philosophy cannot explain one of the most basic acts of cognition: namely, the act of interpretation in which one person explains a second reality to another person. With help from Peirce, Royce saw, quite correctly, that the experience of interpretation requires a triadic rather than a dipolar construct of experience. In *Charism and Sacrament,* therefore, I tried to draw systematically on the American tradition as a whole but especially on the work of Peirce and of Royce, to elaborate such a triadic construct of experience.

I saw that the transformation of a Whiteheadian dipolar construct into a Peircian triadic construct required the redefinition of a number of key Whiteheadian terms. I proposed those redefinitions in the first chapter of *Charism and Sacrament.* At the time I found it fun to play around with Whitehead's language. I developed that language further in *Experiencing God.* I soon found, however, that the majority of my readers did not find Whiteheadian terminology as amusing as I did. Most of them found it jargon. While I would still defend substantially the philosophical positions I developed in both these books, I saw clearly that, if I hoped to communicate with a wider audience, I would have to translate my construct of experience into ordinary language. I did that in *The Divine Mother: A Trinitarian Theology of the Holy Spirit,* in *Grace as Transmuted Experience and Social Process,* and in *Inculturating North American Theology: An Experiment in Foundational Method.* Having made the transition to a more accessible philosophical diction, it made sense to me to attempt a second book on the sacraments, one that hopefully would reach more people than my first one had.

The Forms and Dynanics of Conversion

My understanding of the forms and dynamics of conversion has developed considerably since I wrote *Charism and Sacrament.* I then recognized only four forms of conversion and only two dynamics within the conversion process. Since then I have been led to acknowledge a fifth kind of conversion and five other dynamics which I overlooked in my first excursion into foundational thinking. In the present study, I speak of affective, intellectual, moral, religious, and sociopolitical conversion. In examining the seven dynamics of conversion I attempt to probe how each kind of conversion conditions every other. The advances in my own understanding of conversion have, I believe, allowed me to articulate with greater adequacy than I did in *Charism and Sacrament* the complex and intimate relationship between initial and ongoing conversion, on the one hand, and sacramental worship, on the other.

I regarded my treatment of the sacraments in *Charism and Sacrament* as inadequate for other reasons. I write books so that I can teach them to my students. When I joined the faculty of the Jesuit School of Theology in Berkeley in 1973, the academic calendar followed the quarter system. The constraint of having to present not only a theology of conversion but also a sacramental theology in nine weeks led me to give short shrift in *Charism and Sacrament* to the rites of reconciliation and of anointing. The present volume attempts to make up for that deficiency.

Fallibilism and Alternation

Methodological considerations have also prompted me to undertake this study. In philosophy I espouse both a contrite Peircian fallibilism and William Ernest Hocking's principle of alternation. As an epistemological doctrine fallibilism asserts that one has a much better chance of arriving at the truth through shared systematic inquiry if one admits rather than denies the fallibility of one's own position.

At the same time I recognize the need within systematic foundational thinking for an organizing theory of the whole. I have tried to contextualize my construct of conversion philosophically by developing a metaphysics of experience in the tradition of Whitehead, but a metaphysics of experience that conceives of experience as triadic rather than dipolar in structure. Whitehead discovers two kinds of feelings in experience: concrete physical feelings and abstract conceptual feelings. My own construct of experience, by contrast, contains three generic kinds of feelings: values, actions, and general tendencies.

With Whitehead I recognize the radical fallibility of any metaphysical theory of the whole, including my own. Such theories need to find validation in personal experience, in scientific and scholarly investigations of created realities, and in divine revelation. Moreover, I endorse Hocking's suggestion that in any fallibilistic approach to metaphysics, thought needs to oscillate between the narrow, in-depth investigation of particular questions, on the one hand, and reflection on one's theory of the whole, on the other. In-depth investigation of particular problems can cause one to modify one's theory of the whole. A modified theory of the whole can raise new questions about particular realms of experience that need more in-depth investigation.

This study applies the principle of alternation to my own understanding of the sacraments. I began the construction of a systematic theology of conversion with a study of sacramental theology. As I moved from it to a much more detailed reflection on the person of the convert and on the God encountered within Christian conversion, both my metaphysics of experience and my construct of conversion developed in significant ways that alerted me to inadequacies and oversights in my initial study of the sacraments. The present study attempts, then, to transcend those inadequacies in the light of my own subsequent theological development.

Yet another motive has impelled me to write this study: namely, the fact that I have felt repeatedly called to do so in prayer.

A Comprehenisive Construct

In *The Catholic Sacraments,* Professor Joseph Martos kindly devoted several pages to the approach to the sacraments proposed in *Charism and Sacrament.* He characterized my sacramental theology as "charismatic." I would accept the characterization as valid in the sense that my approach to the sacraments probably insists more on the relationship between sacramental worship and the charismatic action of God's Holy Breath than most sacramental theories. Moreover, as I have indicated, *Charism and Sacrament* addressed itself explicitly to theological and pastoral issues raised by the Catholic charismatic renewal. For that reason alone, one might argue for characterizing such a sacramental theology as charismatic.

Were I, however, to give a label to the sacramental theology contained in these pages, I would use another term than "charismatic." I would prefer to call the approach to worship taken in these pages "foundational and experiential."

As foundational, the sacramental theology presented here aspires to a certain comprehensiveness. In *The Catholic Sacraments,* Professor Martos argues that in an age of theological pluralism like our own one can expect to find a variety of models for interpreting Christian worship. I would agree with the necessity and even the advantage of pluralism in contemporary theology. A variety of legitimate approaches calls attention to different facets of the Christian mystery, and it dramatizes the inability of any theological system to box God in. Nevertheless, nothing prevents theologians from attempting to incorporate into their theories some of the salient aspects of other theological models and constructs.

In point of fact the foundational, experiential approach to the sacraments which I suggest derives something from most of the other major constructs of sacramental worship. From Platonism it derives the insight that through the sacraments we participate in God in a new way. I understand participation, however, very differently from a Christian Platonist, who acquiesces in the unacceptable dualisms of Platonic thought. Dualistic thinking conceives of interrelated realities in such a way that their relationship to one another defies all subsequent conceptualization. Thus, Platonism sunders soul from body, spirit from matter, time from eternity, subjectivity from objectivity. Instead, I interpret graced participation relationally and experientially as the mutual in-existence of two experiences, the divine and the human. [By that I mean that through faith God exists in us and we in God in a new way that transcends natural existence in God because through faith we experience God and God experiences us in a new and transforming manner.] The theology of conversion which follows attempts to anatomize the ways in which faith causes us to participate experientially in God in new and creative ways.

From a scholastic sacramental theology, the following account of Christian worship derives the insight that one can understand the meaning of sacramental worship only by analyzing the significant structure of the rites of the Church themselves. Instead, however, of analyzing the act of worship in categories derived somewhat artificially from Aristotelian cosmology, a foundational, experiential approach to the sacraments interprets contemporary ritual in the light of its historical evolution. It does so on the presupposition that history, rather than some fictive substantial form, finally defines the essence of every created reality including human rituals. Moreover, with the scholastics, a foundational theology of the sacraments acknowledges that, when celebrated with the proper attitudes and commitment, the rites of the Church function as instrumental causes of divine grace and that each rite has a distinctive purpose. Instead, however, of endowing each ritual with a fictive essence made up of matter and form, a foundational, experiential analysis ponders the significance of the ritual as a whole, even though it recognizes the preparatory, subordinate, and supportive character of some parts of the ritual and the definitive, indispensable character of other parts.

With Dom Odo Casel a foundational theology of the sacraments discovers in every authentic act of sacramental worship an encounter with the paschal mystery.

From an existential construct of the sacraments, the following foundational approach appropriates the insight that in the sacraments we encounter in a personally transforming way the God revealed in Jesus and in his sanctifying Breath. A foundational sacramental theology also endorses the idea of primordial sacramentality developed by modern existential theologians. Foundational theology, however, makes both ideas practical by interpreting the idea of encounter in the light of the forms and dynamics of conversion and by identifying the kinds of experiences and commitments that endow Christian living with revelatory sacramentality.

From a liberation theology of the sacraments, a foundational, experiential sacramentalism derives the insight that authentic sacramental worship demands practical commitment to constructing a just social order.

Foundational sacramental theology endorses and builds on the sacramental theology of Vatican II by attempting to advance the council's unfinished sacramental revolution.

Finally, the foundational sacramentalism developed in these pages builds on a modified form of process theology by invoking a metaphysics of experience that replaces Whitehead's inadequate dipolar construct of experience with a triadic construct.

In other words, this study lends indirect support to Lonergan's claim that a theology of conversion provides a comprehensive, authenticating ground for the enterprise of theological reconstruction. In the case of sacramental theology it offers a comprehensive approach to Christian worship that promises to incorporate and validate the best insights of the major models for thinking sacrament: Christian Platonism, Christian Aristotelianism, Christian existentialism, charismatic theology, liberation theology, process theology, and the conciliar tradition.

The Structure of the Argument

This study divides into two volumes. In the first section of the first volume I shall attempt to explore the modalities and dynamics of adult, Christian conversion. In the second, I shall attempt to understand how the three rites of Christian initiation—baptism, confirmation, and first Eucharistic Communion—function as efficacious symbols of the experience of adult conversion.

The second volume contains the third and fourth sections of this study, both of which probe the personal and social dynamics of ongoing conversion. The third section examines the two vocational sacraments—marriage and orders. In it I shall attempt to show that these sacraments both express and deepen the initial conversion to

Christ which the rites of adult initiation symbolize. The fourth section then ponders the other sacraments of ongoing conversion: reconciliation, anointing of the sick, and Eucharist.

Acknowledgements

I owe a debt of gratitude to the friends and colleagues who have helped me with writing this project. I owe the greatest debt to the John Courtney Murray Group, good friends and brothers who have read and criticized in one way or another most of the chapters in this book. I also owe thanks to my friends and colleagues at the Jesuit School of Theology at Berkeley whose friendly criticisms of several of the following chapters both privately and at our faculty colloquia helped me restate and clarify my thought. Finally, I want to thank James Kraft, my research assistant, who helped provide me with bibliographical documentation. With friends and helpers such as these, I must myself take responsibility for any imperfection in what follows.

PART I

Conversion

CHAPTER I

The Ins and Outs of Conversion

Two Converts

For years Jim had been drifting away from religion. The church services he attended bored him. Pious people turned him off. In moments of real honesty he admitted to himself the absurdity of life. "Why pretend?" he asked himself. "I'm at sea, and so is everyone else. They can't admit it to themselves, but I can." If asked, he professed himself a religious agnostic. At first he felt a new sense of freedom in casting off the last tattered rags of an empty childhood faith. He turned to philosophy to find some reason to live; but, as he pondered the futility of the human condition, the prating of the philosophers first filled him with a profound sense of despondency, then with grief-stricken despair. Sensing his misery, a concerned friend invited Jim to attend a Cursillo. As Jim listened to the personal faith witness of the other people there, his heart expanded to the vision of a community of people united by its love for Jesus. He felt the concreteness, the reality of that love. Beside it the abstractions of philosophers paled to insipidity. Despair lifted like a dark curtain rising. One thing only seemed to matter now: knowing Christ. He learned to spend long hours in prayer, but something did not quite fit. He battled depression for several months until, fighting an inner reluctance, he consented to pray with a friend for deliverance from the power of the Evil One and for complete openness to the Breath of Christ. Suddenly the depression he had been battling evaporated. He felt vividly the power of God freeing and filling his heart. He sensed the folly of trying to control his relationship with the Lord. He gave himself over to the action of the Holy Breath of Christ.

Anna experienced conversion differently. Unlike Jim she never abandoned the Church or religious practices. She went to Sunday Eucharist all her life and even read the prayers regularly. Her praying had helped her through the ups and downs of marriage and child-rearing. It had sustained her when her husband died. Still, in quiet moments, she felt a kind of restlessness, a vague malaise she could not name. She felt cheated somehow, like someone who buys a puzzle only to discover some of the pieces missing. She did not blame God. "I'm at fault," she told herself, at a loss to name what ailed her or how life had cheated her. Then, one day while praying with some friends, suddenly something rent the veil that blinded her. She felt the shallowness of her life, the combination of insecurity, judgmentalism, and pride that had imprisoned her in religious formalism. Wracking, uncontrollable sobs shook her. A purifying sense of the Breath of Christ welled up within her. Her heart felt scoured, free, and clean.

Both Anna and Jim experienced conversion in the latter half of the twentieth century; but ever since the crucified and risen Jesus first confronted his astonished disciples centuries ago, countless other Annas and Jims have felt their hearts wrenched, healed, and transformed in a life-giving encounter with the God Christians worship. This book attempts to understand the way such encounters change people's lives and motivate the Church's shared sacramental prayer.

The New Context: The RCIA

Several recent events in the development of Catholic piety support the timeliness of such a study. The Second Vatican Council reestablished the catechumenate. The restored catechumenate attempts to prepare adult converts for the rite of Christian initiation. So did the instructions adult converts received prior to Vatican II, but the restored catechumenate mandated by the council attempts to do so more thoroughly and systematically. It creates a community of shared faith that nurtures in neophytes the kind of commitment that the rites of initiation ought to seal. The restored catechumenate marks a return to an earlier Church discipline. Today's catechumens spend three years of shared prayer, study, and testing before their official admission into the Catholic communion. The restored catechumenate seeks, in other words, to lead adults seeking Church membership through a three-year communal experience of conversion.

The New Context: The New Theology of Conversion

The need to establish such a program of initiation has forced the Church's pastoral leaders to take a fresh look at the experience of conversion itself. Until relatively recently Catholic theology on the whole paid little heed to the forms and dynamics of conversion. The reestablishment of the catechumenate has, however, coincided providentially with the rediscovery of conversion as an important topic for theological investigation. Some contemporary theologians even speak of conversion as an experience that grounds and authenticates the whole of Christian faith and practice. This study takes a similar approach. It attempts to show that sound sacramental worship must express an integral conversion before God.

The New Context: Parish Revitalization

Besides focusing theoretical and pastoral attention on the experience of conversion, the restored catechumenate has also raised some searching questions about existing church communities. The restored catechumenate attempts to insert adult converts into thriving, Eucharistic communities of faith. On the whole, the new catechumens tend to encounter in the course of the years of catechetical preparation a deeply meaningful experience of what membership in such a community ought to resemble. Some neophytes, however, discover in the parishes they eventually join only pale copies of the more vibrant experience of community they knew as catechumens. Others find their future parishes utterly diffident to the catechumenate itself. Such facts raise serious questions about the degree of conversion present in our parish communities and about the way we have institutionalized much of our parish life. We ought in principle to expect seasoned Christians to exhibit more, not fewer signs of conversion than neophytes. We ought to expect closer bonding in longstanding communities than in communities of recent converts. We ought to find in our Eucharistic communities concrete signs of openness to the sanctifying, gift-giving Breath of Christ that distinguish them from those who lack faith, not fragmented communities of bourgeois individualists. Until we raise existing Eucharistic communities to at least the level of conversion we expect of recent converts and until we structure parish living in such a way that it adequately nurtures the faith of neophytes, we cannot claim to have responded adequately to the challenge that the new catechumenate poses. We shall reflect on this challenge in greater detail in another chapter. Here we merely note its existence.

The sacramental theology developed in these pages addresses, therefore, not only those seeking adult baptism but also those already baptized. It concerns itself not only with preparing people to participate in the shared worship of the Church but also with the quality of life in Christian sacramental communities. It studies not only initial but ongoing conversion as the indispensible precondition for authentic Christian worship. It deals not only with the conditions for entering the Christian community but also with the lifelong challenge of living as its fully converted member.

The New Context: Implementing Vatican II

Another development in contemporary Catholicism suggests the timeliness of this study. The Second Vatican Council closed over twenty years ago. While other councils of the Church have addressed the question of liturgical reform, only Vatican II attempted to revolutionize the way Christians pray. The council sanctioned virtually all the changes in Church ritual demanded by the liturgical movement. The structural changes in official prayer that the council mandated have to most intents and purposes happened. Catholics now worship in the vernacular. They listen to homilies on a revised lectionary. They celebrate the feasts of the Church according to a revised liturgical calendar. They worship together in streamlined sacramental rites that seek to communicate their significance without the need for extensive explanation. Nevertheless, one continues to hear complaints about the quality of sacramental worship: its tedium, its irrelevance to people's lives.

The fact that not all Catholics have greeted Vatican II's liturgical reforms with enthusiasm does not call into question the theological appropriateness of the council's liturgical revolution, although it does raise questions about the way that liturgists and pastoral leaders effected that revolution. The malaise that continues to haunt official Church worship points rather to a fundamental truth that the council insisted upon over twenty years ago: liturgical renewal requires much more than ritual reform. It demands as well the integral conversion of the entire Christian community. *Sacrosanctum Concilium,* the Constitution on the Sacred Liturgy, makes the point clearly:

> The sacred liturgy does not exhaust the entire activity of the Church. Before people can come to the liturgy they must be called to faith and conversion. . . . Therefore the Church announces the good tidings of salvation to those who do not believe, so that all people may know the true God and Jesus Christ whom He has sent, and may repent and mend their ways (cf. John 17:3; Luke 24:27; Acts 2:38). To believers the Church must ever indeed preach faith and repentance, but must also prepare them for the sacra-

ments, teach them to observe all that Christ has commanded (cf. Matt 28:20), and win them to all the works of charity, piety, and the apostolate. For all these activities make it clear that Christ's faithful, though not of this world, are the light of the world and give glory to the Father in the sight of men (*Sacrosanctum Concilium*, 9).

This profound insight enunciates one of the fundamental presuppositions grounding this study of sacramental worship. The malaise haunting the revised liturgy of the Church dramatizes a serious pastoral problem that we must address if the liturgical reforms mandated by Vatican II hope to advance beyond mere formalism. Christian worship comes alive when it expresses integral conversion before God. It languishes in the absence of conversion. Both clerics and laity who complain of the tedium of sacramental worship need, then, to rend their hearts, not their monthly missalettes. Accordingly, the present investigation of sacramental worship insists that the rites of the Church must express an ever deepening commitment that only an integral, ongoing conversion before God can effect.

The need to ground sacramental worship in a sound insight into the forms and dynamics of conversion has theological as well as pastoral implications. It means that liturgical history alone never suffices as a norm for how contemporary Christians ought to worship, for a normative insight into the Church's public prayer rests finally upon a validated and adequate understanding of the conversion experience that sacramental prayer fosters and celebrates. In other words, this study proceeds on the methodological presupposition that only a sound foundational theology of conversion finally rescues liturgical scholarship and practice from the dogmatism of taste in which both too often currently languish.

The New Context: Faith and Justice

A third development in contemporary Catholic piety testifies to the timeliness of the present study. *The Challenge of Peace,* the North American bishops' pastoral on the arms race, and *Economic Justice for All,* their pastoral on the United States economy, represent a major effort on the part of the National Conference of Catholic Bishops to implement a different document of Vatican II, namely, *Gaudium et spes,* the Pastoral Constitution on the Church in the Modern World. These two letters have inaugurated a new style in episcopal teaching, one that emphasizes widespread consultation and public debate of pastoral letters before they reach final promulgation. In the process, the North American bishops are rediscovering a truth that the patristic Church knew well: concern with the popular acceptance of official Church teaching in the course of its promulgation enhances the authority of the official pastoral magisterium. One can only hope that the rest of the episcopal college would profit from the experience of the American episcopacy in this matter.

The new pastorals also exemplify for the theological community an effective technique for pursuing liberation theology in a North American context. True to the method of liberation theology, both pastorals begin with an extensive analysis of a concrete situation of serious institutional sin, then criticize that situation in the light of biblical teaching and of the Church's magisterium. They conclude with specific, practical policies for effecting institutional reform. The letters prescribe no concrete policies for actualizing those policies and leave that to the initiative of the people of God.

Moreover, the recent pastorals also dramatize another important insight popularized by liberation theology: integral conversion before God has a sociopolitical dimension. It demands not only the turn to the subject but a turn to the Others, to the poor, the marginal, the victims of institutional sin and injustice. In an age and culture corrupted by individualism and narcissism, our bishops have challenged us North Americans individually and ecclesially to advance beyond privatized piety to the kind of religious commitment that forces us to grapple with pressing questions of faith and justice.

The analysis of the foundations of Christian sacramental worship in the following pages attempts to advance in the spirit of the recent episcopal pastorals. It recognizes distinct moments within the experience of integral conversion before God. It distinguishes clearly between personal and sociopolitical conversion. It insists that authentic Christian worship must embody both types of conversion. This study attempts, then, to raise and to answer the following question: *How ought a community of thoroughly converted Christians to worship sacramentally?* Its response divides into four sections.

The Division of the Chapter

The present chapter begins to explore the forms and dynamics of conversion. It divides into four parts. The first examines some traditional interpretations of the conversion process. The second reflects on a disturbing fact: not every experience of initial conversion ends well. As we shall see, an examination of the forces that subvert conversion forces us to expand the more traditional account of conversion. Accordingly, part three attempts to describe five forms of conversion, while part four analyzes the ways in which they mutually condition one another. The chapter ends with a few concluding remarks.

1. Traditional Approaches to Conversion. A traditional Catholic theology of conversion insists on its universal necessity. God calls everyone to conversion. Without it no human can hope to achieve salvation.

Conversion as Turning

Converts turn from something and to something. A traditional analysis of conversion distinguishes three kinds of turning. Moral conversion turns the will from a life of sin to the pursuit of moral goodness. Religious conversion turns one *from* ignorance of or indifference to the God revealed in Jesus and through the action of his Breath. It turns one *to* a life of faith. Confessional conversion incorporates the convert into the one, true Church.

Conversion effects a personal transformation of the convert. Catholic theology traditionally interprets that transformation as ontological, as real, and not merely as extrinsically imputed. Conversion results from the action of divine grace, which not only heals and sanctifies converts but perfects their natural powers of operation by creating within them the capacity to act supernaturally. Through conversion and the action of divine grace one passes from a state of sin to one of justification. Conversion effects a supernatural enlightenment.

Conversion and the Sacraments

Traditionally, Catholic theology links conversion to two sacraments: baptism and reconciliation. Both sacraments give access to Eucharistic Communion. Baptism completes the process of initial conversion. The rite of reconciliation functions as a "second baptism" in the case of baptized Christians who have separated themselves from the Church through serious sin.

Traditional Catholic theology regards the process of conversion as incomplete until it reaches sacramental embodiment in the rite of either baptism or reconciliation. That insistence expresses a conviction about the way divine grace operates: individuals come to grace through the mediation of the Church. It also expresses a belief in the incarnational and ecclesial character of both sin and grace: since, when we turn from God, we use our bodies to sin and harm both ourselves and others, the complete renunciation of sin and return to God should also find embodiment in a physical act that expresses the social, ecclesial dimensions of divine grace. In addition, the public confession of sin symbolizes the convert's passage from the dark secrecy of sin to the open light of grace.

The Effects of Conversion

Conversion, then, effects multiple changes in the lives of converts. It mediates the forgiveness of their sins. It begins the process of their sanctifying assimilation to Christ. It gives them a share in his victory over sin and death. It gathers together and augments the people of God. It grounds the convert's hope for ultimate salvation when Christ will return to judge the living and the dead.

Catholic and Protestant Approaches to Conversion

Initially, a Catholic approach to conversion contrasted with a classical Protestant approach at significant points. The first Protestant theologians sniffed suspiciously at medieval Scholasticism and attempted to link Christian doctrine to identifiable religious experiences. As a consequence, they tended to emphasize the psychological transformation that conversion effects. Catholic theology never denied the psychological impact of conversion but tended to insist on the ontological transformation that grace and conversion effect. Catholic theologians have traditionally insisted that the action of divine grace within conversion equips the convert with completely new supernatural powers of operation: faith, hope, love, gifts of sanctification, gifts of service. In its classical formulation, a Protestant theology of grace tended by contrast to speak of extrinsically imputed grace and justification rather than of the efficacious infusion of new supernatural powers. Finally, while traditional Catholic theology insisted on the Church's mediatorial role in the conferring of grace, classical Protestant theology tended to emphasize more the subjective gracing of individuals.

One can even today find echoes of these differences in the writings of Catholic and Protestant theologians, even though, as we shall see, history and ecumenical dialogue have blurred the differences between a Catholic and a Protestant theology of grace. The position developed in these pages reflects the emerging ecumenical consensus. It questions the need to contrast the ontological and the experiential. In this regard it seeks a middle ground between the classical Catholic and Protestant positions, although in other respects it favors a classical Catholic approach to the dynamics of grace as truer finally to the actual experience of conversion.

In the course of the following chapters, we shall have repeated occasion to reflect on the foundations of a traditional theology of conversion. For the moment, however, we need to note some of the ways in which a traditional Catholic theology contrasts with more recent theological reflections on the conversion process.

New Approaches to Conversion

First, a traditional theology of conversion tends to speak of conversion primarily as a religious event with moral and ecclesial consequences. Contemporary theology by contrast portrays religious conversion as only one form of conversion. As we shall soon see, one may legitimately distinguish five kinds of conversion in all: affective, intellectual, moral, religious, and sociopolitical.

Except for religious conversion every other form of conversion can occur naturally. A conversion happens naturally when it transpires in complete abstraction from the action of God's historical revelation. For example, neurotic or psychotic pain and conflict may convince one of the need to deal responsibly with one's personal emotional development without God, Jesus, or the divine Breath ever entering into the picture. Similarly, the experience of deceit and of institutional oppression may convince one of the human need to deal responsibly with persons and to seek a just social order without even a hint of faith in the triune God ever entering one's head or heart. Moreover, having distinguished the different forms of conversion, the construct of conversion that I shall propose also attempts to understand their dynamic interplay.

Initial and Ongoing Conversion

Second, a traditional theology of conversion focuses primarily on initial conversion or on subsequent experiences that resemble it, like repentance after serious sin. The theology of conversion I shall try to develop distinguishes initial from ongoing conversion in the case of all five forms of conversion.

Third, a traditional theology of conversion links it to two sacraments: baptism and reconciliation. I shall attempt to show that either initial or ongoing conversion grounds and authenticates all the official rites of the Church.

Let us explore these contrasts in greater detail, for they shall demonstrate that a traditional theology of conversion fails to ground adequately a sound pastoral approach to the restored catechumenate. We begin by examining some of the dangers latent in too narrow a focus on the religious dimensions of conversion.

2. Religious Conversions That Turn Sour. Some religious converts mature into saints. Like aging wines, sanctification takes time, often an entire lifetime. Converts who turn into saints center their lives on God. They open their hopes and their hearts to the healing power of divine grace. Faith purifies their minds and informs their every belief. Love teaches them to serve others faithfully in the image of Jesus and to follow the charismatic inspirations of his Holy Breath. We need only read the lives of the great saints to understand the meaning of total consecration to God. Think of Paul the Apostle, Mary of Magdala, Augustine of Hippo, Perpetua and Felicity, Francis and Claire, Ignatius of Loyola, Teresa of Avila, John of the Cross, and all the men and women whose lives teach us the meaning of the gospel. They glorify God because they reflect in arresting ways the divine beauty manifest in the face of Jesus.

Conversion and Fundamentalism

Not every conversion, however, matures into saintliness. I do not speak only of pretended conversions in which individuals undergo baptism, not because they believe sincerely in Christ but because they seek through baptism to achieve some other advantage. The first missionaries to China had, for example, to distinguish "rice Christians" from genuine converts. Contemporary missionaries face analogous problems in judging the sincerity of converts. When I speak of religious conversion turning sour, I refer to individuals who at one point gave every evidence of having experienced an authentic initial conversion to Christ but whose subsequent lives lack the signs of true holiness.

I think, for instance, of a woman convert I knew in New Orleans. In her early twenties she passed from agnosticism to a living faith in Jesus. In personal and shared prayer she experienced the power of his Breath. Her initial conversion gave every sign of authenticity.

She devoted long hours to meditation and to reading the Bible. She reached out to others with a sincere and practical religious love. Almost four years after the initial conversion, however, she professed atheism. What had gone wrong?

I can only guess, but I think I know. Her faith had claimed every facet of her life except her mind. After her conversion she chose to interpret her religious experiences fundamentalistically. She defended fiercely the literal inerrancy of the Bible and resisted, for what emotional reasons I can only guess, a more theologically nuanced interpretation of her relationship with God. She did not, however, lack for intelligence. When therefore she finally understood the folly of fundamentalism, she fallaciously concluded that religious faith demands mindless assent to indefensible propositions and that in order to believe she needed to renounce her mind. Rather than do that, she chose not to believe at all.

Conversion and Neurosis

I think of other converts who began well but whose deep-seated conflicts blighted their maturation into genuine holiness. I remember a religious brother active in the Catholic charismatic renewal who seethed with repressed animosity but resisted seeking therapy on the grounds that any attempt to rely on human healers would only manifest a lack of trust in God. Eventually the rage storming deep within him drove him from the religious life and from the Church. I also think of devout people who have taken neurotically motivated impulses that surfaced during prayer for the manifest voice of God informing them how *others* should live their lives. I recall all of the ways in which religious folk can abuse religious language in order to avoid facing their unconscious anger, guilt, and fear. I think of a religious superior I knew who eventually had to leave office because he claimed an exclusive hot line to God that justified habitual pious acts of oppression.

Conversion and Moral Selfishness

Like neurosis, selfishness can also don the vestments of piety. I think of television evangelists who use the religious media to amass personal fortunes. I think of affluent and of upper-middle-class Christians who frequent worship with devout fidelity but who would never dream of divesting themselves in any significant way of their possessions in order to alleviate the suffering of the poor. I think of the

Catholics I knew as a small child in New Orleans who received Holy Communion daily even as they fought tooth and nail to preserve an unjust system of racial segregation. I think of worshipping Christians who pray devoutly on Sunday but who from Monday to Saturday think primarily of number one.

Conversion and Privatized Religion

When I think of a religious conversion gone sour, I also think of Christians whose privatized piety blinds them to the impact of institutionalized injustice on their own consciences and on the lives of others. In this country we live in a materialistic, commercialized culture that protects aggressively the vested interests of big business but abandons the poor to sink or swim in the treacherous waters of a free market economy. The mass media din into our very souls a gospel of *machismo,* chauvinism, national security, and individualism irreconcilable with the gospel of Christ. Naive belief in our own innocence as a people blinds us to the ways our national leaders use this nation's power for exploitative ends. Converts who close their eyes to the fact of institutional injustice not only in human society but even within the Church itself may at an interpersonal level learn how to deal in a Christlike manner with others; but by refusing to deal in any systematic way with institutional injustice they end by turning a deaf ear to the miserable cries of the poor, the marginal, the exploited. In the process they collaborate in the violation of personal rights that as religiously committed people they stand committed to defend.

At least four major forces can, then, conspire to suffuse an authentic initial religious conversion to God with a corrosive hypocrisy that can in the end not only undermine but even destroy the commitment of faith itself. Mindless religious fundamentalism can discredit an initial conversion and make religious truths seem incredible. The religious rationalization of deep-seated neurosis and psychosis can confuse faith with varying degrees of madness. Moral hypocrisy can transform religious practice into pious self-seeking. Privatized piety can blind converts to their connivance in the violation of human rights that they otherwise stand committed to defend.

Authentic Conversion

Religious converts need not, of course, succumb to the onslaught of these four forces. They can cultivate an intelligent, reflective faith instead of a fundamentalistic one. They can face deep-seated emotional problems honestly and can with the help of others seek and find healing in faith. They can own the claims that gospel living makes not only on their personal conduct but on the management of human institutions as well.

Moreover, one need not have undergone religious conversion in order to cultivate intellectual, emotional, moral, or sociopolitical responsibility. Anyone who has moved in contemporary academic circles has encountered intellectually responsible people who in religious matters remain agnostic. The pain engendered by neurosis or psychosis can force people to deal responsibly with their emotions in complete abstraction from faith in God. Humanists devoid of any overt religious commitment can live lives of enormous moral and sociopolitical responsibility in active dedication to the search for a just and humane society.

These facts dramatize the complexity of conversion. They suggest that an integral experience of conversion before God contains in addition to religious faith affective, intellectual, moral, and sociopolitical variables that can either advance or undermine religious growth. They also suggest that one can take personal responsibility for one's affective, intellectual, moral, or sociopolitical development in complete abstraction from religious faith.

3. Five Forms of Conversion and How They Happen. Traditionally both Catholic and Protestant theology distinguish between conversion and sanctification.[1] The term "conversion" in such an

---

1. Classical Protestant Pentecostalism also distinguishes conversion and sanctification from baptism in the Holy Breath. In effect it offers a linear construct of conversion in which the convert advances from conversion to baptism in the Holy Breath and finally to sanctification. In addition, this approach to the understanding of conversion interprets the gift of tongues as the normative sign of Breath baptism. I have tried to argue elsewhere that while historically understandable to anyone who studies the history of the Pentecostal Churches, this particular construct of conversion suffers from interpretative inadequacy. Like the more traditional constructs of conversion, it contrasts conversion and sanctification; but even initial conversion sanctifies. Moreover, any theological construct of conversion that equates baptism in the Holy Breath with the reception of a particular gift tends to instill an unfortunate and divisive elitism. In point of fact, a careful reading of the Synoptic Gospels, from which the term "Breath baptism" derives, demands a much broader interpretation of its meaning. Breath baptism effects the total transformation of the believing disciple in the image of Jesus. It begins with one's first contact with the Holy Breath through faith and

approach designates the initial act of turning from sin to justifying faith in God. "Sanctification" designates the graced transformation in faith that follows upon conversion. Such an understanding of the term "conversion" restricts it to those experiences that a more contemporary theology would call "initial religious conversion." Moreover, a more contemporary theology of conversion describes sanctification as "ongoing religious conversion."

A New Theological Idiom

In these pages I adopt a more contemporary theological idiom in speaking of conversion, even though by "initial religious conversion" I intend the same experiences as a traditional theology does by "conversion." Similarly, by "ongoing religious conversion" I intend the same experiences as a more traditional theology of conversion does by "sanctification."

In discussing conversion I prefer the more contemporary idiom for two reasons. First, the newer terminology suggests correctly that the processes of sanctification deepen the commitment effected by initial religious conversion. The newer terminology, therefore, highlights in helpful ways the fiducial, moral, and vital continuities that link initial religious conversion to its practical consequences. Second, the new terminology also suggests the dynamic link between religious conversion and the other forms of conversion.

In order to do speculative justice to the complexities of conversion, we need to distinguish at least five kinds of conversion. The five forms of conversion resemble one another analogously.

How then ought one to understand the term "conversion"? Of what does "initial" and "ongoing conversion" consist? How does each form of conversion occur? How do the other forms of conversion resemble one another? How do they differ? Let us respond to each of these questions in turn.

a. What Does Conversion Mean? A traditional theology of conversion, as we have seen, correctly recognizes that in an initial Chris-

culminates in bodily resurrection. See Donald L. Gelpi, S. J., "Conversion: The Challenge of Contemporary Charismatic Piety," in *The Reasoning Heart: Toward A North American Theology,* edited by Francis Oppenheim, S. J. (Washington, D.C.: Georgetown University Press, 1986) 25–47; *Pentecostalism: A Theological Viewpoint* (New York: Paulist, 1971), and *Charism and Sacrament: A Theology of Christian Conversion* (New York: Paulist, 1976), *Experiencing God: A Theology of Human Emergence* (New York: Paulist, 1978).

tian conversion converts turn from unbelief to belief, from sin to the attempt, with the help of divine grace, to live a sinless life, from exclusion from sacramental communion with the community of Jesus Christ to full sacramental communion with its members. In effect, then, a traditional theology of conversion recognizes that the commitment of faith entails both moral and ecclesial consequences.

The construct of conversion that I shall develop sanctions all these insights but questions their adequacy. I shall try to show that besides moral and ecclesial consequences, initial religious conversion entails affective, intellectual, and sociopolitical consequences as well.

Some Initial Definitions

Most readers will, I suspect, find terms like "affective," "intellectual," "moral," and "sociopolitical conversion" baffling and unfamiliar. Even the term "conversion" itself needs clarification. Allow me then to offer a few preliminary definitions and to begin to explore some of their implications.

Conversion: the decision to pass from irresponsible to responsible behavior in some distinguishable realm of human experience.

Affective conversion: the decision to turn from an irresponsible resistance to facing one's disordered affectivity to the responsible cultivation of a healthy, balanced, aesthetically sensitive emotional life.

Intellectual conversion: the decision to turn from an irresponsible and supine acquiescence in accepted beliefs to a commitment to validating one's personal beliefs within adequate frames of reference and in ongoing dialogue with other truth seekers.

Moral conversion: the decision to turn from irresponsible selfishness to a commitment to measure the motives and consequences of personal choices against ethical norms and ideals that both lure the conscience to selfless choices and judge its relapses into irresponsible selfishness.

Sociopolitical conversion: the decision to turn from unreflective acceptance of the institutional violations of human rights to a commitment to collaborate with others in the reform of unjust social, economic, and political structures. Sociopolitical converts seek to empower the oppressed to demand and to obtain their rights from their oppressors.

Religious conversion: the decision to turn from either ignorance of or opposition to God to acceptance in faith of some historical, revelatory self-communication of God and its consequences. Christian conversion exemplifies a particular normative form of religious conversion. In Christian conversion, converts turn from ignorance of and opposition to God to adult faith in the God definitively and normatively revealed in Jesus Christ, the incarnate Son of God the Father, and in the Holy Breath whom they send into the world. Christian converts also accept the consequences of that decision.

Personal Conversion

Let us begin to explore some of the implications of these definitions. In every form of conversion the convert turns from irresponsible to responsible behavior in some identifiable realm of human experience. Realms of experience differ from one another by the kinds of habits that govern them. When we respond emotionally and irrationally, intuitive habits govern our behavior. When we respond rationally and logically, inferential habits govern our behavior. When we respond morally to other persons, prudential habits govern our behavior. When we respond religiously, habits of faith govern our behavior. In the forms of conversion that correspond to each of these realms of experience, the convert decides to act responsibly in making personal decisions. I therefore designate these four forms of conversion—namely, affective, intellectual, moral, and religious—by the term "personal conversion" because in each of them one takes new responsibility for oneself.

Sociopolitical Conversion

In "sociopolitical conversion," however, converts take responsibility for influencing decisions governed by habits other than their own. Sociopolitical converts take responsibility not for the motives and consequences of individual, personal decisions but for collaborating with others in order to ensure that the motives and consequences of the habitual decisions of those who lead large institutional structures both express and foster integral conversion before God. Sociopolitical converts at the same time seek to empower the oppressed to demand and receive their rights from their oppressors. In other words, while personal conversion involves a turn to the self, sociopolitical conversion involves a turn to the Others, whether oppressed or oppressors.

Conversion and Responsibility

Through conversion converts pass from irresponsible to responsible behavior. "Responsibility" means accountability. Responsible persons acknowledge a duty to render an account of the motives and consequences of their decisions to someone or to some community of persons.

In the first instance, responsibility requires converts to answer to themselves. Conversion commits one to espouse ideals and principles of conduct that both attract one by their beauty and stand in judgment over any act that contradicts them. Each kind of conversion commits one to a specific set of ideals. The affectively converted aspire to emotional health and aesthetic sensitivity. The intellectually converted aspire to a true understanding of reality through obedience to sound logical and methodological procedures. The morally converted aspire to interpersonal behavior that transcends selfish or crudely pragmatic considerations and acknowledges ideals or principles that make absolute and ultimate claims. Something claims us with moral ultimacy when we must not only stand willing to live for it but also, if necessary, to die for it. Something claims us with moral absoluteness when it both lures and judges the conscience in every circumstance. Those who have experienced sociopolitical conversion aspire to a just social order. The religiously converted aspire to union with God through the obedience of faith. Christian converts aspire to union with the Father through transformation in the image of his Son and in the power and anointing of their Holy Breath.

In initial conversion converts acknowledge that in all their subsequent actions they must measure the motives and consequences of their conduct against the ideals and principles of conduct required by each form of conversion. In ongoing conversion converts accept responsibility for the practical consequences of initial conversion.

Responsibility and Accountability

In the first instance, converts stand accountable to themselves. In the second instance, converts must answer to others for the motives and consequences of their actions. We live in communion with other persons. Through affective, intellectual, moral, and sociopolitical conversion I live accountable to other human persons and to the human community, for irresponsible conduct in each of these realms of experience brings incovenience and suffering into the lives of others. Through religious conversion I live accountable also to God and to the Church. Through Christian conversion I live accountable as well to the three persons who comprise the Trinity and to the community of believers who confess faith in them.

Both the motives and consequences of our acts make a difference to others. The consequences make a clear and palpable difference. A careless smoker may, for example, with one smoldering cigarette ignite a fire that destroys several homes. A wealthy philanthropist may endow a hospital or a university chair. Indeed, every act makes a difference to those it affects directly. Its motives, however, also make a difference. Parents, for example, accept with pleasure the gifts of their small child with no care for the crudity of the giver's artistry because they value the love that motivates the gift more than the gift itself. Similarly, acts of hatred and spite wound us even though they fail to effect the evil they intend.

Responsible people live in dialogue with those affected by their own choices. Personal conversion creates social accountability in interpersonal dealings with others. Those who experience sociopolitical conversion take responsibility for doing whatever they can to ensure that the decisions of those who shape the policies and practices of large institutions express and foster integral conversion. Sociopolitical conversion, therefore, makes one accountable to society at large. Different social contexts require different kinds of institutional accountability. One must account legally for actions that violate the laws of the land. One must account economically for commercial transactions. One must account politically for acts of governance.

Responding vs. Reacting

Responsible people also respond to other persons as persons. When we merely react to other persons rather than respond to them, we take into account neither their needs nor the way in which they will interpret what we say or do. When we respond to others we do take into account their needs and probable response to our actions. In other words, we respond to others when we treat them in the way that we ourselves would in their circumstances want to have others treat us. As a consequence, responsible people seek to perform the "fitting" act. Actions fit a situation when they take into account the relationships that constitute it as well as the history that has produced it. Actions also fit a situation when they advance it creatively to the highest degree of perfection to which it can reasonably attain.

Responsible behavior implies, therefore, social solidarity with others, accountability to them for the motives and consequences of one's behavior, and the willingness to shape one's conduct in ongoing dialogue with others. Responsible behavior recognizes, therefore, the social, dialogic character of the human conscience. It also extends beyond interpersonal encounters to include sociopolitical transactions. It therefore includes accountability not only for persons but for things—for the surrounding environment and the living and nonliving realities in it—both for preserving and enhancing their intrinsic value and for ensuring that their use will have no negative impact upon the lives of other persons. Responsible conduct demands sensitivity to situations and to the history that produced them.[2]

Strictly Normative Thinking

Every form of conversion engages strictly normative thinking. Strictly normative thinking contrasts with explanation. Explanatory thinking (in contrast to merely descriptive) predicts the way in which realities around us ought to behave. In that sense it offers a normative account of the world confronting the thinker. Strictly normative thinking, by contrast, concerns itself with the thinker's own motives and conduct. It measures one's own choices against values and principles personally acknowledged as binding one's conduct.

The different forms of conversion measure conduct by different norms and ideals. Affective converts seek to cultivate a healthy emotional life. Intellectual converts submit to sound principles of logic and to sound methodological, artistic, or literary procedures. Moral converts apply prudential norms to interpersonal interaction and collaboration. Sociopolitical conversion extends moral concern to questions of policy and of institutional reform. Religious conversion judges conduct in the light of the demands of divine revelation.

In each form of conversion, therefore, responsibility takes on different connotations because a different kind of "ought" governs its occurrence and development. Affective conversion measures the authenticity of conduct by norms of health. Intellectual conversion judges personal authenticity by norms of consistency, coherence, truth, and adequacy. Moral conversion decides the authenticity of interpersonal transactions by prudential moral norms. Sociopolitical conversion, in addition to invoking prudential moral norms judges complex situations in the light of sound economic, political, and

2. Those familiar with the work of H. Richard Niebuhr will recognize that the preceding account of responsibility owes much to his pioneering reflections on this complex subject. Cf. H. Richard Niebuhr, *The Responsible Self* (Harper & Row: New York, 1963).

social analysis. Religious conversion measures human authenticity by norms of faith. In religious conversion God always holds the initiative. Here God's free and gracious self-disclosure grounds the religious "ought," and "responsibility" means responding to God on the terms God sets rather than on the terms that we ourselves would prefer.

b. How Does Each Form of Conversion Occur? The two accounts of religious conversion that opened this chapter described highly charged emotional experiences. Any sound theology of conversion must, however, respect the diversity of individuals and the incredible variety of human experience. Conversions can occur in electrifying emotional contexts, but they can also happen in more pedestrian ways. Converts may not even recognize at the time that they have indeed undergone a conversion experience. The order in which the different kinds of conversion occur varies from person to person. We should not assume that every adult has experienced all five forms of conversion.

An Autobiographical Approach

As I look back over my own life, it seems to me that at different points in my own development I did convert in all five ways. I will attempt to describe these experiences briefly in order to illustrate how conversions happen. I narrate my own history of conversion not because I regard myself as a particularly good example of the process of conversion. Quite the contrary, as the reader will soon discover, I often resisted or postponed initial conversion; neither have I accepted the consequences of an initial conversion with the consistency I should have displayed. Far from proposing myself as an exemplar of conversion, I narrate these moments of blindness and of illumination in my life because as a teacher I have found no more effective way to illustrate concretely the different kinds of conversion in a manner that respects the analogy of human experience. No two people come to conversion in exactly the same way. I describe the way my own conversion unfolded, therefore, in the hope that you, dear reader, having heard my story may search your own history for analogous experiences.

Although I have chosen to illustrate the different kinds of conversion from personal experience, the construct of conversion sketched in this chapter does not rest on personal experience alone.

It rests also on a scientifically verifiable, philosophical understanding of human experience; on recent studies in empirical, clinical, and social psychology; on economic and political theory; and on an investigation of Christian theology and spirituality. For a documentation of the speculative grounds for the construct of conversion I refer the reader to the other things I have written on this subject.

I Convert Morally

As I just observed, we have no reason to believe that people experience the five forms of conversion in any fixed order. In my own case moral conversion came first. I was born and raised in that most Catholic of southern cities, New Orleans. A friend of mine once described New Orleans as the northernmost Latin American city in the Western Hemisphere. Both sides of my family professed Catholicism. Nevertheless, we went to Mass every Sunday in racially segregated churches. I attended racially segregated Catholic grammar and high schools. I rode on racially segregated buses and street cars. I ate in racially segregated restaurants and cafeterias. My family numbered no violent racists. Nevertheless, racism permeated my world and poisoned my conscience. I inhaled it with every breath. It seeped through my pores and into my bones.

My parents sent me to Jesuit High School in New Orleans. There my Jesuit teachers launched a series of assaults on my racial self-righteousness. Bristling with indignation at their attack on "our southern way of life," I resisted my teachers' effrontery at first, but with time the cogency of what they said began to penetrate my defenses. By my junior year in high school I had renounced my racism and in my heart at least joined the ranks of integrationists.

Had you asked me at the time I would probably have laughed at the idea that I had undergone a moral conversion, although the term aptly describes what I had experienced. Goaded by my teachers I had faced the irresponsible ethical presuppositions of the society that had nurtured me and found them wanting. In renouncing my racism I had taken a new kind of responsibility for forming my own conscience. Although I did not know it at the time, I still needed to face other immoral attitudes and beliefs that society had bred into my bones. Only years later would I repent of my sexism, my militarism, and my middle-class snobbery. Each new repentance, however, would only deepen the moral conversion I underwent as a teenager.

I Convert Religiously

My decision to join the Jesuits set my feet on a path that eventually led me to an adult religious conversion. My own life plan included a wife, a family, and a medical career in the tradition of the Gelpi family. I had, with the help of an uncle who had connections in city hall, secured a scholarship to Tulane medical school. Having arranged my future to my own satisfaction, I discovered to my dismay that God had other plans. There welled up in my heart a clear call to enter the Society of Jesus. I resisted the call at first; but eventually, after several months of futile wrestling with God, I gave in. I entered the Jesuit novitiate at Grand Coteau, Louisiana, two months after my seventeenth birthday. Although at the time I viewed the consequences of my decision with some apprehension, I deem it in retrospect the best I ever made.

Although a religious vocation changed profoundly my relationship with God, I lacked the maturity at the time to take adult responsibility for my end of that relationship. As a young Jesuit I conformed obediently to the expectations of the order I had joined. Finding those expectations on the whole reasonable enough in practice (if not always in theory), I found no cause to question them. For nine years, then, I lived in oblivion of a fundamental inconsistency that marred my commitment to vowed living. The legalistic spirituality I had learned in my novitiate came from Europe, but over the generations religious in this country had with Yankee pragmatism Americanized the practice of the vows. Only when, through an administrative blunder, I was sent to Louvain, Belgium, to study theology, did I find myself in a situation in which I was actually expected to live out the spirituality I had absorbed theoretically as a novice but had never found myself constrained to practice. I found its practice impossible and even undesirable. Suddenly I realized to my dismay that I had lost whatever rationale I had for living the religious life. At the same time, I knew that God still called me to the Society of Jesus. I decided after considerable soul-searching that I would have to begin to pray my way to a personal understanding of the meaning of vowed living. I now look back on that wrenching decision as my coming of age as a Jesuit and as a Christian, as an adult conversion to Christ. As I searched the New Testament for a new understanding of the evangelical councils, the person and vision of Jesus spoke to my heart in new ways. I stirred to the beauty and sublimity of both. I began to understand something about the kingdom of God.

I Convert Intellectually

I find my intellectual conversion harder to date. I believe, however, that it probably occurred during my philosophical studies at St. Louis University. In those days all Jesuit scholastics had to complete three full years of philosophical study. At first I approached my philosophical courses in the same way I had approached all the others. In my examinations I parroted back to my teachers the material they had given to me in class. Then came the day when I realized that I did not believe some of the things one of my professors taught. The more I pondered his position on the reality of relationships, the sillier it sounded. I finally decided to formulate my own position on the subject. With that decision, I believe, I began to come of age intellectually. I began to take responsibility for my own thoughts. I started organizing them on paper. I published one article, then another.

As in the case of every initial conversion, my decision to take responsibility for my beliefs led inexorably to unforseen consequences. It eventually caused me to abandon the philosophical system I had been taught. With time it also forced me to rethink my most fundamental religious beliefs. My study of North American philosophy transformed me into a contrite Peircian fallibilist. Gradually I came to look upon intellectual self-criticism as a way of life. I even began to enjoy studying logic. My first exposure to logical thinking had, by contrast, only inspired in me the profoundest boredom.

I Convert Sociopolitically

By the time I reached the third stage of my Jesuit training I had advanced to an initial sociopolitical conversion. In the third phase of their preparation for ministry young Jesuits get involved in some form of apostolic work. My superiors assigned me to teach in the high school I had attended. As I moved toward my debut in the classroom, I realized that I would have to advance beyond the personal renunciation of racism to active, public opposition to racial injustice. At the time I welcomed the prospect of joining in the political fray.

A whole series of experiences had brought me to that point. During my second year novitiate, the provincial of the New Orleans province, Fr. William Crandall, S. J., at the prompting of the Superior General of the Jesuits, had called a province assembly in order to formulate a common policy on racism. The delegates met at our novitiate in Grand Coteau, Louisiana. After three days of debate the assembly issued a unanimous denunciation of racial segregation as seriously unjust and promulgated specific province policies for dealing with it. Although the assembly had little immediate practical consequence, it spoke eloquently to us fledgling religious. It told us that as a community we Jesuits had to own our responsibility to oppose institutional injustice. In our province we could also look to the example of courageous Jesuit social activists like Fr. Louis Twomey, S. J., and Fr. Stephen Foley, S. J.

In St. Louis I made my first adult black friends among the scholastics with whom I studied. During the same period, bigoted groups like the White Citizens Councils had formed in New Orleans. Moreover, by the late fifties the Catholic Church there was lurching toward desegregating its churches and schools. I realized as I contemplated returning to my alma mater as a teacher that in a racist environment, political neutrality on the subject of racism amounted to an endorsement. I joined the fight against racial bigotry with some gusto.

That initial sociopolitical conversion would also deepen over the years. In the late sixties I made common cause with conscientious objectors to the Vietnam war. I discovered Christian pacifism. In the seventies, I began to deal with sexism in myself, in society at large, and in the Church, and began to oppose actively the oppression of women. Involvement in Bread for the World has educated me both to the evils born of capitalistic greed and to the massive economic and political injustices that have condemned millions throughout the world to degrading poverty and starvation.

I Convert Affectively

In my own case, affective conversion came last of all. One cannot make the Ignatian long retreat and experience regular spiritual direction without dealing at some level with one's own affectivity. Only the mid-life crisis, however, forced me to face methodically my deep-seated neuroses and to take full, adult responsibility for my own emotional development. Over the years, affective conversion has produced a measure of emotional healing. It has also freed me to acknowledge unhealed areas in my heart and to name longstanding neuroses as old familiar friends.

c. How Do the Other Forms of Conversion Resemble and Differ from Religious Conversion? We have defined five forms of conversion and reflected on how they occur. Let us now begin to reflect more explicitly on the analogy of conversion, on the ways in which the different forms of conversion resemble one another, and on the ways in which they differ.

The Analogy of Conversion

The five forms of conversion all resemble one another in that in each of them the convert passes from irresponsible to responsible conduct. In all five forms of conversion, this passage occurs both initially and in an ongoing manner. All five forms of conversion employ strictly normative thinking, even though each form of conversion invokes different norms appropriate to itself. In all five forms of conversion, ongoing conversion flows from initial conversion with moral inevitability. In all five forms of conversion, when those initially converted resist ongoing conversion, they introduce a measure of inauthenticity into their lives. Converts live authentically when they act responsibly. They live inauthentically when they act irresponsibly despite their professed intention to do the opposite. In all these ways the five forms of conversion resemble one another. How, then, do they differ?

Affective, intellectual, moral, and sociopolitical conversion differ from religious conversion in that they can happen through human initiative alone, whereas religious conversion, because it responds to some gratuitous intervention of God in human history, always results from a divine initiative. By the same token, religious conversion always represents an act of divine grace, a free gift of God. God's offer to enter into a loving union with his creatures invites a free response from them; but that response and everything that flows from it happens under the antecedent impulse of God's free self-donation in love. Affective, intellectual, moral, and sociopolitical conversion can, by contrast, happen naturally. They transpire naturally when they occur in abstraction from God's saving intervention in human affairs.

Natural and Gracious Activity

Contemporary theology has correctly insisted that we live in a world in which grace already operates. The mere presence of grace in the world does not, however, justify characterizing every human act as automatically graced. We define the character of our choices act by act, and the sum total of the decisions that have punctuated our development defines our personal character and identity. Ordinarily, the resulting individual tends in different circumstances to act differently: sometimes naturally, sometimes graciously, sometimes sinfully.

Motivation determines the character of human acts, not some fictive, essential, *a priori* dynamism. When we love, we act compassionately and tenderly. When we defend ourselves, we act fearfully. When we lash out at others, we act angrily. When we interact with our world out of an inferred insight into its predictable behavior, we act rationally. When we deliberate, we act prudentially. When God touches us and we respond in faith, we act graciously. When we interact with created realities in oblivion of God's gracious action in history, we act naturally. If grace functions in our environments but we ignore its presence inculpably, we still respond only naturally. When we deliberately resist the offer of grace, we sin.[3]

Natural responses build only natural habits into the character. Sinful responses build sinful habits; but, since we collaborate with God in defining our religious self-identity, both the initial commitment to a self-revealing God in justifying faith and the sanctifying reaffirmation of the commitment in subsequent faith-motivated actions build graced habits into our characters. Gracious transformation in God demands repentant renunciation of sinful habits and of the acts that both create them and flow from them. Gracious transformation in God also demands that in the light of divine revelation we re-evaluate natural habits and the naturally motivated acts that both produce and flow from them. We shall have occasion to reflect on both these graced processes in greater detail later on. For the moment, however, our concern focuses on trying to understand the analogy of conversion itself.

Natural Conversions

Affective, intellectual, moral, and sociopolitical conversion can occur only naturally; but they need not do so. When a religiously committed person undergoes some other form of conversion than religious, faith can help motivate the new transformation. In my own case, religious motives certainly informed my initial moral conversion.

3. For a discussion of the more technical issues involved in these reflections, see: Donald L. Gelpi, S. J., "Thematic Grace vs. Transmuting Grace: Two Spiritual Paths" in *Grace as Transmuted Experience and Social Process and Other Essays in North American Theology* (Lanham, MD: University Press of America, 1988) 67–95.

Nevertheless, even religiously committed people can also make specific commitments completely apart from motives of faith. Fidelity to the complexity of human life and motivation prevents us therefore from affirming that every conversion undergone by religiously committed people necessarily expresses their graced relationship to God.

Finally, the fact that affective, intellectual, moral, and socio-political conversion can occur naturally endows the human person with an "obediential potency" for religious conversion. What does such a statement imply? Our natural, human capacity to convert makes us persons; for only persons act with self-conscious responsibility. Moreover, our capacity to act responsibly in natural contexts creates in us an ability to act in a responsible manner when confronted with the free offer of divine grace if and when it occurs. One responds to such an offer responsibly only on the terms set by God and therefore only in faith.

4. The Dynamics of a Fivefold Conversion. Every kind of conversion changes experience radically by endowing it with a new kind of selfless responsibility, but religious conversion changes experience more profoundly and radically than other forms of conversion. In every experience of conversion we transcend ourselves by becoming different and better people. Religious conversion, however, begins the enterprise of exploration into God. In religious conversion we transcend not just ourselves but created reality in an encounter with a world-transcending God.

Christian Conversion

Christian conversion endows converted exploration into God with normative concreteness. Christians find the will of God normatively revealed in the person of Jesus and in his vision of the kingdom. Christian converts commit themselves unconditionally to both. Christian conversion also introduces converts into the last age of salvation, when through the incarnation of the Son of God and through the outpouring of his Holy Breath, the triune God reveals to a sinful humanity both the social character of the Godhead and the fullness of human redemption.

Each form of natural conversion changes a distinguishable realm of experience: affectivity, thought, conscience, society. Because Christian conversion requires the reevaluation in faith of every natural experience in the light of divine revelation, it interpenetrates and transvalues the four realms of experience that the four kinds of natural conversion have already endowed with natural responsibility.

Because every kind of conversion changes human experience, the dynamics of conversion follow the dynamics of human experiential development itself. Let us begin then to explore descriptively the ways in which human experience grows, for that description holds the key to understanding the way the different forms of conversion interact. I shall first try to identify three distinguishable but interrelated components of experience: the selves that experience themselves and other realities, the transactions that link those same selves to others, and the evaluative responses that make one self present to another and to its world. I shall then argue that these components of experience all mutually condition one another. Finally, I shall derive from that fact a principle for understanding the dynamics of conversion.

Cognitive Stages

Normal human evaluative responses advance in predictable stages. Until the age of eighteen months, children live immersed in the sensory world around them. They respond to that world emotionally and with increasingly complex memory patterns. At first the child understands its world exclusively in relationship to its own body and its needs. As the child learns to coordinate physical movement, it then develops a sense of its body as a whole. Next children begin to understand the permanence of objects. That understanding then motivates an increasingly persistent search for hidden objects. At none of these early stages of cognitive response, however, do children exhibit the capacity to imagine a world other than the one that they actually sense. For eighteen months, then, sensation, feeling, and memory comprise the full panoply of human evaluative possibilities.

Then, at about the age of two, children develop the exciting capacity to imagine a world other than the one that confronts them. At that moment they enter the rich universe of childhood fantasy. Sometimes the vividness of that universe betrays children into confusing it with the real world around them. As the child matures, however, thinking manifests more and more self-regulating flexibility. The immature mind learns to master concrete problems of position and distance but still shows no capacity for abstract inference.

Normally, children acquire the capacity for abstract, inferential thought at about eleven years. That achievement opens the door to the exciting possibilities of human scholarly, scientific, and mathematical achievement. Moreover, within abstract thinking we can distinguish three different kinds of inference: abductive, or hypothetical, inference; deductive, or predictive, inference; and inductive, or validating, inference.

We discover, then, a spectrum of human evaluative responses in any normal mind. Through sensation we become initially present to the world that impinges upon us. Sensations already possess a vague emotive component, which if allowed to develop yields an initial perception of the kinds of tendencies operative in the persons and things we perceive, as, for example, when one recoils in fright at the sight of a coiled snake. Images—whether remembered, constructed, or archetypal—help clarify our felt perceptions intuitively; and judgments of feeling allow the intuitive mind to grasp reality. The first form of inference, abduction, advances intuitively, since no one can tell the rational mind how to come up with the correct explanatory hypothesis. Deduction and induction, by contrast, develop according to the laws of logic.

Facts—the physical impact of the world upon us—begin our evaluative response; and other facts—our own decisions about how we intend to respond to our world—terminate evaluation. We can, moreover, distinguish three generic kinds of activity: transactions, in which two selves interact autonomously; collaboration, in which several selves cooperate to attain the same end; and coercion, in which one self forces another to act.

The Realms of Experience

If, then, we examine carefully the way human experience normally develops, we can divide it descriptively into three distinct but interrelated realms: (1) the realm of the human self and of the other selves that comprise each self's world, (2) the realm of the concrete interaction that those selves have with one another, (3) the realm of the evaluative responses that motivate those transactions. These three realms of experience all mutually condition one another. Let us reflect on how this happens.

Intuition

The things we sense affect us emotionally. Days of overcast skies tend to depress us. Bright sunny days cheer us. Windowless rooms breed claustrophobia; vistas thrill us. A good meal warms and braces us. Danger fills us with apprehension.

The things we feel emotionally color the way we imagine our worlds. Elation conjures up images of delightful possibilities; depression fills us with foreboding. The fearful imagine strategies for defense. The angry plot revenge. Lovers dream of their beloved. Moreover, images in their turn also conjure up different kinds of associated feelings. Paintings express a variety of moods. Music soothes, saddens, or excites us. A good yarn entertains and delights us.

Models

Not only do sensations, feelings, and images all mutually change and condition one another, but they all also interact with abstract rational thinking. Unless we love the things we investigate in science and scholarship, we soon abandon them out of boredom. We also use images in order to concoct models that make scientific thinking possible. For example, in the early days of atomic research, the decision to imagine the atom as a tiny solar system allowed scientists to start formulating theories about how it worked. Our scientific theories also affect the way we imagine reality and feel toward it. Both Copernican astronomy and evolutionary theory changed the way we feel about ourselves and our place in the universe. So has the discovery of the atomic bomb. In addition, technological advances free the imagination to imagine new worlds to explore and control.

Rational Prediction

Rational beliefs about ourselves and our world also affect prudential thinking. Confronted with any decision of importance, we first need to get our facts straight. We then need to examine the ways in which we respond to those facts emotionally. We need to distinguish imaginatively true from false hopes. We need to predict rationally how the situation we face might change. Then on the basis of all these considerations, we need to decide on the fitting course of action.

Cognitive Transactions

Not only do human evaluative responses all mutually condition one another, but the transactions human selves have with their world leave both the acting self and its world changed. In responding to our worlds evaluatively and decisively we build into ourselves habitual tendencies to act similarly in the future. We call the organic constellation of those tendencies our temperament or our character. Two friends, for example, who know one another well can anticipate how the other will probably respond to particular situations. Similarly, as we master new problems and new situations, we acquire new skills for dealing with them. Years of study produce experts. Years of practice create virtuosos. Our decisions not only change us, but they also change the world in which we live. We can preserve or pollute our environments. We can ravage the wilderness or protect it from commercial exploitation. We can use wealth to create hospitals or slums. Moreover, the environments we live in school us to different kinds of habitual evaluative and decisive responses. Boot camps inculcate physical discipline and blind obedience. Universities communicate appreciation for elite culture.

These reflections on the dynamics of experience allow us to enunciate a principle for dealing with the dynamics of conversion. As we have seen, the five forms of natural conversion seek to transform identifiable components of experience. If, then, the different realms of experience all mutually condition one another, then we can also expect that the different forms of conversion will also mutually change and condition one another within the dynamic growth of experience. Closer examination of the process of conversion validates such an hypothesis. In order to understand fully the ins and outs of conversion, we need, then, to begin to explore those dynamics.

Dynamics Defined

By the dynamics of conversion, I mean the ways in which the different forms of conversion mutually condition one another. Let us begin to examine seven identifiable dynamics. I formulate them in the following manner: (a) Affective conversion animates intellectual, moral, religious, and sociopolitical conversion. (b) Intellectual conversion informs affective, moral, religious, and sociopolitical conversion. (c) Moral conversion helps orient affective, intellectual, religious, and sociopolitical conversion to realities and values that make ultimate and absolute claims on human behavior. (d) Religious conversion mediates between affective and moral conversion. (e) Affective, intellectual, moral, and religious conversion authenticate sociopolitical conversion by supplying it with personal norms that help measure institutional responsibility. (f) Sociopolitical conversion authenticates affective, intellectual, moral, and religious conversion by deprivatizing them. (g) Religious conversion transvalues affective, intellectual, moral, and sociopolitical conversion. In the rest of this chapter we shall examine each of these dynamics in turn.

a) Affective conversion animates intellectual, moral, religious, and sociopolitical conversion. When I reflect on this particular dynamic of conversion, I remember with great fondness and affection a dear friend and former teacher, Clement J. McNaspy, S. J. A man of enormous ability and insatiable curiosity, he transformed himself in an age of specialization into a polymath. Very early in life he decided to master all the romance languages and then proceeded to do so. Having learned a new language, he then set himself to read its great classics in the original. A competent musician, he advanced from a study of the history of music to immersion in world history and in the history of art. He communicated to others his own infectious enthusiasm for everything human. When he celebrated his golden jubilee as a religious, a brother Jesuit correctly described him as "a great man and a great Jesuit who had spent his life praising the achievements of other people."

I think of C. J. in connection with this first dynamic of conversion because he exemplifies so well its key term: "animates." One form of conversion animates another when it endows the latter with emotional zest and enthusiasm, creativity, imaginative flexibility, vision, balance, and an ecstatic absorption in beauty that engenders genuine self-forgetfulness.

Negative and Positive Affections

The affectively converted live such animated lives because they have learned how to face and own their own affectivity in healthy, life-giving ways. The human emotions divide into the negative and the sympathetic affections. Anger, fear, and guilt exemplify basic negative affections. We call them negative because as such they exclude positive appreciation for the realities to which they respond. We respond to threatening persons and situations with either anger or fear. Anger motivates aggressive retaliation; fear begets avoidance. Guilt inspires self-loathing. Love, sympathy, friendship, and affection exemplify the sympathetic affections. Sympathetic affections inspire positive appreciation for ourselves and our world. They open windows on reality. They engender the kind of self-love that inspires appreciation for and sensitivity to both persons and things.

Negative affections cause us the most pain, especially when we repress them. The more we repress them, the more we disintegrate psychologically. The process of disintegration begins with "nervousness," with a slight but perceptible impairment of smooth adaptive control of the way we respond to ourselves and to our world. Nervous people manifest hypersensitivity to noise or to external pressure. They become restless, worried, emotionally volatile. If they continue to repress negative emotions instead of facing them and integrating them realistically into their affective perceptions of reality, nervousness gives way to more serious signs of psychic disintegration: fainting, sleepwalking, phobias, frozen personality reactions, obsessive behavior. At the next stage of psychic disintegration, individuals explode compulsively in violent behavior. Impairment of perception, of judgment, or even of consciousness may precede the violent discharge of aggression. Unless one attends to the deep-seated, negative feelings festering in the unconscious, one then lapses into the kinds of seriously bizarre behavior that require hospitalization. At the end of this spiraling descent into despair often lies morbid fascination with self-mutilation or self-destruction and even the act of suicide itself.

The affectively converted commit themselves to dealing systematically with repressed negative emotions. Negative affections can contribute creatively to human growth and development when they motivate realistic perceptions of ourselves and of our world. Some things should anger us; others should terrify us. We should feel shame at selfish and irresponsible behavior. Repressed negative emotions, however, inhibit such realistic emotional perceptions. They betray us into reacting to the persons and things that actually confront us as though they were ghosts from our past.

Emotional Self-Confrontation

As we face the negative affections we have repressed and integrate them into a realistic, creative response to reality, we enable the sympathetic emotions to play with greater freedom and flexibility. Sympathetic affections inspire love for every expression of beauty: sensible, imaginative, intellectual, moral, religious, interpersonal, institutional. The affectively converted bring, as a consequence, zest, enthusiasm, and emotional verve to all those activities that the other forms of conversion render responsible. Affective conversion animates intellectual conversion by inspiring the search for truth with gusto, with imaginative flexibility, and with playfulness. Affective conversion animates moral conversion by engendering a passionate love of virtue and a heartfelt appreciation for lives that incarnate it. Affective conversion also purifies felt perceptions of reality from misleading projections from the past and thus frees the heart to judge the fitting moral response with realistic and enthusiastic commitment. Affective conversion animates religious conversion by sensitizing the heart to the vision of divine beauty incarnate. Affective conversion animates sociopolitical conversion by suffusing the pursuit of a just social order with reforming zeal, vision, and hope.

b) Intellectual conversion informs affective, moral, religious, and sociopolitical conversion. When I reflect on this particular dynamic of conversion, I think of a friend and colleague who like me pursued doctoral studies in philosophy. Ideas fascinate him. I have even known him to pursue a subtle metaphysical point at the breakfast table. He exhibits an habitual concern to understand the viewpoint of another before criticizing it. He assumes spontaneously that humans can discuss every problem with sweet reasonableness if only they love truth enough. He also displays a willingness to discuss just about any topic about which he might have something to say.

Informing as Ordering

My friend reminds me of the second dynamic within conversion because the way his mind works illustrates what I mean by the term "inform." One kind of conversion informs the others when it orders logically and methodologically one's understanding of the way the other kinds of conversions ought to develop at the same time that it validates that understanding. Intellectual conversion informs the other kinds of conversion by providing the operational tools we need to gather information about them and by endowing one's insights into the dynamics of conversion with lucidity and consistency. Intellectual conversion also informs the other kinds of conversion by contextualizing them, by fostering habits of thought that allow one to situate each conversion within the total process of human growth and development. Finally, intellectual conversion informs the other kinds of conversion by inculcating methodological procedures that allow one to formulate adequate, consistent, coherent, and verifiable accounts of the kinds of conversion and their dynamic interplay.

The Love of Truth

Because they love the truth, the intellectually converted dedicate themselves to understanding the forms of intuitive and inferential thinking that lead to the truth. They therefore bring to human affective conversion a conscious fascination with human psychological development, both personal and social. They bring to moral conversion a concern to understand both the workings of the human conscience and the ideals and principles that motivate and judge personal ethical conduct. They bring to religious conversion a passion for theological investigation. They bring to sociopolitical conversion a consuming interest in social ethics and in the social sciences. Moreover, the intellectually converted manifest a reasonable concern to profit from any scientific or scholarly project that throws light on the experience of conversion. Acknowledging their personal limitations, the intellectually converted acknowledge the dialogic character of human reason and welcome collaboration with others in the exploration of all truth, including the truth about conversion. In all these ways, therefore, those who have experienced intellectual conversion ensure that its fruits inform the other four kinds of conversion.

Personal Rights and Duties

c) Personal moral conversion helps orient affective, intellectual, religious, and sociopolitical conversion to realities and values that make absolute and ultimate claims on human behavior. Moral reasoning concerns itself with the motives and consequences of personal decisions, but it transcends a crude and utilitarian pragmatism. Moral values in the strict sense make absolute and ultimate claims upon the human conscience. Something claims us ultimately when we judge it not only worth living for but, if necessary, even worth dying for. In other words, ultimate values draw us by their beauty at the same time that they stand in judgment on our conduct. Absolute values claim us in every circumstance. Let us try to make these abstract definitions more concrete.

Personal moral conversion seeks to preserve integrity of conscience in interpersonal relationships. It concerns itself with personal rights and duties. By a personal right I mean a human need whose fulfillment makes a claim upon the conscience. By a duty I mean the claim that that need makes.

Children, for example, have a right to expect love, care, nurture, and education from their parents. Parents have the corresponding duty to provide for their children's needs. Nothing ever justifies child abuse. In other words, the rights of children claim their parents' consciences absolutely and ultimately.

Most parents, however, love their children spontaneously. While they acknowledge their parental responsibilities as responsibilities, they shoulder them willingly enough because the beauty of parental love attracts their hearts spontaneously. In other words, the moral ideal of parental love lures them by its beauty even as it stands in judgment over any lapse into parental irresponsibility.

Fulfilling one's parental responsibilities, however, does take its emotional toll. Children make constant demands upon their parents. They test the limits of parental authority and patience. Children's spontaneous egocentrism often leaves them oblivious of their parents' personal needs and limitations. The pressures of adult living can also nurture unconscious rage, anxiety, and guilt in harassed mothers and fathers. Parents who fail to deal adequately with such emotional pressures can end by making their children the scapegoats of their seething personal resentments. In other words, personal moral conversion requires of parents that measure of affective conversion needed to fulfill their duties as parents. In the process, affective moral conversion orients affective conversion to realities and values that make absolute and ultimate claims.

Similarly, parents need to educate their children to love the truth. Parents whose minds remain enslaved by fundamentalism or blinded by prejudice will, however, with moral inevitability instill the same intellectual attitudes into their children. The ethical demands of personal moral conversion require, therefore, that measure of intellectual conversion in parents that they need in order to educate their children properly.

Moral Ultimates, Moral Absolutes

Christian conversion too makes its own absolute and ultimate claims upon the human conscience; for Christian converts must not only live for the sake of the gospel but, if necessary, die for it. The demands of gospel living also claim the conscience in every circumstance. Nevertheless, divine revelation does not provide individual Christians with an automatic formula for gospel living. In their interpersonal dealings with one another, Christians must invoke the norms of prudence in order to make charity practical. They must also face and resolve moral dilemmas for which the gospel offers no clear answer. Are there circumstances in which one may legitimately conceal the truth from another? What constitutes a just ordering of personal relationships within the family? Is masturbation sinful? These and similar moral questions require cultivated prudential insight for their resolution.

Conscience Orients Behavior

Personal moral conversion, therefore, helps orient the consciences of Christian converts toward absolute and ultimate values in two ways: (1) It teaches them the prudence that enables them to translate Christian ideals into practice, and (2) it resolves questions of personal morality for which divine revelation provides no clear answer. For example, the gospel demands of Christians that they love one another in the name and image of Jesus. The gospel alone, however, does not tell Christians how best to care for an ancient and ailing parent, whether to continue life support systems on a comatose child, or how to determine a just, minimum wage. In the concrete, the resolution of such moral dilemmas demands prudential reasoning as well as faith. Better still, their resolution demands prudential reasoning informed by faith.

Personal vs. Public Morality

Does personal moral conversion perform an analogous service for the sociopolitical convert? At first one might feel inclined to answer "no." Personal moral conversion deals with human interpersonal relationships. Sociopolitical conversion deals with the reform of large, impersonal institutions. These two realms of human conduct pose such different moral challenges that on the face of it, they would seem to have little to do with one another.

In interpersonal relationships, faces wear names. Decisions tend to produce immediate satisfaction or pain. We manage our interpersonal relationships more easily than we manage large, impersonal institutions. Finally, in interpersonal relationships we can assign responsibility for decisions with relative ease.

By contrast, in the large, impersonal institutions with which sociopolitical conversion deals, decisions come to pass anonymously: often executives have little or no personal contact with the people affected by their administrative fiat. Large, impersonal institutions tend to postpone both the reward of merit and the punishment of inefficiency and wrongdoing. As a result, such institutions increase the likelihood that justice will miscarry. Large, impersonal institutions baffle us by their complexity. We find it hard to assign responsibility for decisions taken corporately or to devise effective policies and strategies for institutional reform.

The moral questions that confront the sociopolitical convert transcend, therefore, in their complexity those with which the personal convert deals. Nevertheless, personal morality contributes in significant ways to the resolution of problems in public morality. Personal morality obeys three moral principles that apply to every form of human conduct: the principle of benevolence (do good), the principle of non-malfeisance (avoid evil), and the Golden Rule (do unto others as you would have them do unto you). Personal moral conversion also yields an insight into the rights and duties of individuals that large corporate institutions can violate. The same ideals of justice, truth, and integrity preside over both the public and the private realms of human choice, even though public morality deals with questions of greater complexity than private. Moreover, personal morality supplies public morality with a sound insight into how the human conscience reaches moral judgments. By contributing, therefore, to the resolution of issues with which the sociopolitical convert struggles, personal moral conversion helps orient sociopolitical conversion to realities and values that claim the public conscience absolutely and ultimately.

For example, in dealing with a massive structural evil like world hunger, it does not take a great deal of social analysis to realize that Third World countries have no say in setting the economic policies of institutions like the World Bank and the International Monetary Fund. First World nations set those policies ordinarily to their own political and economic advantage. International trade barriers and tariff systems also benefit the affluent nations at the expense of those with developing economies. In the end, these policies translate into the kind of persistent economic depression in the Third World that in turn bears bitter fruit in spiraling infant mortality rates, sprawling slums, and starving masses of people. Informed by one of her courtiers that the people of Paris lacked bread to eat, Marie Antoinette supposedly responded, "Then, let them eat cake." A conscience hardened against the demands of personal morality will tend to confront the starving masses of the world with a similar cynicism.

d) Religious conversion mediates between affective and moral conversion. When I think of this particular dynamic within the total process of conversion, I remember a group of students who used to attend the charismatic prayer group to which I belonged while teaching at Loyola University in New Orleans. After a year of praying together, these students decided that God was calling them as a group to witness more visibly to Christ on the Loyola campus. They decided to rent a house next to the campus and to form there a community that would try to live together in the way that Jesus wanted his disciples to live. As they pondered the New Testament in prayer, they concluded unanimously that a truly Christian community could not tolerate in its midst the presence of haves and have-nots. Like the first Christians in the Acts of the Apostles (Acts 2:42-47), they pooled their financial resources. They also agreed that as a community they should imitate Jesus' own table fellowship and welcome into their home anyone in need. They regularly invited beggars to share their meals. In the course of the first years of their life together, they transformed their community into a center of Christian sharing, prayer, and public witness.

The collective transformation in faith that these students underwent illustrates clearly the way Christian conversion mediates between affective and moral conversion. One kind of conversion mediates between two other kinds when it brings them into a relationship they would not otherwise enjoy.

Christian conversion begins in the heart. It demands first of all that converts renounce the sinful attitudes, whether conscious or unconscious, that separate them from God. As we shall soon see in greater detail, the healing of sinful affections in faith transforms affective conversion into Christian repentance. Repentance in turn frees the heart to respond with greater spontaneity to the divine beauty incarnate in Jesus and in people who resemble him. Consent in faith to that beauty transforms the Christian convert into one of Jesus' disciples.

Christian discipleship, however, makes specific moral demands. As we shall see in greater detail in the following chapter, Jesus bequeathed to his followers a compelling vision of what it means to live together as children of God in his image. He invited and challenged his disciples to create a community of faith whose trust in the Father's providential care would free them to share the physical supports of life with one another on the basis of need and not of merit alone. He challenged and invited them to reach out in compassion to the marginal and oppressed, even to sinners. He taught them to forgive one another and to measure the religious authenticity of their prayer by that mutual forgiveness.

The Lure of Discipleship

This faith-derived ideal of Christian moral conduct both lures and constrains the Christian conscience. It lures the conscience by teaching it to dream of a world transformed according to Jesus' moral vision and to find in God the strength and wisdom to transform that dream into an actuality. Jesus' moral vision also constrains his disciples' consciences, for it reveals to them the will of God and therefore stands in judgment over any action or institution that sinfully contradicts it.

Christian conversion demands therefore that the judgments of conscience that moral conversion sanctions submit not only to natural, prudential norms but also to the will of God that the incarnate Word proclaimed. At the same time, moral conversion teaches Christian disciples prudence in their efforts under grace to build God's kingdom on earth. The two forms of conversion thus mutually interpenetrate and condition one another.

Similarly, affective conversion suffuses Christian moral striving with zest for gospel living. Affectively converted Christians also cultivate an emotional balance that allows them to deal with questions of conscience both realistically and creatively. At the same time, Christian conversion teaches the affectively converted to hope for the universal establishment of God's reign. The charismatic action of the Breath of Jesus also transforms natural, felt judgments of prudence into judgments of discernment. Thus Christian and affective conversion both mutually interpenetrate and mutually condition one another. Finally, moral conversion teaches the affectively converted Christian prudential realism in the living of life, while affective conversion teaches the morally converted Christian the emotional health and integration that ensures the realism of both prudential judgment and the judgments of discernment. Christian conversion for its part teaches the affectively and morally converted to form their consciences not merely with natural prudence but also in a prayerful discernment of God's will informed by the obedience of faith.

Clearly, through the mediation of Christian conversion affective and moral conversion stand in a complex relationship that they would never have enjoyed apart from the obedience of faith. For the believing Christian the demands of gospel living define the meaning of both personal love and institutional justice. The unbeliever, by contrast, judges both only in the light of natural prudence. Similarly, one may weigh one's moral options prudentially in the light of natural reason. One chooses very differently, however, if one prays one's way to a discerning judgment about how concretely God is calling one to act in any given moral circumstance.

e) Affective, intellectual, moral, and religious conversion authenticate sociopolitical conversion by supplying it with norms that help measure institutional responsibility. When I think of this particular dynamic within the total experience of conversion, I remember with both fondness and gratitude the late Fr. Louis Twomey, S. J. Until his final illness and death, he dedicated himself heart, mind, and body to the cause of realizing a just social order in the southern United States. His zeal also led him to reach out to other parts of the country and to the rest of the world. Through *Christ's Blueprint for the South,* which he created, edited, and largely wrote for decades, he informed the consciences and enlisted the collaboration of countless people throughout the world in the search for a just social order. He founded the Institute for Human Relations at Loyola University in New Orleans and used it to battle economic and racial injustice.

Lou Twomey brought to the search for social justice a combination of hope, gusto, vision, realistic prudence, and wise discernment that only the affectively converted display. The other forms of personal conversion also informed his political activism. Although today in the wake of the Second Vatican Council his approach to philosophy and theology would probably seem dated, he used the intellectual tools at his disposal to unmask the oppressive ideologies that degrade and enslave people. Moreover, in confronting institutional injustice he invoked principles both of faith and of prudential reason in order to form his own conscience and help others do the same. In other words, besides affective conversion, intellectual, moral, and Christian conversion all informed and authenticated the activism that his sociopolitical conversion motivated.

The Meaning of Authentication

One kind of conversion authenticates another by fulfilling two interrelated conditions. First, conversion A authenticates conversion B when it facilitates in some way the convert's ability to act with the full measure of responsibility that conversion B demands. Second, without conversion A, converts who have experienced conversion B find that they cannot act with the complete responsibility that the latter conversion demands.

For example, the Christian convert who has experienced affective conversion will discern with greater ease the difference between a genuine divine call and one's own neurotic and psychotic impulses. Religious converts who lack affective conversion will, by contrast, tend to confuse the two. As a consequence, the latter will tend to oppress others by demanding that they conform to rigid, personal, neurotic or psychotic expectations. I think in this context of a thoroughly neurotic religious superior who used to pray in solitude every morning until God revealed to him what his subjects where to do that day. The same superior had an unofficial network of spies in his community who regularly informed him about subjects who transgressed the precepts of the superior's own rigid, Jansenistic conscience. Such oppressive behavior, needless to say, violates the moral demands of gospel living. In other words, it suffuses one's Christian commitment with inauthenticity. Affective conversion, therefore, authenticates Christian conversion by helping the Christian conscience to avoid such abuses.

I am therefore suggesting that a fourfold personal conversion enables sociopolitical converts to act with affective, intellectual, moral, and religious responsibility in their management of large institutions and in their search for institutional reform. I am also suggesting that sociopolitical converts who lack affective, intellectual, moral, or religious conversion find that the absence of one or more of the personal forms of conversion betrays them with moral inevitability into acting irresponsibly in the management and reform of large institutions. Let us begin to reflect more concretely on how the forms of personal conversion authenticate sociopolitical conversion.

For a variety of neurotic or even psychotic reasons, an affectively unconverted politician, executive, or social activist might well support policies that foster racism, sexism, anti-Semitism, and other forms of bigotry. Similarly, the intellectually unconverted will tend to approach complex political problems with narrow-minded bias and simplistic fundamentalism. The morally unconverted will lack the insight into personal rights and duties that would enable them to formulate just laws or make sound executive decisions. The religiously unconverted will tend either to preach a gospel of bland secularism or to persecute religion.

Affectively converted politicians, civic leaders, and social activists who are attempting to deal with their own unconscious aggressions and fears will, by contrast, tend to refrain from enacting legislation or sanctioning policies and decisions that express disordered emotional attitudes. The intellectually converted will tend in complex political and economic situations to distinguish between reality and rhetoric, between truth and ideology. The morally converted bring to the formulation of public policy a sound understanding of prudent and just personal dealings. They understand the personal rights on which impersonal institutions can trample. The religiously converted will tend to promote policies and enact executive decisions that promote both religious freedom of conscience and the reign of God.

Authenticating Sociopolitical Conversion

In other words, a fourfold personal conversion authenticates the activity which sociopolitical conversion inspires by supplying political activists with sound norms for judging between responsible and irresponsible institutional policies and executive decisions, by helping sociopolitical activists understand why situations oppress and depersonalize those trapped in them, and by pointing the way toward institutional reform.

Nevertheless, because sociopolitical conversion extends moral concerns into the realm of public policy and institutional reform, it generates moral principles of its own: principles like the right of all persons to share in the good things of this life; principles of legal, distributive, and commutative justice.

Personal conversion, however, yields its own normative insight into the different forms of institutional oppression. Oppressive situations stifle freedom. I define elementary human freedom as the ability to distinguish and to choose between realistic courses of activity. Ultimately, therefore, elementary human freedom roots itself in human evaluative responses, in the ability to distinguish realistic alternatives of action. Personal conversion enhances elementary human freedom by enabling us to act not only freely but with selfless freedom; for in choosing responsibly, converts take freely into account not only their own needs and desires but the needs and desires of others.

The experience of responsible personal freedom sensitizes converts to recognize situations of institutionalized oppression that thwart and stifle human freedom. The affectively converted have learned to face their own neuroses and to cultivate healthy sensibilities. They therefore recognize as oppressive, situations that breed neurosis and psychosis or inculcate emotional decadence. The intellectually converted have learned to love the truth and to distinguish it from lies, cant, and obfuscation. They therefore recognize as oppressive, situations that bar people from access to the truth through lack of education, through the manipulative use of propaganda, or through any other form of rationalized institutional coercion. The morally converted have learned to love personal virtue and to cultivate it. They therefore recognize as oppressive the institutional exploitation of persons for selfish and venal ends. Religious converts have learned to know and obey the will of God. They therefore recognize instinctively as sinful institutional policies and executive decisions that flout God's will.

Not only does personal conversion enhance elementary human freedom by imbuing it with selfless responsibility, but it also makes human choices personal. Persons differ from animals and from things precisely in their ability to initiate consciously responsible social relationships. In other words persons differ from animals and from things by their capacity for conversion. Personal conversion, therefore, sensitizes one not only to situations of oppression but to depersonalizing situations as well; for situations inevitably depersonalize us when they deter us from conversion.

In other words, a fourfold personal conversion authenticates sociopolitical conversion by teaching the politically active the meaning of responsible freedom and of personal dignity. That insight allows one to recognize situations that stifle freedom and degrade persons. It also helps point the way toward institutional reform by teaching us to transform unhealthy, lying, exploitative institutions into healthy, honest, life-giving ones that embody and inculcate an integral conversion in those persons whose lives they affect.

f) Sociopolitical conversion authenticates affective, intellectual, moral, and religious conversion by deprivatizing them. This dynamic finds most dramatic exemplification in the lives of public figures like Martin Luther King or Dorothy Day. Their commitment to social justice suffuses the whole of their lives with a prophetic character. Concern for the oppressed and marginal in society engages them totally: their hearts, their minds, their consciences, their religious faith. Political activism deprivatizes their personal dealings with others by dedicating them to the reform of the large, impersonal, institutional structures that trample on the rights of the oppressed social minorities. Let us reflect in greater detail on how this dynamic works.

The Distinctiveness of Sociopolitical Conversion

At one time, I did not distinguish between sociopolitical conversion and personal moral conversion. I believed that anyone committed to the moral life would automatically recognize the social and political consequences of that commitment. Two considerations, however, forced me to revise my position: the privatized morality of many people I counselled pastorally and the number of powerful people in the world who manipulate institutions for immoral ends.

I have found that well over half of the people I counsel pastorally resist active political involvement with a tenacity that suggests an absence of conversion. They fear that political activism will take too much time. They argue that the complex issues of public policy defy analysis. They question what one person can accomplish anyway in the face of massive institutional injustice. Almost any excuse will to do to avoid grappling in any practical way with the economic and political structures that hold millions of people in degrading economic and political bondage. Nevertheless, at an interpersonal level the same people who resist public, political involvement live relatively responsible, moral lives. One can then live in a way that testifies to a personal moral conversion but that suggests the absence of any sociopolitical conversion.

Commentators on North American culture in the nineteen eighties have criticized it as individualistic and narcissistic. The negative response of many in this country to the North American bishops' peace pastoral and to their pastoral on the economy gives weight to the criticism.

Those who questioned the right of the bishops to condemn the immorality of the arms race and of many of this nation's economic policies did so because they resented any attempt to judge public policy by religious or moral norms. Many of the bishops' adversaries claim to live personally moral and religious lives, but they want to keep both religion and morality out of the public forum. Nevertheless, not infrequently those same adversaries bear public responsibility for the very policies whose immorality the bishops condemned. One can, then, function in a public manner both politically and economically without having experienced sociopolitical conversion; and one can on the whole act morally at an interpersonal level without allowing ethical or religious considerations to touch one's conduct of public affairs.

For a time I puzzled over the reasons why so many Americans judge moral questions with privatized consciences. Did that fact simply reflect the individualistic bias of North American culture? On reflection, however, I decided that the kinds of moral issues that problems of institutional reform raise differ sufficiently both in complexity and in the kinds of moral principles they invoke that one could make a genuine commitment to ethical responsibility in all that concerns one's interpersonal dealings and simply prescind from the need to act responsibly in the face of questions of public policy and institutional injustice.

Degrees of Activism

Sociopolitical conversion commits one to the cause of dealing with the injustices perpetrated by large, impersonal institutions. I empathize with those who shrink from such a commitment, for my own extreme introversion causes me to resist political involvement and the demands it makes on my privacy. In the course of my life I have, however, espoused different political causes: chiefly the struggle against racism, sexism, and world hunger. Nevertheless, I do not for all that consider myself a professional political activist. I have neither the gifts nor the temperament for such a career.

I nevertheless claim some measure of sociopolitical conversion, because I have, legitimately I believe, come to distinguish four possible levels of political involvement available to people living in this nation. I call those who have reached the first level "civic minimalists." They exercise the right to vote responsibly; but because they prescind otherwise from the impact of large institutions on their own and on others' lives, they fall short of full sociopolitical conversion. It gives one pause to reflect that over fifty per cent of the voters in the United States fail even this minimal test of political commitment. Still, the dwindling number of active voters in this country dramatizes the importance of giving even civic minimalists their due.

I call those who live at the second level of political involvement "teaching activists." They study specific instances of institutional injustice and try to educate their own consciences and those of others to the moral issues that oppressive situations raise. Education empowers the oppressed to demand their rights and prepares the oppressor to cede them once they are demanded. Because education to social activism qualifies as a political act, teaching activists who commit themselves to the cause of institutional reform can perhaps claim to have experienced an initial sociopolitical conversion, even though ongoing sociopolitical conversion will almost certainly require of them more than teaching activism.

I call those who advance beyond teaching activism to the next level of sociopolitical involvement "participatory activists." Participatory activists support in concrete ways public leaders and professional activists who agitate or lobby in the hope of correcting specific institutional injustices. Participatory activists contribute funds to groups that promote institutional reform, support lobbies, and engage in public demonstrations that advance just causes.

Professional activists exemplify the fourth level of sociopolitical involvement. These people undertake institutional reform as a career by becoming, for example, politicians, industrial leaders with a concern for economic justice, or lobbyists for the cause of the poor, the marginal, the oppressed, and other victims of injustice.

Most people cannot function as professional activists. The limitations of time, talent, and temperament, on the one hand, and the pressure of other responsibilities, on the other, prevent them from making a career of institutional reform. Human limitation and the burden of other responsibilities also force one to choose which political or economic causes most deserve one's active support and to decide the level of commitment one can give to them. Nevertheless, I myself believe that virtually everyone can function as a participatory activist by espousing some political, social, or economic cause of universal import, like world hunger, nuclear disarmament, women's rights, the rights of blacks, Native Americans, of *latinos,* and of other minority groups. The double fact that virtually half the people in this country fail even to vote and that only a handful ever advance to the level of teaching activism testifies eloquently to the power of an individualistic, narcissistic culture to subvert and prevent sociopolitical conversion from ever happening.

Deprivatizing Personal Conversion

Sociopolitical conversion deprivatizes personal conversion in two ways. First of all, it actively dedicates the convert to some cause of universal moral import. Second, responsible political activism forces one to confront and identify with the Others, with persons and groups different from oneself whose very difference can pose a potential personal threat. Let us reflect on how these two interrelated dynamics shape the total process of conversion.

Dedication to some specific cause transfers the convert from the familiar world of interpersonal living to public confrontation with institutional injustice. Large institutions baffle and frustrate single individuals who seek to change them because ordinarily they can use the power that comes with size, wealth, and influence to outfox, outguess, discredit, silence, or even crush individual opposition. As a consequence, individuals who make common cause with others stand a better chance than loners of effecting significant institutional change.

Inevitably, however, making common political cause with other people confronts one with the Others, with unfamiliar individuals and groups that challenge our familiar values and presuppositions. Sociopolitical conversion brings together members of different classes, races, political parties, life styles, and traditions. By dedicating them to the same cause it forces them in some measure to face and transcend their differences. It also introduces them into the arena of ideological struggle and conflict. One must face and respond to adversaries whose beliefs and commitments contradict one's own. In the case of the economically and politically advantaged, the Others also include the poor, the marginal, the disadvantaged, the oppressed.

Initially, the human ego tends to resent and resist any challenge to its limitations, including the challenge of facing the Others. Challenge, however, expands our limited perspective on reality and produces personal growth. In the process of providing personal conversions with a broader and more challenging context, the challenge of the Others deepens all four forms of personal conversion.

The Personal Impact of Institutionalized Values

By deprivatizing personal conversion, sociopolitical conversion authenticates it in yet another way, because until we have learned to identify and resist the ways in which unjust institutional structures shape our personal self-awareness, we cannot act with full responsibility even in our interpersonal dealings with one another. Let us reflect on the reasons for this incapacity.

Institutions result from habit. When an identifiable group within human society begins as a group to act habitually in a specific manner and when others interpret that manner of acting as typical of the group's legitimate social behavior, an institution results. For example, in some societies aunts and uncles habitually punish their nieces and nephews; in other societies they do not. The two societies have, in other words, institutionalized differently the behavior of aunts and uncles within the family. As a consequence, in each society aunts and uncles enjoy a different social identity.

Because they organize habitual behavior, institutions also inculcate specific ways of responding to reality. We therefore come to personal self-understanding by learning to play different roles not only in an interpersonal institution like the family but also in larger, more impersonal institutions like schools, businesses, social classes, nations, churches. Some injustice usually infects any large impersonal institution. As we enter them through the processes of socialization, large, impersonal institutions successfully infuse our personal attitudes, beliefs, consciences, and religious faith with the poison of racist, sexual, or religious bigotry, of classist snobbery, of supine acquiescence in the economic exploitation of the disadvantaged and powerless, of narrow bias and chauvinism, of consent to aggressive war and to other forms of violent oppression. When we stereotype, exploit, or oppress other persons, we turn them into objects, into things we can use or abuse as we want. Inevitably, then, the failure to advance beyond personal conversion to sociopolitical conversion subverts all four types of personal conversion and renders them inauthentic. The absence of sociopolitical conversion leaves one vulnerable to the institutionalized injustice that distorts human passion, blinds the human mind with lies and half-truths, perverts the conscience by teaching it to degrade and dehumanize other persons, and transforms the religious person into a pious hypocrite.

Only when we actively confront institutional corruption and injustice do we come to understand the extent to which they have consciously and unconsciously shaped and used us as individual persons to tainted and exploitative ends. Only in dealing with the members of a less advantaged social class do we come to recognize fully our own classist conditioning. Only by dealing with the members of a different race do we learn fully to confront our own racial prejudices. Only by facing the members of other nations we have wronged, can we transcend mindless nationalism. In other words, not only does sociopolitical conversion enable the personally converted to act responsibly in their interpersonal dealings with others; but it also resists the corrupting influence of institutional injustice that betrays the personally converted into treating other persons irresponsibly whether for distorted affective, cognitive, pseudo-ethical, or religiously hypocritical motives.

g) Religious conversion transvalues affective, intellectual, moral, and sociopolitical conversion. This particular dynamic of conversion reminds me of some of the converts in our charismatic prayer group in New Orleans. Like Jim, whose conversion account opened this chapter, they often converted to Christianity from an experience of extreme moral and social disillusionment and cynicism. Their conversion caused them to view the world with new eyes, new hopes, new commitment, new vision. Repentance had brought their former cynicism and sensuality to initial healing. They read the Bible with new, invigorating insight. They viewed their lives and human society with a different set of values, values inspired by faith and informed by the teaching and example of Jesus. In other words, their Christian conversion had transvalued their perceptions of God, of themselves, and of the world in which they lived. Religious conversion transvalues the other forms of conversion by providing a novel frame of reference for understanding how they transpire and develop.

The Meaning of Transvaluation

The term "transvaluation" may sound unfamiliar and technical, but it designates a familiar thought process. We transvalue sensations, feelings, images, concepts, inferences, when, having employed them in one frame of reference, we subsequently begin to use them in a different frame of reference. When that happens the old sensations, images, concepts, and inferences retain some of their former meaning; but they also begin to take on new connotations derived from the new frame of reference. For example, before Columbus discovered America, the term "earth" meant the hard ground on which we live and move. Once, however, Columbus taught people in Europe to think of the earth as round rather than flat, the old term "earth" began to connote some completely new and exciting possibilities, which the first European explorers of the New World began to test.

As we have seen, affective, intellectual, moral, and sociopolitical conversion can all occur naturally, i.e., in complete abstraction from any historical acts of divine self-revelation and self-communication. Religious conversion creates a graced and therefore supernatural frame of reference. A supernatural frame of reference results whenever we enter through religious conversion into a conscious relationship with a self-revealing, self-communicating, world-transcending God. A supernatural frame of reference allows us to conceive of things in ways we never would have if left to our natural resources. We call that frame of reference "faith." Christian converts perceive the divine reality with the eyes of Christian faith. They consent to the unique, normative self-revelation and self-communication of God accomplished in Jesus and in the mission of his Holy Breath.

Three Senses of Faith

In the interests of clarity, however, we need to distinguish at this point three theological senses of the term "faith." In its first and broadest sense "faith" designates an initial global act of consent to God. This kind of initial, global faith grounds any subsequent act of hope, religious belief, love, and service that it helps motivate. In its second and more restricted sense "faith" means the second of the three theological virtues: hope, faith, and love. Theological virtues orient us directly to God and differ in that respect from the moral virtues that govern human intercourse. Taken in its second sense faith, then, contrasts with hope and love, whereas faith in its first and broadest sense would help motivate all three theological virtues. Theologians, however, legitimately use the term "faith" in a third sense, the narrowest of the three. In its narrowest sense, "faith" designates a charism, or gift, of the Breath of Christ. Those possess the special gift of faith whose relationship to God differs qualitatively from that of other believers in its degree of trust, confidence, and generosity.

The "Infusion" of Theological Hope

When Christian faith, in the first and broadest sense of that term, begins to transvalue certain dimensions of affective conversion, it gives rise to the theological virtue of hope. Hope dwells in the heart. It expresses a preferential intuitive perception of the future. As we have seen, the repression of the negative emotions draws the human psyche into the maelstrom of violence and despair. The affectively converted confront those same repressed feelings and bring them to conscious psychic integration. The healing of the dark side of the psyche frees it to hope.

Christian conversion transforms confrontation with the dark, potentially violent side of the psyche into religious repentance of the sinful attitudes that separate us from God. Moreover, it informs the hope naturally born of repentance with an ultimately transcendent goal and with specifically Christian ideals and values. In the chapter that follows we shall attempt to understand in more detail how the gracious transvaluation of this and of other natural forms of conversion occurs. Here, however, it suffices to situate the experience of the transvaluation of natural hopes within the total process of conversion.

The "Infusion" of the Theological Virtue of Faith

The theological virtue of faith transvalues natural human beliefs about reality. We judge reality both intuitively and inferentially. Growth in faith demands therefore the gracious transvaluation of both intellectual and affective conversion. Intellectual conversion commits one to collaborating with others in the human search for truth. Christian converts explore the meaning of divine truth both theoretically and practically in a community of faith unified and inspired by the gift-giving Breath of Christ. As an initial, global commitment of faith informs our intuitive perceptions of reality, that commitment inspires religious ritual, narrative, literature, and art. As it transforms our rational perceptions of reality it inspires creedal professions of faith and speculative theology. In both ways it motivates the ongoing infusion of the theological virtue of faith.

The "Infusion" of Charity

Christian conversion transvalues moral conversion by transforming it into the theological virtue of love. Christian faith in its first and broadest sense demands that Christians form their consciences not only in the light of natural human prudence but also and more fundamentally in the light of Jesus' vision of the kingdom. As the conscience makes judgments of discernment informed by the moral demands of life in the kingdom, it learns the meaning of Christian love.

The Christian Search for Justice

The vision of the kingdom also provides a novel context, one born of an initial global commitment of faith, in which to understand the meaning of social justice. The Christian must judge the justice or injustice of human social institutions by the extent to which they conform to the will of God. Christian converts, however, find God's will finally and fully revealed in Jesus, the incarnate Son of God. By demanding that we evaluate and transform human social institutions in the light of faith-derived values, Christian conversion also transvalues natural, sociopolitical conversion and transforms it into the Christian search for social justice.

5. **Concluding Remarks.** In the present chapter we have discovered that Christian conversion contributes two dynamics to the total process of conversion: (1) It mediates between affective and moral conversion, and (2) it transvalues the other forms of conversion. In the chapter that follows we shall explore in much more theological detail the relationship between these two dynamics.

We began the present chapter by noting the pastoral need for a theology of the sacraments grounded in a sound understanding of the forms and dynamics of conversion. We summarized the insights of a traditional Catholic theology of conversion and decided that it focused too narrowly on religious conversion. We then examined some of the reasons why religious conversions that begin well sometimes go sour. That examination forced us to develop a more complex construct of conversion than theologians have traditionally employed. We decided that we need to distinguish five moments and seven dynamics within the total process of conversion. We also distinguished initial from ongoing conversion and natural from gracious conversion.

Some readers may at this point experience a sense of dismay at the complexity of the conversion process. Suspect such feelings, because they stem from the spontaneous inertia of the human ego, which cowers in the face of novel and complex ideas. The complexity of conversion, however, only echoes the complexity of life itself. Those who flee from the complexities of life do so at their own peril; for, however much we try to avoid it, reality has a way of catching up with us in the long run. Conversion, moreover, takes a lifetime. Each convert can claim to have advanced some distance down the road of responsible living. At the end of that road lies perfect union with God. For the present, however, we must advance toward union step by step with the grace of God and with the support of friends and of the communities to which we belong. We do not, therefore, travel alone. Fellow converts walk beside us, while God encompasses us all and through his Breath empowers us to do and to suffer what we could never accomplish left to our natural resources. In the chapter that follows, we will, then, begin to reflect in more detail on the ways in which the Breath of Jesus guides and strengthens us as together we walk with God and with fellow converts toward the fullness of freedom in Christ.

CHAPTER II

Conversion to Christ

In the preceding chapter we began to consider the ins and outs of conversion. We examined five moments of conversion and seven dynamics that govern the way in which they mutually interpenetrate and condition one another. In the present chapter we begin to study more closely the two dynamics that Christian conversion contributes to the total process of conversion: (1) Christian conversion mediates between affective and moral conversion, and (2) Christian conversion transvalues in faith the natural forms of conversion.

Biblical Foundations

The first part of this chapter examines some biblical foundations for a Christian theology of conversion. It reflects on Jesus' baptismal experience as we find it described in the New Testament. We shall discover in that experience the prototype of Christian baptism, for through baptism Christian converts receive the same divine Breath as descended on Jesus in his baptism. The baptismal Breath comes to them to conform them to him: to teach them to live as children of God in his image and to draw them into his baptismal experience.

If the Breath of God teaches Christian converts to live in the image of God's incarnate Son, then a sound theology of Christian conversion must understand the ways in which the divine Breath inspired and shaped Jesus' own conduct. As we shall see in the course of the chapters that follow, all of the Christian sacraments ritualize some aspect of Jesus' Breath-inspired ministry. In the present chapter, however, we seek to understand not the significance of Christian ritual worship but the practical consequences of conversion to Christ. The first part of this chapter, therefore, probes the New Testament for the insights it yields into the moral consequences of Christian conversion. As we shall see, the New Testament gives us a coherent account of the way Jesus expected his disciples to live.

Finally, our examination of biblical foundations for a theology of Christian conversion will close with a reflection on the Christian experience of Breath baptism as it is described in the New Testament. As we shall see, the Breath of Jesus comes not to isolated individuals but to the Christian community as a whole in order to create a realm of grace in which individual converts can encounter the risen Christ.

The Two Dynamics of Christian Conversion

The second part of this chapter employs these biblical insights in order to illumine the two dynamics that Christian conversion contributes to the total process of conversion. As we have seen, in its first dynamic Christian conversion mediates between affective and moral conversion. As we shall see, this first dynamic which Christian conversion effects inspires faith in the broadest sense of that term, a global commitment that opens every facet of a person to the divine Breath's inspiration. In the course of what follows we shall also explore reasons for affirming that an initial commitment to such a global attitude of faith justifies us in the sight of God.

Moreover, the first dynamic of Christian conversion motivates the second, namely, the transvaluation in faith of the four forms of natural conversion—affective, intellectual, moral, and sociopolitical. This second dynamic gives concrete meaning to what a more traditional theology called "the infusion of sanctifying grace." As we shall see, as Christian conversion transvalues affective conversion, it mediates the infusion of the theological virtue of hope. As it transvalues both affective and intellectual conversion, it mediates the infusion of the theological virtue of faith. As it transvalues moral conversion, it mediates the infusion of the theological virtue of love. As it transvalues sociopolitical conversion, it inspires the Christian search for social justice.

Let us then begin to explore these insights into the dynamics of Christian conversion in greater detail.

1. New Testament Foundations for a Theology of Christian Conversion. We begin our reflection on New Testament foundations for a theology of Christian conversion with an examination of the gospel accounts of Jesus' own baptism, for they hold an important key to the dynamics of Christian conversion.

Mark's Baptismal Narrative

a. The Baptism of Jesus. The New Testament informs us that Christian converts are drawn into Jesus' own baptismal experience. Mark the evangelist interweaves skillfully both narrative and image to make this point at the very beginning of his gospel. The gospel opens with the prophecy of John the Baptizer that a "mightier one" would follow him who would baptize his followers "with a Holy Breath" (Mark 1:1-8). Mark follows the prophecy with an account of Jesus' own baptism. After Jesus rises from the waters, the Holy Breath of God descends upon him to begin his manifestation as the "mightier one" whom John had foretold. The divine Breath's descent follows an apocalyptic rent in the heavens that symbolizes the beginning of the last age of salvation. As the Breath descends upon Jesus, a voice from heaven blends two texts from the Old Testament in order to proclaim Jesus Son of God and Messiah in the image of the Suffering Servant described by Deutero-Isaiah. The voice assures Jesus: "You are my beloved Son; with You I am well pleased" (Mark 1:9-11; Ps 2:7; Isa 42:1). Since throughout the Bible the Breath of God functions as a principle of gracious enlightenment, the fact that the Holy Breath descends on Jesus before he hears the commissioning voice suggests that Jesus hears that voice through the enlightenment that the divine Breath imparts.

The Holy Breath descends upon Jesus under the sign of a dove. The Hebrews kept doves as pets. The prophet Hosea compared Israel to a dove (Hos 7:11; 11:11); and Psalm 74 echoed the image in a context that suggests that God has chosen Israel as his specially beloved, as his "pet." Rabbinic literature also described Israel as the dove of God, as the object of his particular delight. That the descending Breath comes to Jesus under the sign of a dove suggests, then, that the Holy Breath of God comes to Jesus to begin his revelation as the specially beloved of God and the beginning of a new Israel. Accordingly, as the Breath descends, the voice from heaven proclaims Jesus "My beloved Son in whom I am well pleased." Mark reinforces this point by informing us that after Jesus' baptism the Holy Breath drove him out into the desert where he was tempted for forty days. Like the first Israel that wandered in the desert for forty years, Jesus, as the beginning of a new Israel, must also endure a time of desert testing (Mark 1:12-13).

Mark's Gospel addressed a persecuted Church. In the course of it, the evangelist warned his readers that those who follow a suffering Messiah expect that they too would face the same principalities and powers that nailed Jesus to the cross. Indeed, in Mark's Gospel the courage to testify to Jesus in times of persecution distinguishes those who have experienced Breath baptism (Mark 13:9-12).

For Mark, then, those baptized in Jesus' name receive a share of the same sanctifying Breath that descended on him after his baptism by John. Breath baptism incorporates Jesus' disciples into the new Israel that he himself begins. Jesus, then, models for his followers the practical consequences of Breath baptism. The sanctifying Breath of Christ comes to Jesus' disciples in order to conform them to him by drawing them into his own baptismal experience. This the Breath does by teaching them to live and die as children of God in his image (Mark 10:38-40).

Matthew's Baptismal Narrative

Matthew's Gospel reproduces Mark's theological interpretation of the significance of Jesus' baptism, but at three points Matthew interpolates Mark's account of the event itself. First, in Matthew's narrative, Matthew contrasts the way in which the Breath of God comes to Jesus and the way that same Breath will come to his disciples. Second, before the baptism occurs John attempts to dissuade Jesus from submitting to it. Finally, during Jesus' messianic commissioning, the voice from heaven addresses not Jesus himself, as it does in Mark's Gospel, but the reader. Let us try to understand the meaning of these three interpolations that Matthew introduces into Mark's baptismal narrative.

Matthew, citing perhaps an older tradition about the Baptizer's prophecy of a mightier one who will follow him, has John predict that the mightier one will baptize "with a Holy Breath and with fire" (Matt 3:11). In Jesus' own baptism the Breath will come to him under the sign of a dove, but the same Holy Breath will come to Jesus' disciples under the sign of fire. As we have seen, the descent of the divine Breath upon Jesus under the sign of a dove begins his public revelation as messianic Son of God, as the beginning of a new Israel, as the one who begins a new creation and seals a new covenant. Fire, by contrast, symbolizes divine holiness in its capacity to judge and purify sinful humanity. Divine holiness purifies those who believe in God and consumes unbelievers in the fire of judgment.

Besides contrasting the way in which the Breath relates to Jesus and to his disciples, Matthew also prefaced his account of Jesus' baptism by a brief exchange between him and the Baptizer. The fact that

Jesus had received John's baptism seems to have embarrassed the first Christians. It seemed to suggest the superiority of John's baptism to the one administered by Jesus' own disciples. As we have seen, Mark's Gospel vindicated the superiority of Christian to Johannine baptism by citing the Baptizer's own prophecy that a mightier one would follow him who would baptize in a sanctifying Breath. In other words, Mark portrayed John as having acknowledged prophetically the superiority of Christian baptism to his own. Matthew underscored and developed this theological insight in the dialogue between Jesus and John that prefaced his account of the baptism itself.

As Jesus approaches John in order to receive the latter's baptism, John protests that he feels reluctant to administer his own baptism to one whose baptism John himself needs. Jesus replies: "Let it be so now; for thus it is fitting for us to fulfill all righteousness" (Matt 3:14-15).

John's protest clearly asserts the superiority of Christian to Johannine baptism. Jesus' reply to John explains the reason for that superiority: Christian baptism fulfills Johannine. Matthew, who wrote for a community of Jewish Christians, portrays Jesus in his gospel as one who fulfills the Law and the Prophets (Matt 5:17). Already in his infancy gospel, Matthew had introduced the theme of fulfillment by alluding to several Old Testament prophecies that the story of Jesus' birth fulfills (Matt 1:22-23; 2:5-6, 15, 17-18, 23). In Matthew's theology Jesus fulfills the Law and the Prophets by demanding more of his disciples than they did of the devout Jew (Matt 5:21-48). In the same way, for Matthew Christian baptism fulfills Johannine.

In Matthew's eyes John's baptismal ministry performed only a passing function in the history of salvation. Christian baptism replaces Johannine because Christian baptism signifies everything that Johannine baptism signified and more. Not only does Christian baptism summon one to repentance, as John's did, but it also confers on the baptized the same sanctifying Breath of God who descended on Jesus at the Jordan and who comes to Christian converts in order to draw them into Jesus' own baptismal experience.

Moreover, in Matthew's baptismal narrative the voice from heaven addresses not Jesus but the reader. Instead of saying to Jesus: "You are my beloved Son; with You I am well pleased" (Mark 1:11), the voice in Matthew's account says: "This is my beloved Son with Whom I am well pleased" (Matt 3:17). The shift in pronoun from "You" to "this" underscores the fact that Matthew intends by narrating the story of Jesus' baptism to engage the baptismal faith of his reader. The voice from heaven challenges the reader directly to profess faith in Jesus as messianic Son of God, Suffering Servant, and divinely beloved beginning of a new Israel.

Clearly then, the interpolations that Matthew introduced into Mark's account of Jesus' baptism only underscore important aspects of the theological interpretation that Mark offered of that event.

Luke's Baptismal Narrative

Luke, like Matthew, has the Holy Breath come to Jesus under the sign of a dove but to his followers under the sign of the fire of purification and judgment (Luke 3:16, 22). In his baptismal narrative, however, Luke, unlike Matthew, makes no mention of a dialogue between Jesus and John prior to the baptism. Unlike Mark, Luke does not describe the event of the baptism, although he notes that it occurred. Mark, as we have seen, situates Jesus' messianic commissioning not at the moment of the baptism itself but at the moment when Jesus rises from the baptismal waters. Luke for his part postpones the commissioning until John has completely finished baptizing. Apparently, Luke wished to stress even more clearly than Mark had that John's baptism in no way confers the Holy Breath on Jesus in the way that Christian baptism would confer the divine Breath on Jesus' followers (Luke 3:21).

A second motive may have inspired Luke to postpone Jesus' messianic vision. Jesus experiences the vision after his baptism while rapt in solitary prayer (Luke 3:21). In the Acts of the Apostles the Pentecostal Breath will descend on Jesus' disciples in the upper room where they too have gathered apparently for prayer. Seemingly, Luke wished to structure his account of Jesus' baptism in such a way as to suggest that it foreshadows Pentecost. In Acts the event of Pentecost also reveals the Breath baptism that Jesus' own baptism foreshadows (Acts 2:1-41).

Luke also depicts the Breath as descending on Jesus in the "bodily form" of a dove (Luke 3:12). Luke's Gospel, like Matthew's, insists that Jesus stood related to the divine Breath from the first moment of his conception (Luke 1:35; Matt 1:18). Accordingly, Luke's insistence that the dove descended in bodily form softens somewhat the apocalyptic tone of Mark's baptismal narrative and transforms the event into a semi-miraculous public revelation of Jesus' messianic commissioning.

Like Matthew, Luke endorses the main lines of Mark's theological interpretation of Jesus' baptism. Luke reproduces Mark's account of the voice from heaven. The Holy Breath comes to him to begin his public manifestation as Son of God and the beginning of a new Israel, as Messiah in the image of the Suffering Servant, as the one who begins a new creation and seals a new covenant. Because it begins Jesus' revelation as Breath baptizer, Jesus' own baptism foreshadows Christian baptism. Hence, the Breath of God will come to his followers in order to conform them to him by teaching them to live as children of God in his image.

The Johannine Witness

John's Gospel omits all reference to Jesus' baptism, but the fourth evangelist does reproduce the substance of the Baptizer's witness to Jesus, with minor variations. As in the Synoptic Gospels, the Baptizer testifies that he baptizes only with water and that one greater than himself will follow him (John 1:26-27). The Baptizer also prophesies that Jesus will baptize his followers in a Holy Breath (John 1:33). In contrast to the Synoptic Gospels, however, the fourth evangelist for theological reasons makes the Baptizer a personal witness to the descent of the Breath upon Jesus.

The Fourth Gospel, however, like the Synoptics insists that the Breath of Jesus will come to his disciples in order to conform them to his image. The Holy Breath, the Paraclete, will call to their minds everything Jesus taught them with a new and deeper insight (John 14:25-26). They will learn to witness to Jesus in the same way that he witnessed to the Father; and because of that Breath-inspired witness, they will find themselves drawn inexorably into his passion (John 15:18-27).

The Gospels teach us, therefore, that conversion to Christ has important practical consequences. The same divine Breath that descended on Jesus in his baptism descends in Christian baptism on those who turn to him in repentance and converting faith. The Holy Breath comes to Jesus' disciples in order to teach them to live as children of God in his image, in order to seal with them a new covenant, in order to purify them and give them a share in the new creation. If, moreover, we examine the teachings of Jesus contained in the New Testament, we shall discover that living as a child of God in his image makes very specific moral demands of those who profess to follow him. Let us try to understand those demands by examining more closely some of the moral dimensions of the religious vision that Jesus proclaimed.

b. Jesus' Religious Vision. As the voice from heaven proclaims in all three Synoptic accounts, the Holy Breath descends on Jesus in order to reveal him as God's beloved Son. Any devout Jew living at the time of Jesus would have learned from the Law and the Prophets to call God the Father of Israel and therefore of all of his faithful Jewish servants. Jesus, however, endowed this traditional Jewish belief with a new intimacy. He called God "Papa" and dreamed of a community of faith that could pray together "Our Papa in heaven, hallowed be Your name" (Matt 6:9). He wanted his disciples to trust the Father's tender providence over each of them (Matt 6:25-34) and to obey his will (Matt 6:9-10).

The Father and His Children

In the Gospels, moreover, Jesus acting under the Holy Breath's inspiration, transformed traditional Jewish belief in the fatherhood of God in three other novel ways. He interpreted the meaning of the divine fatherhood in the light of his own sense of privileged Sonship. He proclaimed God universal Father, not just of Israel but also of those Gentiles who believe in him. Finally, he demanded that his disciples imitate the Father's forgiving love of sinners by their own mutual forgiveness, by loving their enemies, and by imitating Jesus' own table fellowship with sinners and social outcasts. Let us reflect on these three facets of Jesus' teaching as we find it in the Gospels.

In the Gospels Jesus claims God as his Father in a unique and privileged sense. While he spoke to his disciples of "My Father" and "your Father," we never find him in the Gospels joining the disciples in saying "Our Father." On the contrary, he claims a privileged relationship to the Father that allows him and him alone to interpret to others the truth about the Father. Those who would live as the Father's child must imitate Jesus' own example (Matt 11:25-27; Luke 10:21-22).

Jesus himself seems to have confined his ministry largely to Jews (Matt 10:5). Nevertheless, his encounters with Gentiles of outstanding faith seem to have caused him to make a place for the nations within the Father's kingdom. They would take their seats beside believing Jews at the messianic banquet. They would number among the children of God (Matt 8:5-13; 15:21-28; Luke 7:1-10; Mark 7:24-30). Jesus' inclusion of the Gentiles in his vision of the kingdom extends and deepens a universalist strain within traditional Judaic belief that asserted that God had chosen Israel as his instrument for saving the nations. Jesus, however, warns that unless his people repent and believe the good news he proclaims, the Gentiles will supplant them in the new Israel he has come to found.

Jesus' table fellowship with sinners, his willingness to reach across social barriers to the marginal and outcast, scandalized his pious, conventional contemporaries and dramatized in another way the universality of his vision. The Father's kingdom makes place for all those that human society excludes. It embraces social outcasts almost aggressively, with a divine determination to include them (Luke 14:15-24; Matt 22:1-14).

The universalism of the reign of God that Jesus proclaimed, its startling inclusion within the new Israel of Gentiles and of the legally defiled, roots itself ultimately in Jesus' understanding of the moral conditions for membership in the kingdom. The Synoptic Gospels describe those conditions in considerable detail. Let us begin to ponder them.

Discipleship in Mark

Mark's Jesus repudiates the hair-splitting legalism of the Pharisees of his day and grounds true righteousness instead in purity of intention (Mark 2:23–3:6; 7:1-23; 12:38-40). He teaches his disciples to trust the Father's providential care and to present to him in prayers of petition their every need (Mark 11:24). Mark's Jesus, however, also makes demands of his disciples that go beyond the exigencies of the Torah. Jesus' followers must prove their dedication to the kingdom by selling their possessions, distributing them to the poor, and joining the company of his disciples (Mark 10:21-22). They must abhor hoarded wealth as the greatest obstacle to entry into the kingdom (Mark 12:38-40). Instead, Jesus' disciples must imitate his own table fellowship with sinners and allow the sharing of bread with the needy, marginal, and outcast to give meaning to the great commandment (Mark 2:15-17; 9:37; 10:15-16; 12:29-30). For Jesus such sharing imitates the Father's own forgiving love (Mark 2:5-12; 15:17). It incarnates a mutual forgiveness that measures the authenticity of his disciples' prayer (Mark 9:41; 11:25). Jesus' followers must even imitate his willingness to forgive in advance those who would murder him (Mark 8:3-9; 9:42-50). Those who join the community of his disciples must also renounce the pride of place that the powerful of this world prize. Instead, they must treat the least among them as the greatest (Mark 9:34-35).

Discipleship in Matthew

Matthew's Jesus makes similar demands of those who choose to follow him. Their expectant faith in the Father's providential care must heal their hearts of any anxious tendency to cling to worldly goods. Rather, they should submit in faith and trust to life in God's kingdom (Matt 6:24-36). Instead of clinging to worldly possessions, the true child of God shares them with the needy and the outcast. Such sharing gives entry into the kingdom (Matt 25:31-36). In sharing the physical supports of life with others, moreover, Jesus' disciples must imitate the Father's perfect love by reaching out to saint and sinner, to the marginal and rejected, even to one's enemies (Matt 5:43-48; 9:10-13); for such sharing incarnates a mutual forgiveness that allows one to claim God's own forgiveness even as it authenticates prayer (Matt 6:12). Among the followers of Jesus the haughty conduct of the princes of this world must also yield to a mutual service that imitates the simplicity of children (Matt 18:1-4; 19:13-14; 20:24-28).

Discipleship in Luke

Not only does Luke endorse the ethics of discipleship that Matthew and Mark inculcate, but he radicalizes it and insists on its eschatological significance. Luke's Jesus demands that his disciples renounce their possessions and distribute them to the poor. This act of self-divestment expresses faith in the Father's providential care and introduces one into the Father's kingdom. It also embodies hope in a God who rewards such compassion in the life to come (Luke 12:22-34; 16:9-13; 18:28-30). Luke's Jesus warns his disciples never to trust in wealth as the guarantee of life (Luke 12:15; 16:10-12). On the contrary, riches enslave the wealthy and exclude them from the kingdom. Great wealth prevents one from serving God (Luke 16:13; 18:18-27), while gross avarice with its concomitant indifference to the plight of the poor plunges one with the rich man of the parable into the fires of hell (Luke 16:19-31). Luke even hints that massive wealth engenders a cynicism that prevents belief in the resurrection (Luke 16:31).

The true followers of Jesus by contrast live poorly in imitation of their master (Luke 14:33; 10:57-58). The sharing born of faith in the Father demands more than almsgiving; it includes hospitality toward the poor and the outcast that will merit a special reward when the just rise from the dead (Luke 14:12-13, 21). A sharing born of unconditioned faith places no conditions on its willingness to share with others. It does so by excluding no one in principle and by imitating the impartiality of the Father's love that reaches out to the good and evil alike (Luke 6:32-36; 14:12-14). Finally, Luke's Jesus founds the kingdom of God, not on power politics, but on a worship of the Father whose sincerity is measured by mutual forgiveness (Luke 5:32; 6:35-37; 11:3; 17:4).

The Synoptic Vision of Discipleship

The Synoptic evangelists offer us, then, a consistent portrait of Jesus' understanding of the moral requirements for entry into the kingdom of his Father: a faith in the Father's providential care that frees one to share one's physical possessions with others, the willingness to share with not only on the basis of merit but also and especially on the basis of need; a mutual forgiveness that imitates the universality of God's own forgiving love and that authenticates worship; the willingness to welcome the sinner, the marginal, the outcast.

The Synoptic Gospels also promise that those who follow Jesus will also find themselves drawn inevitably into his passion. Those who crucified Jesus will also persecute and murder his followers (Mark 13:11-13; Luke 12:11-12; Matt 28:18-20). Prophetic confrontation with the principalities and powers of this world flows inevitably from consent to the kingdom, for the values it incarnates contradict the values incarnate in most human institutions. Those who live as children of God in Jesus' image must be willing as he did to denounce economic exploitation and political oppression. They must by implication stand willing like Jesus to flout discrimination, classism, and every other form of social fragmentation.

Echos of the Synoptic Vision

We find in several other documents of the New Testament clear echoes of the ethics of discipleship that the Synoptic evangelists place on the lips of Jesus. In the final section of the Letter to the Romans, for example, Paul the Apostle sketches for the Roman community the substance of his moral doctrine. His exhortation alternates between the enunciation of general principles of conduct and their application to specific pastoral problems. Having described the universal scope of Christian love, Paul addresses the more concrete question of how Christians ought to relate to pagan authorities (Rom 13:1-7). Similarly, having exhorted the Romans to mutual concern for one another in community, Paul discusses how to deal with scrupulous Christians (Rom 14:1-5). If, however, one ignores those parts of Paul's exhortation that deal with application of moral principles and concentrates instead on the ideals of Christian moral conduct that he presents, one will find that those ideals echo the kinds of conduct that Jesus in the Synoptics demands of his disciples.

Paul insists that those inspired by the Breath of Jesus must share in common not only the physical supports of life but her charismatic inspirations as well. They must share on the basis of need and not of merit only. Paul particularly commends the practice of open hospitality. Communal sharing must express mutual forgiveness in Christ. Christians should reach out even to their enemies, for their sharing seeks to unite those whom sin had formerly divided. The Christian community must care especially for the poor, whom they should welcome as friends and without any hint of condescension (Rom 12:9-21; 13:8-10).

The Letter to James speaks in similar terms. Christian assemblies must abhor social distinctions between rich and poor (Jas 2:1-4). Their faith must take concrete shape in good deeds, especially in their willingness to share the physical supports of life with others (Jas 2:14-16). They must banish from their midst the divisions born of slander and dissension and live instead reconciled in love (Jas 2:8-9). They must recognize that those who hoard their wealth draw down upon them the righteous judgment of God (Jas 4:12–5:6).

The Fourth Gospel shows less concern to detail the moral teachings of Jesus. Like the Synoptic evangelists John grounds Christian practice in faith. He demands that the followers of Jesus must offer to God a pneumatic worship in truth. They must trust the Father's providential care. They can expect to find themselves drawn into Jesus' passion (John 3:18, 21; 4:23; 6:29; 10:27-28; 15:26-27; 16:7-10, 23-24).

The Fourth Gospel was written, however, for a community in conflict with the synagogue and divided by an early form of docetism that denied the incarnation, the redemptive character of Jesus' death, and the reality of his presence in the Eucharist. These doctrinal concerns rather than the details of Jesus' moral teaching preoccupy the fourth evangelist. As a consequence, John simplifies the moral consequences of Christian discipleship to three fundamental maxims: believe that Jesus is God incarnate, love one another in his image, and find in his redemptive death on the cross the full expression of his love (John 13:15-16, 34-35; 15:9-17). The fourth evangelist also measures the authenticity of Christian worship by one's willingness to believe in Jesus' Eucharistic presence (John 6:48). In the Synoptic Gospels, as we have seen, mutual forgiveness authenticates Christian worship.

Nevertheless, the Johannine epistles provide some evidence that the community of the beloved disciple espoused and practiced the ethics of discipleship that the Synoptic tradition inculcated. The First Letter of John warns against worldly pomp and the pride that riches inspire (1 John 2:15-17). It insists that Christian love must express itself concretely in care for the needy (1 John 4:20-21). The Johannine community also valued the hospitable sharing of one's goods with others (3 John 5, 10).

Clearly, the Synoptic tradition provides us with a more detailed account of Jesus' moral teaching than does the Johannine. Moreover, the fact that that vision informed the conduct of Pauline, Palestinian, and Johannine Christians gives us sound reason for tracing this Christian code of conduct back to Jesus himself.[1] In other words, under the inspiration of God's Holy Breath, Jesus not only proclaimed the reign of God but also predicated entry into God's kingdom on one's willingness to submit to its moral demands in faith: an unconditioned trust in Papa's providence that frees one to share with others the physical supports of life on the basis of need and not of merit only. Such sharing expresses our willingness to forgive others as God has forgiven us. Mutual forgiveness, moreover, authenticates the worship of Papa that in turn grounds his reign among those who believe.

c. The Experience of Breath Baptism. All the evangelists tell us that the Breath of Christ comes to converts in order to conform them to Jesus, the founder and beginning of a new Israel; but only Luke describes the way in which this transformation of Jesus' disciples began. He depicts the arrival of the Holy Breath on Pentecost day as the fulfillment of the Baptizer's prophecy that a "mightier one" would

---

1. One would ground an argument that the ethics of discipleship which the New Testament proclaims derives from Jesus himself by invoking the principle of the "cross-section." One could also appeal to the principle of consistency. Cf. Edward Schillebeeckx, *Jesus: An Experiment in Christology*, translated by Hubert Hoskins (New York: Seabury, 1979) 95–96. The principle of the "cross-section" validates sayings and acts of Jesus which appear in divergent and independent New Testament traditions. The principle of consistency validates those sayings and actions of Jesus to which both historical research and exegesis mutually testify. This principle also appeals in a secondary way to the consistency between Jesus teachings and actions as a way of validating both.

appear who would baptize with a sanctifying Breath and with fire. At the close of the third gospel just before the glorified Jesus ascends into heaven, he tells his disciples to return to Jerusalem where he will bestow upon them the "promise" of his Father (Luke 24:49). The term "promise" refers to the Baptizer's prophecy that the Holy Breath's arrival on Pentecost will fulfill. The risen Christ speaks in similar terms to his disciples at the beginning of the Acts of the Apostles (Acts 1:4).

Pentecost

Luke describes the fulfillment of both Jesus' and the Father's promise in the second chapter of Acts. We all know the story. As the disciples gather presumably for prayer in the upper room, the sound of a rushing wind fills the house. Tongues "like fire" descend on them. They burst into glossolalic utterance, rush from concealment, and begin to proclaim the risen Christ with power to the startled pilgrims gathered in Jerusalem to celebrate the feast of Pentecost (Acts 2:1-4). The appearance of the gift of tongues under the sign of "tongues like fire" foreshadows not only the universal proclamation of the gospel in purification and judgment that the Acts of the Apostles narrates but also the outpouring of the other gifts of the Holy Breath upon the community of disciples: gifts of prophecy, teaching, healing, exorcism, witness, and leadership.

Luke, then, insists more explicitly than the other evangelists on the communal character of Breath baptism, even though one could tease a similar insight from Matthew's portrayal of the risen Christ commanding his disciples to go forth and baptize every creature in the triune name (Matt 28:19). The Pentecost narrative in Acts, however, makes it quite clear that the risen Christ baptizes in his Breath the community of disciples as a community and not as isolated individuals. The risen Christ thus creates a realm of saving grace that can welcome neophytes through the baptismal bath that communicates to them the experience of Breath baptism. In other words, for Luke once the Breath of Jesus has arrived, Breath baptism consists in sacramental incorporation into the community of the Breath baptized (Acts 2:38-41).

This basic Lukan insight finds a strong echo in the Apostle Paul's understanding of the action of the Breath of Jesus in the Christian community. Jesus sends the Holy Breath not to isolated individuals but to the community as a whole. Each member of the community participates to some degree in the one Breath, who creates and commissions the Church by empowering its shared life and public witness to Jesus (1 Cor 12:1–14:40).

Breath-baptism and Christian Conversion

Let us pause and ponder this complex truth and its implications: Breath baptism effects Christian conversion. It also creates the Christian community. Of its very nature, then, Christian conversion cannot occur in social isolation. If conversion happens at all, it must transpire within the community of the Breath baptized whose common faith creates a matrix of grace that invites and nurtures conversion. In this manner Christian conversion yields personal access to the same sanctifying Breath that descended on Jesus of Nazareth on the banks of the Jordan. Only he possesses the divine Breath personally in absolute fullness. The Christian convert shares only a measure of pneumatic life and enlightenment and grows in knowledge by openness to the Breath's activity in Jesus and in the other members of the Christian community.

The time has come to begin to relate these biblical insights to the construct of conversion that we developed in the preceding chapter. First, we need to examine in greater detail the specific ethical consequences that flow from the fact that for an adult convert, Christian conversion mediates between affective and moral conversion. As we shall see, in the experience of initial conversion, this first dynamic of Christian conversion grounds the experience of justifying faith. Second, our argument will explore the precise manner in which Christian conversion transvalues affective, intellectual, moral, and sociopolitical conversion and is in turn transformed by them. This second dynamic, as we shall see, grounds the experience both of ongoing conversion and of what an earlier theology called the "infusion" of sanctifying grace. More specifically, I shall argue that in transvaluing affective conversion, Christian conversion gives rise to the theological virtue of hope; that in transvaluing both affective and intellectual conversion Christian conversion gives raise to the theological virtue of faith; that in transvaluing personal moral conversion Christian conversion gives rise to the theological virtue of love; and that in transvaluing sociopolitical conversion Christian conversion gives rise to the Christian search for social justice. Let us reflect on each of these points in order.

2. The Dynamics of Christian Conversion. In the preceding chapter we saw that Christian conversion contributes two important dynamics to the total process of adult conversion. (1) It mediates between affective and moral conversion. This first dynamic affects both initial and ongoing conversion. Within an initial conversion it helps ground the experience of justification by faith. Within ongoing conversion it transforms judgments of natural prudence and other natural judgments of feeling into judgments of Christian discernment. (2) Christian conversion transvalues all the other forms of conversion. This second dynamic functions primarily within the experience of ongoing conversion, where it effects personal sanctification through the infusion of the theological virtues and the Christianization of the human search for a just social order. Let us, then, begin to explore some of the theological implications of these two important dynamics.

a. The Faith that Justifies. Two factors shaped Paul the Apostle's doctrine of justification by faith: his repudiation of the pharisaical piety in which he had been nurtured and his concern to vindicate the legitimacy of baptizing uncircumcised Gentiles. Paul discovered at the heart of pharisaical legalism an illegitimate demand for the "right to be glorified in God's sight" (Rom 3:27). In other words, pharisaism perverted love of the law into sinful self-righteousness. It misinterpreted the Law as the means of human self-justification before God instead of recognizing that God alone works fidelity to the divine will in those who believe.

Justification in Paul

Paul's encounter with the risen Christ had, moreover, convinced him that Jesus had risen from the dead in order to effect our justification (Rom 4:25). In rising, Jesus, the new Adam, became "a life-giving Breath" who enjoys both functional and vital identity with the Holy Breath of God. Because he sends the divine Breath into the community, wherever the Breath acts the risen Christ acts. In addition, however, the risen Lord and the Breath share an identity of divine life with the consequence that whoever shares in the Breath of Jesus already experiences union with God and possesses a present share in his risen life (1 Cor 15:45; 2 Cor 3:1-18).

Paul did not associate our justification by faith in Jesus Christ with a legal verdict of pardon or acquittal by God, for that would imply a corresponding legal right to justifying grace. Instead, Paul attributed justification to God's merciful condescension. In Christ God had willed to manifest his own justice and to justify anyone who puts faith in the crucified and risen Christ (Rom 3:26). Not only did Jesus' perfect obedience to the Father "even unto death" reveal Jesus' own justice in the sight of God, but it also merited justification and justice for sinful humanity.

In thus saving us God acts justly toward himself, for the deity yields to none the honor and glory that belong alone to God. At the same time he justifies sinners by the gift of the Spirit of the risen Lord who empowers them to live as the children of God in Jesus' image (Rom 4:25; 5:16-19; 8:14-17).

Faith binds us to the risen Lord by teaching us to recognize the savior whom God has sent. We know the risen Christ in the course of being assimilated to him in the power of his Breath, an assimilation that will culminate one day in our own resurrection (Rom 3:27–6:23). Because the power of the resurrection, the empowering enlightenment of the Breath of the risen Christ, effects our justification, it also reveals the Law's inability to justify us. The Law heightens our consciousness of sin; but because it remains an external norm of conduct rather than an inner, empowering presence, it lacks the capacity to effect our justification. Only the baptismal Breath communicated to us through faith in the risen Christ transforms the human heart in ways that conform it to the justice of God revealed in Jesus (Gal 3:1–4:31; Rom 2:1–3:20; 6:1–8:39).

Controversies Over Justification

Reformation controversies transformed justification by faith into a bone of contention between Protestants and Catholics. Protestants accused Catholics of lapsing into works righteousness for endorsing the medieval notion that graced acts merit eternal life in the sight of God. They denounced the abuse of selling indulgences as a sinful attempt to buy salvation. Moreover, their doctrine of justification by faith sought to calm the anguished consciences of Christians terrified by their inability to merit eternal salvation with the consoling assurance that trust in God's saving promises itself suffices to justify us.

The acrimony of Reformation debates often blinded both Catholics and Protestants to the areas of agreement and convergence in their respective positions. The Council of Trent, for example, reaffirmed the all-pervasive influence of original sin and taught that baptism remits both original sin and the punishment due to it. It taught that after baptism, however, concupiscence, which comes from sin and leads to sin, continues to afflict the baptized (DS 1510–1516). The latter doctrine has obvious affinities with Luther's insistence on the fact that one should regard the baptized Christian as *"simul justus et peccator"* (at the same time both justified and sinner).

Moreover, the decree on justification issued by the Council of Trent, in contrast to its later decrees, manifested an ecumenical openness that invited dialogue with Protestants. The council reaffirmed the unique saving role of Christ who grants grace "through the merits of his passion" to those reborn in him. Trent also taught that without rebirth no one experiences justification. The council denied absolutely that anything prior to justification, whether faith or works, in any way merits the grace of justification. God's righteousness justifies us by making us righteous.

In the case of the adult convert, Trent attributed the process leading to justification to the predisposing grace of Jesus Christ. Sinners achieve justification by cooperating with that grace. A merciful God effects justification by cleansing and purifying sinners. Jesus merits our justification by his passion and by atoning for our sins. Trent insisted on the primacy of faith in the process of justification. The council also taught that as faith cooperates with good works the work of justification advances (DS 1520–1583).

Trent's teaching on justification did indeed provide foundations for ecumenical dialogue on this vexed issue. Unfortunately, however, by the time the council convened, the time for dialogue had passed. Moreover, real issues did indeed divide Catholic and Protestant. Catholics resisted the initial tendency of Protestants to interpret justification as the forensic imputation of justice that fails to effect a real transformation of the believer. Catholics insisted instead that justification by faith effects a renovation of the human person. In addition, Catholic teaching rejected the deterministic denial of human freedom that it discovered in the Reformers' Augustinian interpretation of human depravity and of divine predestination.

Ecumenical dialogue between Catholics and Lutherans in the wake of Vatican II acknowledged that theological reflection on the question of justification had evolved in both Churches to the point where they could now identify broad areas of agreement uniting them in faith. Not only had Catholics come to acknowledge the legitimacy of many Protestant criticisms of medieval faith and practice, but Protestant theology had also mitigated its rhetoric of depravity and predestination in ways that accorded with Catholic teaching. Both Churches agreed that justification involves more than a legal fiction, for "God in justifying, effects what he promises; he forgives sin and makes us truly righteous."[2]

The First Dynamic of Christian Conversion

A theology of conversion seeks to probe the religious experiences that lie at the basis of sound doctrinal affirmations. Within an experience of initial, adult conversion, the first dynamic that Christian conversion contributes to the total process of conversion grounds an experience of justification by faith. Let us reflect on how this occurs.

A dynamic of conversion, as we have seen, defines the way in which different kinds of conversion mutually condition one another. When one form of conversion mediates between two others it causes them to condition one another in ways that they would not do so if left to themselves. How, then, does Christian conversion establish a new relationship between affective and moral conversion, and how does that relationship ground justification by faith?

Repentance

Adult Christian conversion begins with repentance; and repentance, while it requires the renunciation of sin, begins in the heart: in a confrontation with the disordered passions and attitudes that prevent one from consenting wholeheartedly and without reservation to God. As we have seen, affective conversion also requires confrontation with the dark side of oneself, with the snarl of both conscious and unconscious negative feelings like rage, fear, and guilt that prevent the free flow of the sympathetic emotions of affection and love. Repentance changes the context within which affective conversion occurs. In and of itself, affective conversion transpires naturally. It happens when the felt need to deal with emotional disorders forces itself upon the reluctant, conscious ego. Natural affective conversion abstracts from God's historical self-revelation. One, however, always repents before God. The Christian acknowledges sinful, disordered

2. For the Common Statement on Justification by Faith issued by Lutheran World Ministries and the Bishops' Committee for Ecumenical and Interreligious Affairs, see *Justification by Faith: Lutherans and Catholics in Dialogue VII,* edited by H. George Anderson, T. Austin Murphy, and Joseph A. Burgess (Minneapolis: Augsburg Publishing House, 1985) 15–74.

attitudes in confrontation with the God historically revealed in Jesus Christ. In other words, by demanding that sinful humans face their disordered hearts in confrontation with an incarnate God, Christian conversion transforms affective conversion into repentance.

One may, for example, quite apart from faith decide to face with professional help one's unconscious, debilitating, neurotic resentments. In that case, one converts affectively and naturally. One repents, however, when one recognizes that those same resentments prevent one from trusting God and when one seeks from God the healing that leads to faith.

The God who summons us to repentance and to faith in Jesus Christ reaches out to us in our sinfulness and need: despite the collective burden of institutionalized sin that perverts our own hearts, minds, and consciences, despite our own contribution to the shared misery of humanity through personal sin. As a consequence, we experience both the summons to repentance and faith itself as a pure gift. We experience the summons to repentance as a grace because standing under God's merciful judgment creates for us the possibility of transcending our own sinfulness in faith. As we advance in the life of faith, we grow beyond our sinful past into a future whose possibilities God creates as we collaborate in response to his graced initiatives in our lives. Through Christian conversion God becomes the future that reaches out to us more eagerly than we respond.

The Slavery of Sin

Sin enslaves us to habitual patterns of death-dealing behavior. Vice kills life in us and in others. Sin, however, never totally eliminates elementary human freedom, the ability to distinguish naturally and opt between realistic alternatives for choice. Nor does sin totally obliterate the human capacity for natural conversion, whether affective, intellectual, moral, or sociopolitical, even though unrepented sin suffuses all forms of natural conversion with a debilitating inauthenticity that threatens to subvert them. By bringing sinful disorders to healing in faith, not only does initial Christian conversion create the possibility of a new kind of human freedom, one both rooted in the saving and healing action of the Breath of Christ and oriented toward the future that God would create for us; but by inaugurating the healing of the inauthenticities with which sin corrupts natural conversion, Christian repentance and conversion enhance the responsible freedom that natural conversion effects.

Repentance as Liberation

Left to ourselves, we can never transcend the historical burden of sin that oppresses us. Sinners dissent from God and from one another. Institutional sin and the personal sins of others stand within experience and shape us subtly, more or less consciously, but nonetheless effectively. The victory over sin requires more than the reversal of our own individual sinful decisions. Our sin flows out of a history of human sin and oppression whose sheer massiveness overwhelms us. The removal of that cosmic burden requires a worldwide reversal of dissent in an atoning and redemptive love that only a world-transcending God can effect with merciful condescension.

Repentance heals the heart of sinful emotional disorders. The healing of negative emotions frees the sympathetic affections and in the process enhances the heart's sensitivity to beauty. We experience beauty when we grasp in a single, simultaneously intuitive insight both truth and goodness. The repentant heart touched by the Breath of Jesus perceives the divine beauty incarnate in him and in people whose lives of faith resemble his. That beauty, its simultaneous reality, truth, and goodness, lures the heart spontaneously with the promise of healing and of new freedom in God.

We grasp truth both intuitively and logically. We grasp the good with our consciences, which grapple with issues of personal and public morality. As a consequence, initial personal consent in faith to the beauty of God incarnate in Jesus, to divine truth and goodness simultaneously perceived, engages the consenting convert totally. It opens every aspect of human experience to the saving action of divine grace. It opens the intuitive mind to divine beauty, the intuitive and rational mind to divine truth, and the personal and public conscience to divine goodness.

Moreover, as we have just seen in the first part of this chapter, consent to Jesus as the normative, human embodiment of God brings with it specific moral consequences. It commits one to living as a child of God in Jesus' image. It therefore commits one to the ethics of faith that he proclaimed and lived. In other words, the initial consent of faith transforms one into a disciple of Jesus committed to his vision of the kingdom, concerned to submit to its moral demands in all one's personal decisions, and committed to laboring as the instrument of God in transforming human society according to the moral demands of life in God's kingdom. Since the Breath of the risen Christ effects justifying faith by an empowering enlightenment, that faith terminates ultimately at the one who sends the divine Breath, the Christ whom the Father has raised to his right hand. As a consequence, the consent of justifying faith encompasses not only commitment to the kingdom of God but consent in eschatological hope to the paschal mystery.

Justification and Discipleship

Through the faith that justifies, therefore, Christians find God's will normatively revealed in Jesus and in the morality of discipleship that he lived and proclaimed. His religious vision fulfills the Law and the Prophets by demanding more, not less, than they did, by holding up to humanity the ideal of a human community reconciled in God and through God, a vision that lures us by its beauty even as it stands in judgment on finite human moral perceptions and on every human social arrangement. The initial act of faith justifies us when we acknowledge that Jesus' religious vision claims us and the whole of humanity unconditionally and totally. It claims us because the one who proclaimed it stands eschatologically revealed in his risen glory as Lord, as God incarnate.

The initial consent of justifying faith does not effect the instantaneous transformation of all the habits of sin and disorder that past decisions have built into our personality and into our world. We shall reflect in greater detail on this point when we examine the experiences of original sin and of concupiscence. The initial consent of faith does, however, begin the process of our personal transformation in the Breath of Christ, who teaches us to put on his mind, his attitudes, his conscience. In this sense, the first dynamic of conversion inevitably demands the second, the transvaluation in faith of all one's natural and sinful tendencies, including those that result from genuine natural conversions.

Before we pass, however, to consider the second dynamic that Christian conversion contributes to the total process of conversion, we should note that besides mediating between affective and moral conversion within an experience of initial conversion in the ways we have just described, the first dynamic of Christian conversion also contributes to the process of ongoing conversion. It does so by ensuring that every subsequent responsible decision that a convert makes submit to the moral demands of discipleship. It therefore provides norms derived from faith, both from Jesus' ministry and teaching and from the paschal mystery, for the ongoing transvaluation of the other forms of conversion. Moreover, Christian conversion demands that every subsequent responsible decision submit to the divine Breath's leading, that it express more than natural prudence, that it embody a prayerful discernment of the will of God.

If the first dynamic of Christian conversion grounds the initial convert's experience of justifying faith, the second dynamic mediates the infusion of sanctifying grace. Let us, then, begin to reflect on how this occurs.

b. Sanctifying Grace. Over the centuries Christian theologians have developed a traditional language for talking about the graced transformation of converts. Let us try to understand this language for the light that it throws upon the experience of Christian sanctification.

The Meaning of Divine Grace

The term "grace" designates the free and gratuitous self-gift of God to those who believe in him. It implies the generous benevolence of God in communicating himself to his creatures, the shared awareness of the gift that unites divine giver and human receiver, and the transforming consequence of God's gift, consequences that suffuse human experience with divine beauty.

The grace of God reveals his graciousness: his compassion in the face of human suffering and misery, his fidelity to his promises, his inexhaustible and loving justice, his love, his desire to enter into communion with his creatures. God blesses those whom he graces by uniting himself to them in a creative, life-giving bond that requires of the graced creature an absolute and unconditioned response of love.

The incarnation of the Son of God and the outpouring of his Breath on all flesh reveals to us the fullness of divine grace. The incarnation effects the most intimate union between the divine and the human that God ever effected. By his sinless obedience even unto death on a cross, God's incarnate Son responded to the Father's commissioning will and to the Holy Breath's illumination with that absoluteness that the perfect self-communication of God requires. His resurrection embodies the fullness of graced transformation in God and mediates the charismatic outpouring of the Breath of God on all flesh. The divine Breath's coming creates a realm of grace, the Church, in which gracious transformation in the image of Jesus transpires.

God gives grace, gives himself, to a sinful humanity. He therefore gives gratuitously, freely. Even were we sinless, we could not merit such a gift. Far less can we merit it in our sinfulness. Because he graces us freely, God in Christ chooses, or elects, those whom he desires to gift. Ultimately, that divine election embraces all humanity.

Over the centuries theologians have grappled with the simplicity and complexity of God's free self-gift to his creatures. They distinguish uncreated from created grace. The term "uncreated grace" designates God himself, the divine reality that the gift of grace communicates. The term "created grace" designates the difference that the free self-communication of God makes in the lives of his creatures.

Created grace elevates, heals, and perfects its human recipient. Created grace elevates because it enables us to relate to God in ways we never could, if left to our own power. It heals because it undoes the consequences of sin in our lives. It perfects because in becoming Godlike we also become more perfectly and fully human.

The Forms of Created Grace

Traditionally theologians have distinguished different kinds of created grace on the basis of the kind of change that the action of God makes in those who accept his revelatory self-gift. The term "actual grace" designates a concrete invitation to respond to God in some particular circumstance: for example, an impulse to prayer, to some act of compassion, to pronounce a prophetic word. "Habitual grace," by contrast, designates a generalized tendency to respond to God that previous responses to actual graces have built into one's character. Actual grace creates habitual grace because when we respond to a concrete intervention of God, that response builds into our personalities a generalized tendency to say yes to grace, a tendency that subsequent acts of faith will reinforce and deepen. By the same token, as we grow in habitual grace, we respond to actual grace with greater ease.

Besides actual and habitual grace, theologians have also traditionally distinguished between operative grace and cooperative grace and between sanctifying grace and gratuitous grace. To what experiences do these distinctions refer?

The term "operative grace" designates the gracious action of God who intervenes in our lives with a sovereign and loving initiative. The term "co-operative grace" designates our human collaboration with that divine initiative.

The distinction between sanctifying grace (*gratia gratum faciens*) and gratuitous, or common, grace (*gratia gratis data*) roots itself in the thirteenth chapter of the First Letter to the Corinthians, where the Apostle Paul distinguishes two ways in which the Breath of Jesus transforms those who believe. He describes God's Breath as inspiring the faith, hope, and love of Christians, on the one hand, and their mutual ministry to one another in community, on the other.

The Pauline Charisms

Paul looked upon such ministry as charismatically inspired. By the term "charism" Paul meant some concrete manifestation of the Breath's saving action in the community. Paul included among the charisms gifts of teaching, leadership, healing, miracles, prophecy, discernment, faith, tongues, the interpretation of tongues, helping, administration, almsgiving, works of mercy, and apostolic ministry (1 Cor 12:8-10, 28-31; Rom 12:6-8; Eph 4:9); but he clearly regarded the hope, faith, and love that the Breath inspires in every believer as a more fundamental manifestation of her presence and saving action, at least in this sense, that concrete acts of charismatic service that fail to incarnate hope, faith, and especially love lose their power to unite us to God in a saving relationship.

This Pauline insight led subsequent Christian theologians to distinguish between a created grace, which sanctifies the believer and gratuitous, or common, grace, which inspires human acts that benefit others without necessarily sanctifying the one who performs them. For example, theologians argued that one could not grow in hope, faith, or love without growing in holiness. One could, however, exercise a charismatic ministry of teaching that benefits the Christian community but do so from egotistical motives. In that case, one's teaching benefited others but failed to advance one's own sanctity. As we shall see, sometimes theologians have overdrawn this distinction; for concrete acts of service inspired by the Breath of Jesus do sanctify those who perform them in hope, faith, and love. Moreover, the charismatic act itself, and not just the hope, faith, and love that motivates it, sanctifies.

Sanctifying Grace

How then does grace sanctify us? Persons and things become holy when God sets them apart for his service. God sanctifies things either by claiming them directly through some action or by sanctioning an act that claims them for him. We call Israel "the Holy Land" because of the saving acts God has performed there. We regard Lourdes and similar pilgrimage centers as holy places because of the divine miracles wrought there. We look on pictures and medals as sacred objects when someone who speaks for God has set them aside in a special way for his service.

When God sanctifies persons, he also claims them for himself and for his service. Personal sanctification, however, involves a more complex process of transformation than the blessing of a holy card or picture. God sanctifies persons by transforming them in the image of his incarnate Son through the inspiration of his Holy Breath. By so transforming them God claims them for his own and sets them apart from others for his service.

Sanctification and Transvaluation

That transformation engages especially the second dynamic of Christian conversion: namely, the transvaluation of the other kinds of conversion. The first dynamic begins the process of transvaluation by changing affective conversion into repentance and by informing the natural conscience and every subsequent responsible decision that a convert makes with norms and values derived from faith. As we have just seen, justifying faith together with the first dynamic of conversion that grounds it begins one's transformation as a faithful disciple of Jesus. Discipleship, however, demands obedience to the moral vision that Jesus lived and proclaimed. Faith therefore commits one to living in Jesus' image in the hope of one day sharing in his resurrection. It commits one to putting on his "mind": his attitudes, hopes, beliefs, values, commitments. Jesus' human mind developed in response to the anointing of the Holy Breath. As her inspirations conform Jesus' disciples to him, she draws them into Jesus' own *Abba* experience.

The first dynamic of Christian conversion leads, then, with moral inevitability to the second. Because conversion claims the convert totally, it demands the reevaluation, the transvaluation in faith, of all the values that motivate personal choice, whether affective, intellectual, or moral. We transvalue sensations, emotions, images, intuitions, abstract concepts, or inferences when, having employed them in one frame of reference, we transfer them to another that endows them with new connotations. For example, once Columbus had proved that the earth we walk on has a round and not a flat shape, the term "earth" continued to mean the hard surface of the planet on which we walk; but after the discovery of America the term "earth" took on new connotations in the minds of Europeans, connotations that the first explorers of the New World set out to investigate.

Faith in Jesus Christ creates just such a frame of reference. Without faith we see reality more or less as it exists: beautiful, nurturing, violent, destructive. Once, however, we recognize that this same world stands in a redemptive relationship with an incarnate God who seeks to recreate it in atoning love, we begin to see nature, human society, ourselves, the entire cosmos with new eyes.

We need to examine four specific ways in which faith transvalues natural and sinful human experiences. Christian hope springs from the graced transvaluation of our affective perceptions of the future. Christian faith results from the graced transvaluation of our intuitive and rational perceptions of reality. The graced transvaluation of the human conscience gives rise to Christian love. The graced transvaluation of ethical concern for institutional reform motivates the Christian search for social justice. Let us begin to examine each of these processes of transvaluation in greater detail.

b. Christian Hope. Christian hope transforms natural and sinful human hopes. It heals, elevates, and perfects them. In order therefore to understand the growth of Christian hope, one needs to understand both how human hope develops naturally, in abstraction from the action of divine grace, and how sin mars its growth. We also need to distinguish personal hopes from shared hopes. Personal hopes express individual aspirations; shared hopes express the aspirations of some community.

1) NATURAL AND SINFUL HOPES. An examination of the dynamic structure of human experience shows that we perceive reality in two ways: intuitively and rationally. Intuitive perceptions develop spontaneously and imaginatively, not rationally and logically. We associate intuitive perceptions with the heart rather than with the head. We express them in artistic lyrics, in stories, and in prudential judgments. Rational perceptions, by contrast, obey the laws of logic. We express them in validated hypotheses. When we focus our intuitive perceptions on the future, we experience hope. (When, by contrast, we focus our rational perceptions on the future, we engage in deductive reasoning.)

Hope and Intuition

Our natural hopes root themselves in our biological and personal histories. We hope to avoid painful experiences that either we ourselves or our acquaintances have endured. We hope to enjoy things that have delighted us before or joys that we can imagine or have heard described.

Our natural hopes express judgments of feeling we choose to endorse. Our feelings pass judgment on the potentially beneficial or noxious character of the people and things that fill our worlds. Judgments of fear tell us that we cannot cope with some threat. Judgments of anger tell us that we can. Prudential judgments express our felt sense of complex situations. Judgments of guilt or complacency determine our sense of ourselves. Aesthetic judgments shape our creative attempts to communicate our intuitive perceptions to others.

Because natural hopes express felt judgments, they either conform to reality or do not. Each time we hope, we prefer one possible future over another. True hopes anticipate an actual future. False hopes dream of impossibilities. We can usually explain rationally why some hopes prove true and others false. Such explanations can even nurture hope, but the hope itself springs finally from the affections rather than from their subsequent rationalization. When we hope we aspire to a future. Passionate aspirations differ from dispassionate predictions.

We must also distinguish healthy from unhealthy hopes, inflated from deflated hopes, selfish from unselfish hopes, and liberating from oppressive hopes. Healthy hopes spring from a balanced, integrated affectivity; sick hopes express neurotic and psychotic impulses and can mask deep-seated despair. Inflated hopes spring from a psyche whose conscious ego has lost touch with its own limitations and potentially destructive subconscious tendencies. Deflated hopes spring from defeat, disappointment, suffering. Self-centered hopes motivate egocentric behavior, whether legitimate or irresponsible; selfless hopes breed altruism and concern for others. Oppressive hopes manipulate persons and situations to one's private advantage regardless of the pain and misery they bring to others; liberating hopes create situations that foster life at the same time that they express and nurture integral conversion in others.

Situations of oppression and the repression of negative affections conspire to stifle hope. Oppression angers the oppressed but violently forbids them either the expression of that rage or escape from the tormenting situation. Some suffer oppression mutely, patiently, or with stoic fatalism; but as rage accumulates, others either explode in acts of violence or turn their anger inward as they descend into the maelstrom of psychic disorder, despair, and suicide.

Stages of Natural Hope

As humans advance through life, natural hope faces predictable challenges. Humans begin to hope when as infants they learn to trust their parents. Between the ages of two and three, young children struggle with feelings of shame and doubt. Between four and six they learn the meaning of guilt. The school-age child needs to transcend feelings of inferiority. The adolescent needs to create a personal adult identity. Young adults need intimacy and fear loneliness, isolation. The mature adult needs to find satisfaction and avoid stagnation through nurturing life in others. In their declining years humans struggle to preserve a sense of personal integrity against the temptation to despair.[3]

Personal hopes express an individual's sense of identity. What individuals hope for discloses their character and temperament, their sense of their own person and potential. Shared hopes express a group or community's sense of its identity and potential as a community. Groups come to a sense of identity through complex processes of interpretation: by understanding the events that brought the group into existence and the history that links those events to the present. Communities achieve self-understanding and self-definition by myths that create the world in which they live, by sharing stories of its past, by rituals and customs that express its history and self-perception, and by the scholarly retrieval of its past. A shared sense of identity creates the possibility of reaching communal consensus about the future to which a community ought to aspire collectively.

Shared hopes, like personal hopes, can evolve naturally. When they do so, they display all the limitations of personal human hopes. They can prove true or false, healthy or sick, inflated or deflated, selfish or altruistic, liberating or oppressive. Selfish and oppressive hopes

3. The reader will, of course, recognize in this paragraph Erik Erikson's stages of emotional development. If one locates hope in affective perceptions of the future, then Erikson's stages depict predictable crises in the natural development of human hope. In this context it helps to note that the challenges of the earlier stages persist in the later ones. One must in Erikson's scheme sufficiently surmount the challenge of one stage in order to advance to the next. Nevertheless, the mature adult still struggles with moments of distrust, shame, inferiority, and fractured identity.

indicate an irresponsible absence of conversion, which, when culti-vated in contradiction to the known will of God, transforms irrespon-sibility into sin.

2) GRACED HOPE. Christian hope elevates, heals, and perfects natural and sinful hopes. All hopes root themselves in some reality. Natural hopes rely on personal prowess and on the availability of the means to realize one's aspirations. Christian hope roots itself in Jesus Christ and in his empowering Breath. Christians hope for personal and collective transformation in the Breath and image of Jesus and for the recreation of the world in the power of the risen Christ. Let us begin to reflect on the implications of these specific Christian hopes.

Sharing Jesus' Hopes: The Our Father

The petitions of the Our Father give us a sound insight into the hopes that the historical Jesus had for his disciples. He hoped for the day when all could share his reverence for the Father, when all would obey the Father's will and submit to his reign. He hoped that all might trust in the Father's providential care, that all might escape divine judgment, and that all would know deliverance from the power of Satan.

Those who pray the Our Father share in Jesus' own hopes for them. In embracing the kingdom, they hope that the Breath of God will teach them to live the ethics of discipleship that Jesus lived and proclaimed. They hope for healing from enslavement to material pos-sessions and for a growing freedom to share the physical supports of life with others, especially with those in greatest need. They hope to grow in a capacity to forgive others. They hope to grow in union with God in prayer. They hope for the strength to enter into Jesus' atoning passion and death. They hope to share in his resurrection.

The Effects of Christian Hope

Christians hope for these things not just individually but col-lectively. Indeed, the shared hope of the Church engenders Chris-tian hope in individual believers and neophytes. Moreover, authentic Christian hope reflects the missionary zeal and universal scope of Jesus' own aspirations. Christians hope for the day when not just the Church but the entire human race will experience graced transformation in the image of Jesus. They hope for one another, for the common good of the Church and of human society in general.

The content of Christian hope derives in part from the ministry of Jesus and from his vision of the kingdom, in part from his resurrection. Christians hope for the day when all will acknowledge the Lordship of Jesus that his resurrection reveals. Because they hope for complete transformation in his image, they hope that the same divine power that raised him from the dead will one day raise them up as well. They hope therefore for the re-creation of their mortal bodies and of the world in which they live in the power of the risen Christ.

Christian hope lives stretched, then, between this world and the next. It anchors the heart simultaneously in both. Christians hope for risen glory because in sharing the Breath of Christ they already possess his risen life. They yearn for the new creation even as they labor to embody Jesus' vision of the kingdom here on earth, for they regard moral transformation in Jesus' image as the indispensible condition for sharing his glory. Indeed, as the Gospel of Luke insists, ministering to the needs of those who cannot repay one in this life gives concrete shape to Christian hope (Luke 12:33-34; 16:9; 18:28-30). Christians rely on the salvation already and definitively accomplished in Jesus even as they yearn for complete union with the triune God who has become their future through faith.

Christian hope *elevates* natural human hopes by focusing them on the triune God. Christian hope therefore transcends human history and its limited possibilities. It transcends creation as a whole, for its fulfillment rests finally on the absolutely certain fidelity of God and on his omnipotence. As a consequence, while Christian hope engages human feeling, it expresses much more than natural human intuitions or natural judgments of feeling; for it expresses the saving will of God. What Christians hope for, then, will certainly happen; for God, who has promised it, will do it.

Christian hope also *heals* naturally distorted and sinful hopes. Christian hope teaches the disciples of Jesus to seek emotional healing not just from created remedies but also and ultimately from God. It heals unhealthy hopes, inflated hopes, deflated hopes, selfish hopes, and oppressive hopes through repentance and the dark night of sense. The term "dark night of sense" derives from the writings of St. John of the Cross. It refers to the healing in faith of disordered human affections. During the dark night one faces one's own demons in a process of ongoing purification; but as healing advances the night of fear and struggle turns into the night when two lovers, God and the God-seeker, meet. Repentance creates the possibility of healing twisted human hopes by raising their distortions to consciousness and by opening the heart to the healing power of God. The dark night of sense prolongs the fruits of initial repentance through the process of ongoing conversion.

Unhealthy hopes spring from repressed rage, fear, and guilt and produce bondage, affective paralysis, deeds of violence and self-destruction. Inflated hopes produce either self-idolatry or ruthless exploitative behavior. Deflated hopes express cynicism or despair. Oppressive hopes distort the oppressor sinfully and stifle hope in others. All of these impulses contradict the fundamental thrust of Christian hope because they contradict the mind of Jesus and his vision of the way God's children ought to live. That vision demands, then, that distorted and sinful hope be brought to healing through transvaluation in faith.

Finally, Christian hope *perfects* natural human hopes. Natural hope reflects the limitations of the human psyche: limitations of biology, history, race, sex, class, region, and nation. As humans learn to see the world with the eyes of others, they learn to mitigate the spontaneous egocentrism of natural hopes but rarely transcend it altogether. Christian hope teaches the human heart to share God's own hopes for each person and for the world. As we grow in sanctification, the saving divine wisdom incarnate in Jesus teaches us to put aside the pettiness of our own egos and to embrace the world with God's own selfless, atoning love. Christian hope teaches us to transcend the limits of history, race, sex, class, and nation, and by universalizing our natural hopes, renders them more truly human and humane.

The Healing Power of Christian Hope

Christian hope also simultaneously perfects and heals human hope in yet another way. Natural hopes often reflect the limitations of the human ego that engenders them. Jungian psychology suggests that, as the human ego matures, it acquires a fundamental attitude toward reality. Introverts focus on the problem of meaning and display an increasing fascination with their own psychic processes. They need leisure to respond to the abrupt intrusions of the world. Extroverts, by contrast, develop fascination for the persons and things around them and figure out their responses in the process of interacting with others; but they run the risk of losing themselves in the demands of other persons and events.

The hopes of the inflated introvert flow from a rebounding imagination. The imagination rebounds from reality when it equates the real with human interiority. The inflated introverted ego as a consequence fallaciously hopes to find ultimate reality within its own psyche. Platonism gives classical philosophical expression to this kind of imagination. Withdraw from the external world, it counsels, retire within yourself, and there discover the real, the true, the good. The hopes of inflated extroverts by contrast flow from an exploitative imagination. Opaque to their own ultimate motives, inflated extraverts tend to use others more or less ruthlessly for their own purposes.

Deflated introverts face the specter of despair; unable to find meaning in the world around them, their personal, psychic fragmentation prevents them from finding it within themselves either. The hopes of the deflated extrovert tend, on the other hand, to reduce reality to ultimately meaningless facts.[4]

Christian hope perfects natural human hopes by teaching the human imagination to transcend the biases of the natural human ego. It does so by sacramentalizing the human imagination. By a sacrament in the broadest sense of the term I mean an event that both reveals and conceals the presence of God. All events of divine grace qualify as sacramental events. When faith transforms human experience, the very process of transformation reveals the divine reality in which it occurs and the vectors that structure the divine experience. Since, however, finite human experience differs finally from the all-encompassing reality of God, its gracing fails finally to reveal God totally.

Christian hope teaches the imagination to perceive sacramental events and to respond to them affectively and intuitively. It thus teaches the rebounding imagination to look for ultimate realities in concrete sensible things and not just in the labyrinthine corridors of the human psyche. It teaches the exploitative imagination to reverence both persons and things for their capacity to reveal the divine and not to use them ruthlessly for personal ends. Christian hope teaches the deflated introvert to find ultimate meaning in God and thus to transcend despair. It teaches the deflated extrovert that concrete sensible facts not only enjoy significance but even ultimate sig-

---

4. For a further discussion of these insights into the dynamic structure of the human imagination, see William Lynch, S. J., *Christ and Apollo* (New York: Mentor, 1960) and Donald L. Gelpi, S. J., *Experiencing God: A Theology of Human Emergence* (New York: Paulist, 1978).

nificance. In all these ways Christian hope perfects natural human hope.

Moreover, as Christian hope elevates, heals, and perfects natural human hopes by transvaluing them according to the mind of Christ, they in turn enliven and animate the Christian enterprise with contagious zest and enthusiasm.

c. Christian Faith. As Christian conversion transvalues affective and inferential judgments about the nature of reality, it infuses into the human mind the theological virtue of faith. In the preceding chapter we distinguished three different senses of the term "faith." In reflecting on the faith that justifies, we invoked the first and broadest meaning of faith: a commitment to divine beauty incarnate that opens the entire person to the saving reality of God. In the present discussion the term "faith" corresponds to its second meaning. In its second sense, faith contrasts with the other two theological virtues of hope and love. Viewed as a theological virtue, faith engages the ongoing fixation of religious beliefs through active participation in a community of faith whose members seek personal and shared self-understanding. As we have seen, human beliefs express both judgments of feeling and rational inference about the nature of reality.

1) NATURAL, VICIOUS, SINFUL, AND GRACED BELIEFS. Natural beliefs about reality express both intuitive judgments of feeling and validated rational inferences reached in abstraction from God's historical self-revelation in Jesus and in his Holy Breath. We formulate intuitive beliefs in stories, lyrics, myths, ritual, and works of art. We express inferential beliefs in scholarly and scientific reflection on ourselves and on the world in which we live. We believe something when we stand committed to accept the consequences of what we assert about reality.

Vicious beliefs rationalize irresponsible behavior. They express perceptions of reality distorted by passions like greed, lust, pride, hatred, sloth, gluttony, and envy, passions that prevent us from relating to other persons as persons and that betray us into using them manipulatively for selfish ends.

Sinful beliefs contradict the historical self-revelation of God in Jesus and in his Breath.

Faith and Belief

The theological virtue of faith transforms natural beliefs by transvaluing both intuitive and inferential judgments about the nature of reality in the light of divine revelation. Christian faith demands that we perceive all created reality in God. Christian faith never replaces scientific and scholarly investigations into the human person and the nature of the cosmos. Such investigations advance with their own autonomy and in accord with their own methods. Indeed, Christian reflection on the meaning of divine revelation needs to keep pace with new developments in science, scholarship, literature, and the arts and when necessary to revise its perceptions of created reality in the light of important artistic, scholarly, and scientific breakthroughs. Christian faith demands, however, that religious beliefs about God conform to the historical revelation of God made visible in the Word incarnate; for the incarnation of God provides us with definitive empirical evidence concerning both the reality of God and the deity's saving intentions in our regard. In demanding that we understand all created reality in the light of divine revelation, the theological virtue of faith elevates natural beliefs to the transcendent reality of a self-revealing God. Christian faith also corrects and perfects religious beliefs derived from mere rational reflection of created realities by measuring them in the light of God's own word to us about himself.

Christian faith also heals vicious and sinful beliefs. Repentance demands that converts renounce the vicious passions that distort their perceptions of human relationships. It corrects human misconceptions about God and demands that all religious beliefs conform to both the historical and practical demands of divine revelation.

In a sense the theological virtue of faith transcends any particular formulation of Christian belief just as the other habits of the human mind transcend the particular propositions they generate in their search for a satisfactory account of reality. Christian faith, however, transcends particular creedal affirmations in yet another way, because it terminates, not at them, but at the ultimately mysterious and all-encompassing reality of God itself. No finite mind, however devout, can comprehend or express adequately that reality in propositions, whether intuitive or inferential. The critical believer therefore approaches God humbly, by the path of analogy, acknowledging that God both resembles and differs from his creation and from any propositional affirmation we make of him.

Faith and Analogy

The sacramental character of the revelation we have received also demands that we approach the triune God by way of analogy.

An event, as we have just seen, takes on a sacramental character when it both reveals and conceals the reality of God. The incarnation of the divine Word provides a perfect example of a sacramental event. When we contact the Word of God through his humanity, we contact a divine person. The humanity of Jesus discloses his divinity; but, to the extent that it remains finite and human, Jesus' humanity fails to reveal to us the full reality of the Son of God or of the Godhead as a whole. Because the incarnation both reveals and conceals God, it qualifies as a sacramental event. It yields a definitive and normative insight into God's triune life and saving intentions toward us, but it by no means yields an exhaustive account of the divine experience. In speaking of the events of Christian revelation, we must, then, in order to understand them aright, grasp both the way in which they reveal God to us and the way in which they fail to do so. We must in other words acknowledge that they give us only a limited and analogous insight into the transcendent reality of God.

Even though the full reality of God will always transcend the propositional affirmations we make about it, nevertheless religious beliefs have importance because they define the quality of the faith of both individuals and communities. Faulty or misleading formulations of Christian belief place obstacles between us and the revealed reality of God instead of orienting us toward it. Creedal affirmations can, then, either foster or thwart religious growth.

2) CHRISTIAN CREEDS. As in the case of Christian hope, the shared faith of Christians measures the faith of individual believers, for it provides the matrix of grace that nurtures individual faith to maturity. The shared faith of Christians expresses itself most fundamentally in the way they live and pray, but it also finds classic formulation in Christian creeds. Typically, Christian creeds express a Trinitarian, incarnational, narrative faith.

The incarnation and mission of the divine Word and the Pentecostal mission of the Holy Breath together reveal the Trinity. The Son and Breath enter history as divine persons sent to save us. Their distinct historical missions reveal their difference from the Father and from one another. The Son whom the Father sends stands in an interpersonal relationship with the one who sends him. Both the Father and his risen, glorified Son send the Holy Breath to create the Church. She, being divine and coequal with the Father and the Son, enjoys like them personal existence. Moreover, all three stand historically revealed as possessing an identity of divine life that they impart to those who believe in them. The Son's perfect obedience to the Father who sends him and to the Breath who illumines him reveals the total mutual self-donation in love that unites the divine persons in perfect identity of life.

If the incarnation and Pentecost together reveal the Trinity, the Trinity contextualizes both revelatory events. Since the third century, Christian theology has tended to focus somewhat narrowly on the second person of the Trinity; but the Trinity, rather than the incarnation, ranks as the fundamental Christian mystery, the mystery of God in his transcendence. Trinitarian faith, therefore, provides the ultimate theological context for understanding the incarnation and the mystery of Church that the divine Breath creates, not vice versa.

Typically Christian creeds begin by equating the God who created all things with the Father of our Lord Jesus Christ. All three divine persons act simultaneously in their dealing with their creatures; and all three acted simultaneously in the creation of the world. Nevertheless, we attribute creation in a special way to the Father because within the Godhead itself he functions as the aboriginal efficacious source of the other two divine persons and therefore as the divine source of all creative efficacy. The Son, on the other hand, through his perfect obedience to the Father's missioning will and to the Breath's inspirations stands historically revealed as the one through whom the Father and Breath act. Christian creeds, therefore, also assert that the Father creates and saves the world through the Son.

Having professed faith in the Father creator, Christian creeds then typically narrate the principal events in the life, death, and resurrection of Jesus. The narrative character of Christian faith roots it in history: in the history of God's people, in the story of Jesus, and in the saga of the Church.

The narrative character of Christian faith also ensures that faith like hope derives its content both from the ministry of Jesus, on the one hand, and from his resurrection and sending of the divine Breath, on the other. Because it roots itself in Jesus' ministry, his vision of the kingdom of God supplies Christian faith with some of its most fundamental tenets. That same vision makes faith practical. It demands that Christians believe in God and not merely that God exists. We believe in God when we affirm his providential care of us, a care that frees us to share with others the material supports of life as well as the fruits and graces of the Holy Breath. We believe in God when we allow the Breath to teach us by the charisms how to serve others in the name and image of Jesus, how to build up and reform the Church, and how to proclaim the good news to every creature. We believe in God when we act toward others with the same love, forgiveness, and compassion that God has revealed to us in Jesus. In a word, as Christians we believe *in* God when we allow his Holy Breath to teach us personally and collectively to put on the mind of Christ. We therefore believe *in* God only when we value orthopraxis as much a orthodoxy.

Ultimately, the paschal mystery reveals the divine reality in which Christians believe. The risen Christ confronts the believer as Lord and God. Jesus' resurrection also reveals the destiny of all those who believe in him. Like him they shall one day rise in glory. By revealing the incarnation, the resurrection therefore gives decisive shape to Christian Trinitarian faith and to Christian beliefs about the afterlife.

Faith in the paschal mystery also demands orthopraxis of the believer. The risen Christ confronts those who believe in him as "a life-giving Breath" (1 Cor 15:45), as Breath-baptizer, as the efficacious obediential source of gracious illumination. One cannot, as a consequence, believe in the paschal mystery without believing in the Holy Breath. Belief in the Holy Breath includes belief in the Breath's saving action: in the forgiveness of sins, in the communion of all the saints that the Holy Breath effects, in mutual charismatic service, in every form of graced enlightenment, in the promise of future glory with Christ.

The narrative character of Christian faith flows from the fact that it derives its content not only from the human attempt to understand God rationally but also and more fundamentally from intuitive perceptions of the triune God. As we have seen, when intuitive perceptions of God focus on the future they become Christian hope; but we perceive more than the future with our feelings and imagination. We also grasp historical events intuitively, including the sacramental events that reveal the Trinity. Accordingly Christian faith expresses itself not just in theological affirmations but also and more fundamentally in ritual, narrative, myth, art, and lyric. Indeed, since, as we have seen in reflecting on the experience of justifying faith, faith in the broadest sense flows initially from the heart rather than from the head, intuitive perceptions of the meaning of salvation history hold a privileged place in the Christian community. We have enshrined these intuitions of faith in the Bible, in the worship of the Church, and in Christian art and literature. Rational reflection on the meaning of Christian revelation attempts to endow intuitive perceptions of divine revelation with inferential precision. The intuitive perceptions, however, come first; theology as normally practiced comes second.

3) THE CERTAINTY, TRUTH, AND FREEDOM OF FAITH. These insights into the creedal character of Christian faith shed light on the certainty, truth, and freedom of the act of faith. They also illumine the relationship between faith and reason.

A more traditional Catholic explanation of the theological virtues rests on a very different understanding of human nature from the one presented in these pages. That traditional explanation derives its anthropology from Thomas Aquinas and presupposes that human persons relate to God through the two spiritual faculties of intellect and will. Accordingly, it locates the three theological virtues exclusively in these two powers of the soul. Faith transforms the intellect, hope and love transform the will. The position developed in these pages, by contrast, locates hope in intuitive perceptions of the future. Hope, therefore resides in the affections, while faith engages both intuitive and inferential perceptions of divine revelation. Christian love as we shall see, results from the transvaluation in faith of prudential perceptions of one's interpersonal responsibilities.

Two Pardoxes

The theological attempt to locate faith in the intellect alone led to some unresolved paradoxes. Having exalted reason to the position of the highest human faculty, a traditional theology found itself hard put to explain the superiority of supernatural faith to natural forms of rational understanding. Through the judgments of reason one grasps reality itself, it was argued; but in the act of faith, one accepts someone else's account of reality as the truth instead of grasping the transcendent object of faith directly. Given a choice between these two ways of knowing, should not one prefer reason to faith?

Besides seeming to degrade supernatural faith to a position inferior to the judgments of natural reason, the intellectualization of faith also raised some problems about its certitude. A traditional theology of faith defends its absolute certitude on the basis of the fact that faith participates in the absolute infallibility of the God who commands it. Having asserted so much, however, a traditional theology of faith then found itself hard pressed to explain how a fallible intellect could posit such an act. God does not lie; but when does a fallible, developing mind know that it has grasped divine truth?

Transcending the Paradoxes

The first of these two paradoxes results in part from an inadequate understanding of both faith and revelation as assent to propositional truths on the authority of another. In fact, the act of faith consists in consent to a God whom one encounters in events charged with sacramental significance. As a consequence, revelation consists in more than assent to propositions, and faith involves more than the assent to propositions. Moreover, the consent of faith engages more than just the perceptions of the rational intellect; for it also includes, more fundamentally, a felt, intuitive perception of the action of divine grace.

With such an expanded understanding of both faith and revelation, one can, I believe, circumvent both of the preceding paradoxes. In the theory of knowledge defended in these pages, one grasps reality most fundamentally in an initial judgment of feeling and only subsequently through rational inference. In an initial judgment of feeling, one encounters concretely and sensibly some reality that one desires to understand further. Further understanding may come in the form of either imaginative or inferential insight. Subsequent insights enhance the clarity and precision of the experience of initial encounter but never replace it.

The initial consent of faith consists, then, in consent to a felt encounter with the Holy. In the passage from unbelief to religious faith, one recognizes that one in fact stands in a felt relationship with a self-revealing God, a relationship that demands acknowledgment and requires further exploration. One thus grasped by God knows the divine embrace for a fact, even though the consequences of acquiescing in that embrace may require a lifetime to explore. As one advances through the different stages of faith, that initial judgment continues to provide believers with their most fundamental cognitive contact with God, a contact that perdures as the intuitive and rational mind grapples with the significance of one's encounter with the Holy. The certitude of faith, when viewed from the standpoint of the one who believes, anchors itself here.

Interpreting the Encounter

The growth of faith involves both intuitive and inferential perceptions of the character of one's relationship with the deity and of the partners in that relationship. Moreover, since faith ambitions an integrated and integrating insight into reality, it also commits the believer to a specific view of the world. Because, however, faith flows from receptivity to divine grace, in a very real sense religious thought accords better with intuitive thinking, which proceeds with more spontaneity and with less conscious ego-control than logical inference. Such thinking, however, far from playing second fiddle to inferential reason provides humans with a more fundamental contact with reality than the abstract inferences that seek to endow intuitive perceptions with logical clarity and control. Through both intuitive and inferential reflection, however, faith, as Augustine saw, seeks self-understanding.

Even the initial assent of faith offers, of course, an interpretation of a religious experience. Moreover, the ability to identify a religious experience as religious presupposes minimally a certain number of appreciative insights into the meaning of the term "God" and into one's own human condition. The term "God" acquires its initial meaning through contact with religious people. A potential believer needs some sense both of who God would be, if the divine reality does exist, and of what it would be like to enter into relationship with such a reality.

Potential believers also need some insight into the human need for salvation. Salvation becomes a problem when the religious question arises. The religious question asks whether human life has an ultimate purpose and whether or not one can miss that purpose. Those who answer both parts of the religious question positively admit their own need for salvation.

The human need for others in order to grow teaches the intuitive mind to search for salvation in community. Eventually, however, an insight into the inability of human communities to extricate themselves totally from their own folly and malice leads the religious seeker to look for salvation in some reality that transcends the human. As a consequence, salvation also demands moral transformation in accord with God's transcendent, saving will.

The human heart that has reached these intuitive insights needs only to experience God's efficacious touch in order to know it and respond in faith. The consent of faith emerges, then, from the human heart's felt encounter with the one reality capable of giving human life ultimate meaning and purpose. That consent expresses most fundamentally a belief in that reality, a belief motivated, as we have seen, by its inherent beauty; for, as we have also seen, when we experience beauty, we grasp both the truth and the goodness of reality simultaneously with our hearts.

Believing in God and Believing God

Belief in the God we encounter in initial faith teaches us subsequently to *believe God*, to accept divine revelation on the terms demanded by the events of salvation history, insofar as we can interpret them correctly. The correct interpretation of divine revelation results from participation in the ongoing attempt of a community of faith to understand the religious events that found it and to live out collectively the consequences of commitment to God.

The Certitude of Faith

The certitude of faith exceeds, then, rational certitude because it roots itself in a felt perception of the direct action of God upon the believer that commands assent. Faith involves much more, therefore, than assent to a proposition about God on the authority of another person. Rather it identifies at least in a preliminary fashion a concrete religious experience as divinely authoritative. That act of identification leaves the believer with the subsequent task of understanding both intuitively and inferentially the significance of that felt encounter with the divine. Such understanding engages fallible human hearts and minds but hearts and minds also capable of reaching valid insights into the action of God in human history. Those insights develop but never replace the initial sense of having been grasped by God in a way that commands one's consent.

The Freedom of Faith

Such an approach to the act of faith also allows us to understand better its inherent freedom. Freedom under grace degenerates into an inexplicable conundrum if one restricts the human capacity to respond to God to the two powers of intellect and will; for, if one explains freedom as an essential trait of the spiritual will, one must then offer a plausible account of how God can move efficaciously an essentially free power of the soul without coercing it.

Human freedom, however, roots itself not in the spiritual essence of the will but in the power to differentiate conceptually viable alternatives for action. Moreover, God touches persons rather than moves wills. Persons touched by God perceive consent to the divine as one course of action among others; but they also know that they can choose to exclude God from their lives, if they so desire. All consent to God, therefore, advances freely because the unbeliever touched by God perceives not only the possibility of faith but also the possibility of unbelief. Moreover, when it occurs, faith expresses initially a spontaneous leap of the heart rather than an inferential judgment of the intellect.

4) STAGES OF FAITH. We may expect that as Christians grow in faith they will probably advance through identifiable cognitive stages of religious belief. James Fowler has distinguished six such stages. He calls the first stage "intuitive-projective faith." Typically, this stage occurs in children from three to seven years of age. At this early age, children's thought patterns lack the stability to produce a unified vision of the world, even through stories. Instead, the child empathizes with numinous religious images that will tend in later life to color positively or negatively mature religious perceptions. The religious attitudes of significant adults also shape early faith attitudes profoundly.

By the age of seven children develop the ability to think in an organized fashion about concrete realities and thus advance to the stage of "mythic-literal" faith. Images of God at this second stage take on a decidedly anthropomorphic cast. Moreover, these young believers tend to accept as literally true the religious stories that give ultimate meaning to their lives.

Clearly, in the first two stages of Christian faith development, the attitudes of other Christians, their worship, and their retelling the Christian story provide the faith of children with the categories they need for understanding the reality of God and the meaning of salvation.

With the onset of adolescence, children can begin to advance to "synthetic-conventional" faith. At this stage the young understand religious realities as traditionally explained whether they consent to them or rebel against them. Hence, as young Christians advance to conventional faith they need a solid grounding in the Christian tradition, a heartfelt appropriation of its fundamental symbols, an appreciation for a Christian worldview and for Christian morality, and a solid grasp of Church history.

Toward an Autonomous Faith

The conflict of religious authorities, official changes in Church doctrine or discipline, or personal exposure to previously unfamiliar religious communities and belief systems can advance young believers beyond synthetic-conventional faith to "individuative-reflexive faith." Typically, this transition occurs in late adolescence or young adulthood. At stage four believers begin to assume personal responsibility for their religious attitudes, beliefs, and commitments. Young Christian adults advancing to individuative-reflexive faith need a familiarity with the methods and categories of critical theological thinking that will allow them to appropriate the Christian tradition in a personally adequate manner.

The personal rationalization of faith that occurs at stage four can advance in oblivion of one's unconscious motives and attitudes. The need to confront those motives later in life may combine with the limitations of one's personal creed in order to force a reevaluation of one's personal religious view of the world. When that occurs, believers advance to the fifth stage of faith, which Fowler calls "conjunctive faith." At stage five, one discovers religious affectivity in a new way and with it a new facility in responding to traditional religious symbols. Religious thought now advances dialectically. Sensitivity to the limitations of one's personal religious vision suffuses belief with a healthy sense of paradox. Christians of conjunctive faith need to learn how to deal both with the doctrinal contradictions within the Christian tradition and with the challenges of comparative religion. They need, therefore, to master the techniques of theological dialectic and of ecumenical dialogue. They also need a sound insight into the dynamics of Christian conversion, for that insight provides the norms for judging the soundness or unsoundness of different doctrinal positions.

Fowler calls the sixth and final stage of faith "universalizing faith." Only rare individuals advance to this stage, which takes on the characteristics of extraordinary saintliness. At stage six believers do not so much seek the transcendent as the transcendent grasps and possesses them. Their loyalty to ultimate realities heightens their sensitivity to injustice. They resonate profoundly with religious symbols because they commune with the living realities those symbols manifest. They perceive all things as reconciled in God. Christians of universalizing faith will find nourishment in any source of sound religious insight but will probably find special help in the writings of great saints and mystics.[5]

Stages of Faith and Conversion

In dealing with converts, one should not, however, confuse the transition from one stage of faith to another with the experience of conversion itself. The two experiences may coincide but need not. One may experience a conversion within a given stage of faith with-

5. For a more detailed exposition of Fowler's stages, see: James Fowler, *Stages of Faith: The Psychology of Human Development and the Quest for Meaning* (San Francisco: Harper & Row, 1976).

out advancing to the next stage. Similarly, passage from one stage of faith to another need not coincide with conversion.

I have defined conversion as the decision to pass from irresponsible to responsible behavior in what concerns one's relationship with a self-revealing, self-communicating God. At what stage in the development of faith does such a response to God become humanly possible? Surely children who respond to God with mythic-literal faith lack the capacity to take full personal responsibility for their religious beliefs and attitudes. Even those who have passed from mythic-literal faith to synthetic-conventional faith lack the conceptual equipment needed to assume adult responsibility for consent to God; for as long as one accepts without question a conventional creed or conventional religious discipline, one runs the risk of acquiescing blindly in the sins and inadequacies that mar it. Religious conversion, therefore, in the sense in which I have defined it cannot occur until an individual has passed from conventional to individuative-reflective faith.

The passage to individuative-reflective faith need not, however, coincide with conversion, for the simple reason that one can make the transition from synthetic-conventional faith to individuative-reflective faith in an irresponsible manner. One could, for example, choose to live by self-defined religious standards rather than by those demanded by an integral response to self-revealing God. When, however, one makes the transition to individuative-reflective faith in a way that responds to God on God's own terms, then one would experience an initial adult religious conversion in the sense in which I have defined the term "conversion."

d. Christian Love. Christian hope transvalues our intuitive perceptions of the future. Christian faith transvalues our intuitive and inferential beliefs about reality. Christian love transvalues our consciences.

1) NATURAL LOVES AND THE NATURAL CONSCIENCE. Natural human love expresses itself in deeds. A sense both of personal need and of gratitude to the adults who fill those needs colors the love of small children. With the processes of socialization, the needy love of children matures into friendship. Sexual maturation brings the capacity for erotic love. Marital love blends the affection that unites family members, profound friendship, and romantic attraction. Beauty in nature and in persons motivates a natural contemplative love. When self-sacrificial, love embodies the love of atonement.

Love and Conscience

Love seeks to effect the good of another. Nevertheless, like every human act, love terminates an evaluative response that specifies it. Deeds of love express attitudes, hopes, and beliefs. They also express more immediately prudential judgments about the way persons ought to act toward one another.

We perceive our moral obligations both intuitively and inferentially. We are drawn intuitively by certain kinds of rational conduct and repelled by others. In analyzing moral situations rationally we formulate principles that allow us to discriminate between virtuous and vicious conduct.

Judgments of conscience invoke moral values. Moral values claim us absolutely and ultimately. They claim us ultimately when we are willing not only to live for them but, if necessary, to die for them. They claim us absolutely when we acknowledge that they bind us in every circumstance. Moral values, however, do not only bind the conscience, they lure it. They hold up an ideal vision of the way that persons ought to deal with one another, a vision that attracts the conscience by its beauty and challenges the creative imagination to effect its actualization.

Creative ethical thinking begins, then, by coming to clarity about the moral ideals relevant to a morally perplexing situation. The conscience must then reach a positive appreciation of those values already incarnate in the persons and things involved in the situation. Normally, we find it hard to appreciate anything that threatens us in any way. In order to appreciate any situation ethically, we need, then, to deal with its threatening aspects and bring to as full a resolution as we can personal attitudes that would cause us to misprize it. Having appreciated positively the values ingredient in situations of moral conflict, we need then to regret any facet of the situation that falls short of the ideals that judge it. Finally, we need to use our imaginations creatively to advance the situation the next possible step toward the realization of those ideals. Moreover, we form our consciences responsibly when we do so, not in isolation, but in ongoing dialogue with those who can help us to form it correctly.

2) THE CHRISTIAN CONSCIENCE. Christian love transforms the workings of the natural conscience by informing them with gospel values and ideals. Imagine, for example, that some acquaintance has slandered you seriously. Hurt and anger may tempt you initially to enroll the slanderer at the top of your hate list; but even brief reflection on the moral claims that the gospel makes on your conscience

tells you that such conduct would fall far short of the ideals to which Jesus calls you. Jesus not only summons his disciples not to respond to evil with evil but even to deal lovingly with one's enemies. You realize that you will not even begin to approach that ideal of conduct until you deal with the legitimate hurt and anger you feel over the injustice you have suffered. In the course of dealing with your animosity toward your antagonist, you begin to put his slanderous attack into some kind of perspective. You begin to appreciate that this single act does not exhaust his character and that he can and has behaved more justly and lovingly in the past. You recall past acts of kindness he has done. You decide then that instead of retaliating spitefully, you will appeal to his better part and seek some kind of reconciliation with him. You decide, on some reflection, not to let the sun set on your anger. Moreover, you decide in approaching your slanderer that you will follow the gospel pattern (Matt 18:15) and first seek him out individually.

The Shape of Christian Love

This homely example illustrates the way in which the ethics of discipleship that Jesus lived and proclaimed helps give Christian love its content. Those who seek to love others in the name and image of Jesus seek actively to share their possessions with others, especially with those in need. They labor, therefore, not in order to heap up possessions but in order not to burden others and at the same time in order to have something to share with the needy. They try through sharing to bring into existence a community of people mutually reconciled in Christ. Like Jesus himself they reach across social barriers to the marginal and outcast, even to sinners. They let their own willingness to forgive others measure the authenticity of their own prayer.

Like Christian hope and faith, Christian love embraces this world and the next. It seeks out the triune God as the transcendent object of its love. It longs to dissolve and abide with Christ in God. Christian love discovers in Jesus' passion, death, and resurrection the supreme revelation of divine love, and in the final outpouring of the Holy Breath on all flesh Christian love recognizes divine love's universal scope. Nevertheless, while it longs for union with God Christian love acknowledges that such union flows from one's willingness to imitate in this life the atoning character of divine love. The atoning divine love incarnate in Jesus reconciles humans to one another and to God by forgiving in advance any wrong, by sustaining that forgiveness even in the moment of rejection, and by offering to others the possibility of reconciliation even before they repent. Divine atoning love seeks to redeem the present sinfulness of humankind, but because that effort plunges one into the passion of Jesus, such atoning love never knows complete fulfillment in this life.

Needless to say, not every effort to love others in Jesus' name ends in frustration. Moreover, the mutual love of Christians for one another in the image of Jesus creates the matrix of divine grace that nurtures love in individual believers and frees them to reach out in love to others.

Natural Love and Christian Charity

Christian charity informs all the natural forms of human love. It teaches the maturing Christian to imitate the free gift of divine love that claimed us first and sought us out in our sinfulness and need. Charity teaches natural human love to put on the mind of Christ, to obey the moral vision he proclaimed, and to reach out to others with his forgiving compassion.

Because charity transforms natural human love, it never transcends utterly human need. Christians need to love others, but like the small child they need to receive love in return. Shared enthusiasm for the work of the kingdom binds friends together in Christ. Charity teaches Christians to love others with the forgiving love of Christ and to gift with love even those who do not merit it. We shall consider in a later chapter how Christian love endows marital love with sacramental significance. Moreover as charity deepens it matures into contemplative union that gives one the eyes to find God in all things. Authentic charity, then, blends needy human love with contemplative love of divine beauty and with the redemptive love of atonement.

Christian charity expands the limited scope of natural loves and loyalties to include everyone, even one's enemies. In the process it perfects natural love and heals its spontaneous limitations. Charity elevates natural love by focusing it on the infinitely lovable reality of the triune God.

e. The Christian Search for Justice. In teaching the conscience to submit to the moral demands of life in the kingdom of God a Christian ethics of discipleship transforms human interpersonal relationships into an embodiment of charity. When the Christian conscience judges human institutions in the light of that same New Testament morality, it begins the Christian search for a just social order.

The Kingdom: A Program for Social Reform

Christian conversion transvalues sociopolitical conversion by teaching the social activist to measure the justice or injustice of institutional structures by Jesus' vision of the moral consequences of submitting to the reign of God. Jesus seems to have rejected Davidic messianism as the equivalent of idolatry (Matt 4:8-11; Luke 4:5-8). In the course of his public life he resisted every attempt to transform his ministry into a political power play. He rejected the path of violent revolution (Matt 26:51-53) and founded the kingdom of God instead on the obedience of faith, on mutual forgiveness, on humble service, and on prayer.

Yet the kingdom Jesus proclaimed issued a radical challenge to the economic, political, religious, and social structures of his day. He seems to have derived his vision of the kingdom in part from the Jewish year of jubilee. During the jubilee year, the land was supposed to lie fallow, renewing itself, while the people of God experienced a renewal in faith that changed the economic order of society. The jubilee year called for the cancellation of debts, for the liberation of slaves, for active care and concern for the poor, and for a reordering of society in ways that expressed the justice of God (Deut 15:1-18). Jesus seems to have conceived the kingdom as a time of perpetual jubilee. He summoned his disciples to the cancellation of their debts (Matt 6:12) and to the same practical compassion for the poor that marks the year of jubilee. The kingdom that he proclaimed challenges the avarice of the rich and demands an economic reordering of society that imitates God's own justice.

Moreover, while the kingdom of God does not rest on coercive political power, it does relativize the claims of every humanly contrived political structure because it demands a more fundamental commitment than any state can require. Christian martyrs in every age have, like Jesus, witnessed to that truth with their blood. Submission to the kingdom has, then, important political consequences.

Jesus' table fellowship with sinners and his insistence that his disciples share their material possessions in ways that break down social barriers challenge every form of social elitism. His vision of the kingdom undercuts every claim to privilege or to self-righteous superiority as incompatible with divine justice. In this way the kingdom demands a radical reordering of the institutions that legislate human social relationships.

Finally, Jesus' vision of the kingdom challenged the religious hypocrisy of his day. His cleansing of the Temple made a clear statement about his estimate of the extent to which the Jewish priestly caste's administration of Temple cult expressed obedience to God's reign. His denunciation of pharisaical self-righteousness flouted the going sense of religious propriety and complacency.

In other words, while Jesus eschewed founding the reign of God on power politics, his vision of the kingdom nevertheless stands in judgment on the justice or injustice of every humanly contrived economic, social, political, and ecclesiastical system. It also judges religious hypocrites who sanction injustice and who then foolishly try to justify themselves before God.

The Christian Meaning of Justice

The converted Christian, therefore, finds in the ethics of discipleship that Jesus lived and proclaimed not only the ultimate meaning of love but also the ultimate measure of social justice. For the Christian, justice means much more than giving others their due. It includes more than the observance of the commandments. It transcends legalistic definitions of justice or philosophical definitions based in some theory of the natural law. Christian justice orders human society in accordance with God's revealed will and finds that redemptive will definitively manifest in the life and teachings of Jesus. The divine justice that Jesus embodies expresses God's merciful compassion and persistent will to save us in spite of ourselves. That divine justice works our justification by summoning us to the obedience of faith and by teaching us to measure human justice by God's own merciful compassion and forgiveness.

Christians can, then, judge no society just that fails to reach out in compassion to the poor and needy. They can call no society just that fails to seek the common good by encouraging its marginal, alienated, and oppressed members to contribute to and share in the benefits to which the better advantaged enjoy easy access. Christians can call no society just that engages in aggressive war and that tolerates or perpetuates situations of oppression.

In the preceding chapter we pondered the moral inevitability of sociopolitical conversion. We say that the failure to confront institutional injustice and oppression will with moral inevitability betray the personally converted individual with a privatized conscience into irresponsible behavior even at an interpersonal level.

The Christian convert must, however, face the challenge of institutional reform for yet another reason. As we have seen, Christian conversion results from baptism in the Breath of Christ; and Breath-baptism draws one into Jesus' own baptismal experience. As Breath-baptized Christians learn to put on Jesus' mind, their conversion to Christ transvalues every dimension of their lives. Breath-baptism thus creates a social matrix of divine grace that fosters the graced transformation of individual believers.

Christian Mission

The Acts of the Apostles makes it clear, however, that Breath-baptism has other important consequences as well. Having created the Christian community, Breath-baptism launches it on the enterprise of prolonging the historical mission of Jesus by proclaiming his gospel to all creatures. Moreover, the universal scope of the salvation revealed in Christ demands that all finally submit to the divine reign. Christians must summon to repentance and to faith not only the lowly and oppressed but also the rich and powerful whose decisions create situations of institutional oppression. Inevitably, then, Breath-baptism brings the Christian convert into conflict with the same economic, social, political, and religious forces that conspired to nail Jesus to the cross.

Integrally converted Christians need, then, to draw upon the insights born of their personal conversion to Christ in order to diagnose the causes of institutional injustice and oppression. In the process of doing so, they must summon those responsible for those oppressive injustices to repentance and to the obedience of faith. More specifically, converts need to draw on the insights born of an affective conversion transvalued in Christian hope and faith in order to confront prophetically the disordered attitudes embodied in oppressive institutions. They need to invoke insights inspired by an intellectual conversion transvalued in Christian faith in order to unmask the oppressive ideologies that rationalize situations of social injustice. They need to derive from a moral conversion transvalued in Christian love and from a sociopolitical conversion informed by a vision of divine justice the norms that both measure the immorality of unjust situations and validate just social arrangements. Finally, they need to challenge in Jesus' name and image every form of religious hypocrisy that would conspire with institutionalized oppression. Let us reflect on each of these points in order.

1) THE DISCIPLES OF JESUS NEED TO DRAW ON INSIGHTS BORN OF AN AFFECTIVE CONVERSION TRANSVALUED IN CHRISTIAN HOPE AND FAITH IN ORDER TO CONFRONT PROPHETICALLY THE DISORDERED ATTITUDES EMBODIED IN OPPRESSIVE INSTITUTIONS. As we have seen, the structures

of human society root themselves in human habits. Subgroups develop typical patterns of habitual behavior that society at large first recognizes as typical, then sanctions, then inculcates. Oppressive hopes and attitudes habitual to a culture can, then, breed oppressive institutions. Moreover, sometimes such hopes and attitudes spring from deep within the unconscious mind. In our culture, for example, racism, sexism, and militarism all give evidence of rooting themselves in deep-seated emotions, many of them unconscious.

Oppresive Hope and the Archetypal Imagination

Often the oppressive hopes that create situations of injustice engage the archetypal imagination. As we have seen, the intuitive mind perceives reality in images, some remembered, some created by fancy. Among the images that organize intuitive perceptions archetypal ones also function and play an important role, for they organize the human imagination and endow its otherwise chaotic spontaneity with identifiable patterns. Archetypal images recur in different individuals, in different cultures, and in different human epochs. They channel enormous emotional energy. They tend to organize other images into a unified imaginative perception of reality. Carl Jung first called attention to the presence of archetypal images in human intuitive perceptions, but studies of mythology and comparative religion have validated his suggestion.

Jungian theory places special importance on five recurring archetypes: heroic images of the masculine, images of the feminine, clothing (which symbolizes social relationships), shadow images of the dark side of the psyche, and images of contextualizing wholeness.[6]

Racism

Racism seems to engage the archetype of the shadow. When the shadow surfaces in dreams, it always has the same sex as the dreamer and symbolizes the dreamer's feelings of hostility, fear, and shame that need conscious healing. Befriending the shadow by facing one's disordered and potentially destructive unconscious tenden-

---

6. For a popular introduction to Jungian archetypal theory, see C. G. Jung and others, *Man and His Symbols* (Garden City, N. Y.: Doubleday, 1964). For a more detailed analysis of two major archetypes, see Erich Neumann, *The Origins and History of Consciousness* (Princeton: Princeton University Press, 1954); *The Great Mother: An Analysis of the Archetype* (Princeton: Princeton University Press, 1963).

cies can enhance one's personal psychic integration. Refusal to face the shadow, however, breeds shadow possession. Then, instead of dealing with the shame, rage, and terror festering in their own hearts, the shadow-possessed tend to project those same feelings onto other persons, especially those of darker skin. In this country blacks symbolize subconsciously to racists all of those shameful, fearful, and potentially violent aspects of themselves that the racists fear to face. Racists tend, therefore, for unconscious motives they probably do not understand, to project onto blacks their own subconscious self-loathing. They therefore deride and insult blacks, avoid them socially, segregate them from the rest of society by legal or economic means, persecute them, and in extreme cases lynch them.

Sexism

An analogous psychological process helps motivate the battle of the sexes. Sexism engages another archetype, that of the male hero. The typical hero of folklore and myth is born in obscurity but is called by destiny or by the gods to some momentous quest in which he must slay a dragon, rescue an imprisoned maiden, and return home triumphant, where he weds the rescued damsel and lives with her happily ever after. Hero myths interpret the experience of masculine coming of age and help motivate institutionalized behavior in male-dominated cultures. In the patriarchal myths that shape every culture we know, women find themselves cast in passive roles: they need rescuing in their helplessness before marriage; after marriage they recede into the obscurity of the home, from which they gaze in admiration on the hero as he savors his exploits. In sexist societies like our own, these nursery images take sinister institutional form. Sexist institutions school both men and women to acquiesce in rigid sex roles that deny women the same cultural opportunities as men, bar them from economic and political competition, and by relegating them to social passivity often reduce them to degrading poverty. Witness the growing feminization of poverty in our own country during the neocapitalist era of Reagan and of Bush.

Militarism

The archetype of the *macho* hero also gives unconscious motivation to militaristic social structures. In militaristic societies the armed forces exert decisive influence over public policy. Militarism breeds and draws sustenance from bellicose nationalism, chauvinism, ethnocentrism, and xenophobia. Militaristic societies seek aggressive expansion, glorify armed might, idealize discipline for its own sake, value regimentation and blind obedience to authority, and prefer violent to diplomatic solutions for economic and political conflicts.

We have good reason to suspect that the atomic arms race engages two archetypes simultaneously. The image of the *macho* hero helps breed the militarism that inspires the frantic search for bigger and better weapons. The collective paranoia that has traditionally divided the superpowers has, however, also bound them in a shadow relationship, as each projects onto the other its own repressed and unacknowledged aggressions. The resulting annual outlay of billions of dollars for weapons research, construction, and deployment has transformed this nation from the humanitarian government that once sponsored the Marshall Plan and the Great Society to an international arms merchant and supporter of oppressive anticommunist dictatorships that protect our economic interests abroad. At the same time funds that might have been used to eliminate hunger, poverty, and ignorance create instead weapons that threaten the very survival of life on this planet. As we Americans point self-righteously to the violation of human rights that occur under a totalitarian Russian regime, we close our eyes to the human rights of the poor that our neocapitalist economy systematically violates both in this country and abroad.

Racism, sexism, militarism, and the arms race all illustrate large, impersonal institutional structures that spring in part from archetypally motivated emotional disorders. Christians need to use the insights born of an affective conversion transvalued in Christian hope in order to raise to social consciousness the unconscious affective disorders that engender and perpetuate these oppressive social structures. Christians also need to summon those whose hopes and attitudes oppress others to repentant healing in faith. Finally, Christians need to draw upon Jesus' vision of the kingdom in order to advance human society the next possible step toward a social order that incarnates divine justice rather than human oppression.

2) THE DISCIPLES OF JESUS NEED TO DRAW UPON THE INSIGHTS OF AN INTELLECTUAL CONVERSION TRANSVALUED IN FAITH IN ORDER TO RE-FUTE THE IDEOLOGIES THAT SANCTION SITUATIONS OF OPPRESSION. In *Economic Justice for All,* their recent pastoral on the United States economy, the North American bishops cite, quite correctly, the achievements of our economic system. The United States ranks as one of the most economically powerful nations in human history. It boasts of

rich natural resources, fertile soil, and a climate that favors agricultural development. Moreover, the people of this nation have created the American economic wonder by sweat, self-sacrifice, and collaboration.

The Bishops and the Economy

The bishops find signs of hope in the contemporary North American economy: parents who successfully integrate work with the responsibilities of married life; families who resist the allure of materialism and consumerism; conscientious business executives who seek to organize work and commerce equitably; young people who value the service of others more than wealth; workers who seek to ennoble toilsome and repetitive labor; immigrants who come to these shores seeking to make a new life for themselves.

Nevertheless, the bishops quite correctly remind us that for many the American dream goes unfulfilled, while for others it has turned into a nightmare. The bishops point out that for two hundred and fifty years this nation wrested its wealth from the sweat of slaves. The bishops call attention to the swelling ranks of the urban poor and homeless, to the feminization of poverty, to unacceptable levels of unemployment, to the deterioration of family life as a result of economic pressures on the poor and middle class, to the questionable future of the family farm, and to serious economic threats to farming communities. In our cities thousands of poor and homeless people sleep in churches, subways, on the streets and line up for doled food at soup kitchens. The specter of unemployment haunts many of those currently employed. Dwindling social supports plunge more and more individuals and families into poverty, hopelessness, and despair. Beyond our borders eight hundred million people languish in absolute poverty, while four hundred and fifty million people face death by starvation. Even within our own borders twenty million people, including twelve million children go to bed hungry.

As a people, we Americans resist facing the dark side of our economic system; and we have generated a variety of ideologies to blind ourselves to its ugliness. Ideologies offer pseudo-rationalizations of injustice while simultaneously masquerading as self-evident truths. We can distinguish three common kinds of ideology that function within our own culture and in other cultures as well: ideologies of isolation, ideologies of exploitation, and ideologies of domination. Let us consider a few indigenous examples of each.

Ideologies of Isolation

Ideologies of isolation fragment society in oppressive ways. Individualism, classism, and racism, and anti-Semitism all exemplify ideologies of isolation. Individualism assures selfish and egocentric people either that concern for the common good makes no claims on their consciences or that the pursuit of private interest will automatically secure the good of all. Classism assures the rich and economically advantaged that since the poor have through sloth and other vices caused their own economic misery and degradation, those who enjoy the good things of life have no responsibility to extricate the poverty-stricken from their misery. The rationalization of racism, of sexism, and of religious bigotry offers endless reasons why its victims deserve an inferior social status and even prefer it.

Ideologies of Exploitation

Ideologies of exploitation rationalize the unjust ways in which large institutions manipulate and abuse other people to their own political and economic advantage. Both neocapitalism and totalitarian communism have spawned ideologies of exploitation. Capitalist economies posture as the guardians of democratic liberty and as the protectors of the good life. Capitalism and democracy grew up side by side historically, but the facts belie the claim that capitalism fosters democracy. At best democratic systems of government can temper the economic injustices that capitalism engenders as it concentrates increasing wealth and power in the hand of a shrinking capitalist elite. At worst in capitalistic societies big business manipulates the democratic processes of government to its own economic advantage. We have yet to see whether in this nation the democratic process can survive the capitalistic manipulation of the mass media. In addition, capitalism cannot justify its claim to guarantee the good life. It arranges the economy to the advantage of the rich and the upper middle class, leaving the poor to sink or swim in its powerful economic currents. Capitalism commercializes and trivializes culture (consider the vapidity of most commercial television shows); and it fails to provide efficiently goods and services that do not wear a price tag: education, local government service, public health. Contemporary capitalism suffers, moreover, from a worldwide malaise motivated by unstable markets, periodic stagflation (economic stagnation combined with inflation), and fiscal instability. "Reaganomics" with its bailouts for floundering corporations and tax breaks for the rich, on the one hand, and its unrelenting assault on the New Deal and the Great Society, on the other hand, practiced for its part a peculiar kind of socialism toward the affluent combined with a ruthless capitalism toward the poor. To date the Bush administration offers no significant improvement.

Marxism, on the other hand, although it began as a revolutionary doctrine, evolved into a form of bureaucratic collectivism in which the state owns the means of production and the party bureaucracy owns the state by its totalitarian monopoly of power. By forcing workers to surrender "surpluses" as a free gift to the state, communist collectivism ironically exploits the working class in exactly the same sense that Marx originally decried when he denounced the exploitation of the German peasant classes. We have yet to see whether *perestroika,* the "new thinking" of the Soviet high command, will rectify such abuses.

Ideologies of Domination

Ideologies of domination rationalize the forceful subjugation of one group or nation to another. During the nineteenth century belief in "manifest destiny" helped rationalize the conquest of Native Americans, the annexation of Texas, the multiplication of slave states, and the war with Mexico in 1846. As late as the 1890s, manifest destiny joined forces with both national chauvinism and racism to "justify" annexing Hawaii and other Spanish possessions. The doctrine of *lebensraum* lent an aura of fleeting respectability to Nazi expansionism. Today the superpowers have transformed *lebensraum* into an ideology of national security. Both ideologies portray the state as a living organism justified in doing whatever it needs in order to expand and survive.

An intellectual conversion informed by faith frees the human mind from blind submission to ideologies of isolation, exploitation, and forceful domination by exposing their deceptions critically and in the light of Jesus' vision of the kingdom. Such a critique frees the mind to devise principles, policies, and strategies that serve the interests of divine justice rather than the vested economic and political interests of power elites. Faith teaches the intellectually converted activist to measure social justice by the mind of Christ and to advance practically toward the actualization of God's reign on earth as in heaven.

3) CHRISTIANS NEED TO DERIVE FROM A MORAL CONVERSION INFORMED BY AN ETHICS OF DISCIPLESHIP AND FROM A SOCIOPOLITICAL CON-

VERSION COMMITTED TO THE CAUSE OF DIVINE JUSTICE THE NORMS THAT AUTHENTICATE INSTITUTIONAL POLICIES AND DECISIONS. Personal moral conversion, sociopolitical conversion, and Christian conversion each make a distinctive moral contribution to the human search for a just social order.

Personal moral conversion yields an insight into personal rights and duties that institutional injustice violates.

Sociopolitical conversion supplies the conscience with prudential norms and ideals of institutional justice. Sociopolitical converts acknowledge that all persons have the right to share readily in the good things of this world and to live a humane life. They understand the meaning of legal, commutative, distributive, and social justice.[7] They subordinate the actions of both business and government to the common good. Together these two forms of moral conversion— personal and sociopolitical—instill in converts the insight and courage to denounce oppression, exploitation, and violence.

When, however, in addition a Christian moral commitment informs the human search for a just social order, the conscience invokes Jesus' vision of the kingdom in order to measure the ultimate justice or injustice of institutional decisions and policies. It finds in that same vision the ultimate moral ideal that gives overall direction to the search for a just world peace. In order to begin the process of translating Jesus' vision into an actuality, believers need to derive from that vision principles that define public policies that advance society toward the vision of the kingdom. Christians then need to devise strategies that turn policy into actuality.

4) THE DISCIPLES OF JESUS NEED TO CHALLENGE EVERY FORM OF RELIGIOUS HYPOCRISY THAT WOULD ATTEMPT TO CONSPIRE WITH INSTITUTIONAL OPPRESSION. Religious people conspire with oppression when they allow oppressors to coopt religious language in the interests of exploitation and violence. They conspire with oppression when they invoke the blessing of God on unjust actions and policies. They conspire with oppression when they remain silent in the face of manifest institutional inequity. In this country slave owners and racists have piously quoted the Bible to justify the legal and economic en-

---

7. Legal justice regulates the responsibilities of individuals to the body politic. Commutative justice regulates transactions among individuals and groups in the private sector of society. Distributive justice regulates the reponsibilities of the body politic toward each of its citizens. Social justice provides norms and principles for the right ordering of social institutions.

slavement of blacks, and for generations religious leaders failed to protest the abuse with sufficient vigor. Television evangelists and other religious supporters of the political right invoke the divine blessing on a government that turns a blind eye to the poor and homeless in this country and pursues policies that ensure the economic enslavement of the Third World to the First. Jesus had no truck with such religious hypocrisy, and neither should his followers.

We shall return to a consideration of the sociopolitical dimensions of Christian conversion in subsequent chapters, when we consider the meaning of original sin and concupiscence. For the moment, however, it suffices to have underscored the fact that the missionary thrust of Christian conversion forces a gracious transvaluation of sociopolitical conversion that in turn gives rise to the Christian search for a just social order.

In the course of reflecting on the theological virtues, we discovered that each of them roots the Christian convert simultaneously in this world and in the next. The Christian search for justice on earth as in heaven never ends. In the public arena, we win at best only partial and temporary victories. That fact demands of those who struggle against institutional oppression a certain quality of patience and commitment. Christian patience must express an eschatological commitment. We must stand ready to endure any temporary setback or reversal in our attempt to embody God's own justice in the social fabric of our lives because our commitment to the cause of justice is motivated by more than pragmatic considerations of personal success or failure. As Christians we seek to actualize the kingdom in our institutions because God wills it, and not for personal aggrandizement or success. Indeed, Christian longing for the second coming springs from a radical commitment to embody the kingdom both personally and institutionally; for that longing expresses a holy impatience to get on with the work of redemption.

In reflecting on the theological virtues we found that the shared hope, faith, and love of the Christian community takes precedence over the hope, faith, and love of individual Christians in this sense, that the shared hope, faith, and love of the community creates a matrix of divine grace that nurtures individual aspiration, belief, and love to graced maturity. We must say the same for the Christian search for a just social order. The Christian community's prior justification by faith ultimately motivates the Church's corporate search for institutional justice. That search in turn nurtures in individuals and groups the gifts of prophecy and political activism that advance the cause of divine justice.

3. Conclusion. In the present chapter we have attempted to understand the dynamics of an adult conversion to Christ. We have examined some of the biblical foundations for a theology of Christian conversion. We have probed the experiences that ground the idea of justification by faith and sanctifying grace; and we have used an insight into Jesus' moral vision in order to illumine the two dynamics that Christian conversion contributes to the total process of conversion: its mediation between affective and moral conversion and its transvaluation in faith of the natural forms of conversion. We have reflected on the ways in which these two dynamics mediate the infusion of the supernatural virtues of hope, faith, and love. Finally, we have seen that Jesus' vision of the kingdom judges human social, economic, and political institutions and inspires the Christian search for a just social order.

In the course of these reflections we have repeatedly insisted that the social dynamics of divine grace take precedence over the personal. The Breath of God comes first, not to isolated individuals, but to the Church as a whole. We have described the Church as a matrix of grace that nurtures individual believers to Christian maturity and advances them toward a share in the glory of the risen Christ. The rites of adult initiation incorporate the convert into that matrix of divine life. Before we consider the process of initiation itself, we need, then, to take a closer look at the social dynamics of ongoing justification and sanctification. To this consideration we turn in the following chapter.

CHAPTER III

The Social Dynamics of Sanctification

We began these reflections on adult conversion by examining the dynamics of conversion in general. In the preceding chapter we focused on the two dynamics that Christian conversion contributes to the total process of adult conversion. We saw that Christian conversion mediates between affective and moral conversion. In the process it opens the entire person of the convert in faith to the God revealed in Jesus and in his Holy Breath. This first dynamic motivates the second; for the commitment of the total person to the triune God demands the transvaluation in faith of human hopes, beliefs, prudential judgments, and sociopolitical involvement.

We saw too that for the adult Christian convert, the religious vision of Jesus creates the context within which that transvaluation occurs. More specifically, we saw that through the process of transvaluation the ethics of discipleship that Jesus both lived and proclaimed reorients affective, intellectual, moral, and sociopolitical conversion toward realities and values that lure the convert by their beauty even as they stand in judgment over human folly and sinfulness. We reflected on the ways in which the transvaluation of personal conversion effects what a more traditional theology called the infusion of the theological virtues. We considered too how Christian conversion transforms sociopolitical conversion into the Christian search for social justice.

In reflecting on the infusion of the three theological virtues, we insisted that the shared hope, faith, and love of the Christian community takes precedence over that of the individual Christian. By that we meant that the community's shared orientation to God provides a matrix of divine grace that teaches its individual members to hope, believe, and love as Christian adults and so in their own turn to contribute to the shared hope, faith, and love of the Church as a whole.

That same matrix of grace supports Christians as they learn to hunger and thirst actively after God's justice in human society.

The Matrix of Conversion

The time has come to examine more closely the social processes that create this matrix of divine grace into which the rites of initiation introduce the adult Christian convert. Christian conversion results from baptism in the Breath of Jesus. The Acts of the Apostles tells us that on Pentecost the Holy Breath transformed Jesus' disciples into the Church, into a realm of grace capable of expansion through the baptism of new converts. In the vision of Luke the Holy Breath created the Church through an abundant outpouring of the charismatic gifts.

The New Testament gives us some reason to believe that prior to Pentecost those who encountered the risen Christ had experienced a personal enlightenment effected in them by the Breath of Jesus (1 Cor 15:45; John 20:21-23). The Breath's arrival on Pentecost differed, however, from these earlier illuminations in its ecclesial, charismatic character. On Pentecost the Breath came to the community of disciples as a community. Moreover, she constituted them a community, a Church into which others could be admitted, precisely by empowering them through her charisms to minister to one another and to proclaim the risen Christ fearlessly.

The Charisms in Medieval Theology

Medieval theologians used two terms to designate the Breath's charismatic activity in the Christian community. They spoke of two different kinds of gifts: gifts (*dona*) of sanctification and gifts (*gratiae gratis datae*) of service, or gratuitous graces.

They equated the *dona* with the different "spirits" that Isaiah anticipated that the Breath-filled, messianic king of Israel would one day possess: "spirits" of wisdom, understanding, counsel, fortitude, knowledge, piety, fear of the Lord (Isa 11:1-2). The pious interpretation of the seven "spirits" of which Isaiah spoke has generated a large body of devotional literature. By the Middle Ages theological reflection had transformed them into seven habits infused into the soul through sacramental initiation, habits that facilitated personal sanctification by rendering one docile to the Holy Breath's inspirations. As we have seen, however, one would do better to equate the grace of ongoing sanctification with lifelong docility to the Holy Breath in putting on the mind of Jesus.

Medieval theologians equated the other gifts, the *gratiae gratis datae* (or gratuitous graces), with the charisms of which Paul the Apostle spoke and that Luke described in the Acts of the Apostles. In this chapter I restrict the meaning of the term "gift" to the Pauline gifts, or charisms. By the term "charism" or "gift" I mean a particular manifestation of the Holy Breath's illumination that builds up the Christian community through concrete acts of service.[1]

Medieval theology also portrayed the gifts of service (*gratiae gratis datae*) as effecting the edification of the Christian community rather than the personal sanctification of those who exercised them. This idea roots itself in Paul's reflections in 1 Corinthians 13 on the difference between faith, hope, and love, on the one hand, and the charisms, on the other. One can, however, exaggerate this distinction. True enough, one may possess a genuine charism and misuse it. One gifted with the charism of teaching might, for example, exercise that gift for motives of vanity and arrogance rather than as an expression of one's personal commitment to Christ. Such teaching, if true in content, could help build up the Christian community's shared faith without uniting the teacher any closer to God in the process. Nevertheless, the charismatic gifts of teaching, prophecy, administration, leadership, etc. do sanctify those who exercise them when that exercise embodies the mind of Christ. Moreover, as we shall soon see, growth in the theological virtues matures with moral necessity into the charismatic service of others in Jesus' name and image.

A traditional theology of the charisms contrasts them with the theological virtues in yet another way. The virtues allegedly empower one to act as a Christian while the gifts endow the believer with docility to the Holy Breath's inspirations. This distinction points to a fundamental condition for growth in one's commitment to Christ: one advances in holiness and in the graced service of others not only through deeds that express commitment to God but also and more fundamentally by listening to the inspirations of divine grace. Nevertheless, one may question the legitimacy of associating too nar-

---

1. In *Charism and Sacrament: A Theology of Christian Conversion* (New York: Paulist, 1976), I contrasted the charismatic action of the Holy Breath with her actual graces and defined a charism as "a more or less permanent, enabling call of the Spirit of Jesus" (29). I have since concluded to the arbitrariness of the distinction. I would now include within the Breath's charismatic inspirations both occasional inspirations and more or less permanent calls to service.

rowly the notion of action with the virtues and of receptivity with the gifts. Both the infusion and strengthening of the theological virtues result from prayerful receptivity to the action of the Holy Breath. Similarly, authentic charismatic service of others involves not only listening to her but also acting on her inspirations; for the charisms empower ministry.

The Challenge of Vatican II

The Second Vatican Council has challenged the Catholic community to renew its faith in the charismatic activity of the Breath of Jesus. For most Catholics that renewal may well make the difference in practice between believing in the Holy Breath and believing in some kind of abstract way that the Holy Breath exists. We believe in the Holy Breath when we respond in expectant faith to her gracious illuminations. She certainly inspires the entire process of sanctification; but, as we shall soon see, she does so in part through her charismatic inspirations. Without them the matrix of divine grace that nurtures both catechumens and baptized Christians to mature holiness simply ceases to exist. This fact, as we shall also see, will have important practical implications for the organization of the new catechumenate. Moreover, it demands that we regard the Breath's charisms as indispensible to the very survival of the Church.

The Argument of This Chapter

Let us begin to examine in more detail the social dynamics that create the charismatic matrix of grace into which Christian initiation seeks to introduce adult converts. Our reflections divide into two parts. The second part has several subdivisions.

The first section of this chapter examines the ways in which the Second Vatican Council has changed Catholic perceptions of the Church. More specifically, it takes a look at the council's teachings concerning the Holy Breath's charismatic activity: how it constitutes the Christian community as a community of faith, on the one hand, and how it inspires its missionary activity and its confrontation with secular society, on the other.

The second section of this chapter begins to examine the ways in which the charisms of service transform the shared faith experience of Christians. It first argues that different charisms correspond to distinguishable moments in human experience, both personal experience and shared experience. It then examines more closely the relationship between the natural gifts of individuals and the divine Breath's charismatic inspirations. Finally, the second section of this chapter focuses on the ways in which the charisms of service not only transform a personal experience of faith into a shared, ecclesial experience but also empower the Church's mission to non-Christians.

1. The Ecclesial Vision of Vatican II. The theological architects of the Second Vatican Council regarded themselves quite correctly as traditionalists. The vision of the Church that they wrote into the council's official decrees retrieved important but long-forgotten insights into the life and mission of the Christian community. The council's architects, however, also understood the revolutionary uses of the Christian tradition. They knew perfectly well that the theology of the Church that they promulgated would challenge many popular assumptions about the Catholic community's mission, life, and discipline. The council fathers felt justified in issuing that challenge because, quite correctly, they saw those assumptions as seriously misleading and saw the need to update Catholic faith and discipline.

In a sense, one needs to understand the entire history of the Church in order to deal theologically with the ecclesiology of Vatican II. The popular assumptions about the Church that the council called into question stemmed, however, from more recent events in Church history. In many ways Vatican II sought to undo misconceptions popularized in the wake of the First Vatican Council.

Vatican Council I

Called in 1869 and disbanded suddenly in 1870 because of the Franco-Prussian war, Vatican I met in a very different atmosphere from Vatican II. A highly Roman and clerical council, Vatican I had practically no lay participants and no Protestant observers at all. Vatican I's ringing anathemas express the siege mentality into which official Church teaching had lapsed at the close of the nineteenth century.

Moreover, the abortive character of this council, the fact that war prevented it from completing its work, produced in the dissemination of its teaching a number of theological distortions that the bishops at Vatican I probably did not foresee. The papal commissions that prepared the council's work drew up fifty-one documents for discussion and debate. Only five reached the floor of the council. Only two came to a vote: *Dei Filius* discussed the relationship between faith and reason, while *Pastor aeternus* defined papal infallibility. Vatican I made no statement about the role of the bishops, priests, laity, or religious in the life of the Church. This council's heavy emphasis on the role of papal teaching and authority combined with modern communications to produce a creeping curialism, a growing and historically unprecedented centralization of Church authority in the hands of the papal curia.

The Integralists at Vatican II

The curial integralists, who formed the small, vocal minority at Vatican II, gave voice in its debates to the vision of the Church that had gained popular credence in the wake of Vatican I. The integralists wanted a highly centralized Church in which virtually any administrative decision of any importance happened in Rome. The integralists looked upon the pope as the only real official teacher in the Church; bishops, they held, exist solely to hand on papal doctrine to the rest of the Church. The integralists tended, too, to equate the unity of the Church with a legal uniformity canonically imposed by the see of Peter. They portrayed the Catholic Church in triumphalistic terms as the one, true Church commissioned by God to defend Christian truth against unbelief and Protestant heresy. They tended to conceive of the Church as a "perfect society," that is, as a society divinely endowed with all the resources it needs to accomplish its supernatural purpose, just as the state, that other "perfect society," has within itself all the means it needs to achieve its natural purposes. Committed to a hierarchical understanding of Church government, the integralists at Vatican II meant by the term "Church" its ordained leaders and demanded of lay Christians strict and passive obedience to the hierarchy's laws and teaching.

The Ecclesiology of Vatican II

The liberal majority of the bishops who dominated Vatican II and gave decisive shape to its teaching espoused a very different vision of the Church. Instead of a Church centralized exclusively in Rome, they pushed for and obtained an initial and partial decentralization of Church government through the establishment of national conferences of bishops as a counterbalance to the inflated authority of the Roman curia.

Against a papalist interpretation of Church authority, they defended the collegial character of Church government. Vatican II endorsed the principle of collegiality, but unfortunately it left its meaning somewhat vague. The principle of collegiality asserts that the college of bishops in union with the pope, who functions as the college's head, rules the Church. The documents of the council failed, however, to make it clear whether in all their actions pope and bishops function as a college or whether in certain areas the pope, on the one hand, and the bishops, on the other, function independently, while in the other areas of Church government they function collegially. The liberals tended to espouse the first interpretation; the integralists, the second.[2]

Against the legal uniformity that the integralists defended, the liberals called for and obtained an inculturated approach to Christian evangelization. Inculturated evangelization respects the diversity of peoples and traditions and tries to communicate the gospel in symbols derived from each culture in which the Church roots itself. It also draws upon the gospel to challenge those elements in any given culture that contradict Christian revelation.

In contrast to the triumphalistic vision of the Church that the integralists defended, the liberal majority at Vatican II committed the Catholic community to ecumenical dialogue with non-Catholic Christians and with other world religions.

Instead of espousing a hierarchical vision of the Church, the liberals at the council depicted the Church as a mystery of grace that transcends its institutional structure and as the entire people of God. They portrayed the hierarchy as standing within the Church and as exercising responsibility for its unity and for the common good of the Christian community.

Instead of looking upon lay people as in all cases bound by obedience to the hierarchy, the liberals regarded baptized Christians as bound to obey under the hierarchy the charismatic inspirations of the Breath of Christ.

Instead of depicting the Church and state as two "perfect societies," the liberals at Vatican II portrayed their relationship in dialogic terms. In the council's vision secular society has something to teach the Church, just as the Church has something of crucial importance to teach secular society.

2. In the discussion of collegiality after Vatican II, it has become clear that the integralists would allow the bishops to act collegially only when the pope gives them explicit permission to do so.

Vatican II on the Charisms

The liberals at Vatican II enshrined their vision of the Church in the council's official documents. Here we need to underscore one facet of that vision, namely, its insistence that the charismatic activity of the Holy Breath constitutes a perennial endowment of the Church. Prior to Vatican II most Catholics assumed, as did the integralists at the council, that the charisms of which the Apostle Paul speaks in his letters and which Luke describes in the Acts of the Apostles had been given to the first generation of Christians but thereafter discontinued. Vatican II set aside this fallacious belief and insisted instead on the charismatic inspiration of all ministry within the Church.

The council documents place repeated emphasis on the Breath's sovereign freedom in dispensing the charisms (*Apostolicam actuositatem*, 3; *Ad gentes*, 23; *Lumen gentium*, 7). The documents also insist on their universal availability: the Breath of Jesus calls all Christians, ordained and unordained alike, to some form of charismatic ministry (*Apostolicam actuositatem*, 3, 28, 30; *Lumen gentium*, 4). In depicting all Church ministry as charismatically inspired, the council rejected as inadequate any attempt to reduce the apostolate of the laity to "Catholic Action," as the integralists tried to do. Had the council adopted the integralist position in this matter, it would have placed all lay apostolic activity directly under the hierarchy, who alone would have had the right to initiate and terminate it. Vatican II, by contrast, saw the lay apostolate as flowing from Christian baptism and as expressing the Church's mission to evangelize the world (*Apostolicam actuositatem*, 1; *Lumen gentium*, 9).

In teaching that the laity should conduct their apostolate in creative responsiveness to the Breath of Christ, although in union with the hierarchy and in responsiveness to its discerning supervision, Vatican II placed genuine limits on the exercise of ecclesiastical authority within the Church. The Church's ordained leaders have the responsibility and therefore the authority to discern and coordinate the Christian community's charismatic ministry. Through their preaching and example they must evoke the gifts. In no circumstance, however, do ordained leaders have the right to suppress the divine Breath's authentic charismatic inspirations. In other words, Vatican II obliged all ordained leaders to respect and encourage the Breath's inspirations in the spontaneous ministry of lay Christians (*Lumen gentium*, 12; *Apostolicam actuositatem*, 3). By implication, the council documents require the ordained to see to it as well that the structures of Church discipline do the same.

The council also endorsed Paul the Apostle's doctrine of the Church as the body of Christ bound together in mutual love and service by the gift-giving Breath of Jesus (*Lumen gentium*, 7, 26, 48, 50; *Ad gentes*, 5; *Perfectae caritatis*, 7; *Presbyterorum ordinis*, 2, 8, 9, 15; *Unitatis redintegratio*, 3; *Apostolicam actuositatem*, 3; *Lumen gentium*, 32). The council, of course, used other images to understand the mystery of the Church, images like the bride of the Lamb, the mother of the human race, the virginal spouse of Christ. Nevertheless, the frequency with which the Pauline image of the body of Christ occurs in the council's teachings underscores the importance of the Holy Breath's charismatic activity in the life of the Christian community, for in Pauline theology sharing the gifts creates the body of Christ.

In the council's teaching not only does the Breath of Christ create the Christian community by dispensing her charisms to its members, but by her gifts she also empowers the Church's missionary activity. The council regarded not only individual missionary vocations but also the formation of missionary organizations as charismatically inspired (*Ad gentes*, 23).

Finally, the council not only insisted on the charismatic inspirations of the lay apostolate but also entrusted to lay Christians the primary responsibility for Christianizing secular society. In other words, in their attempts to inform human family life, culture, economics, politics, and international relations with gospel values, Christians need to seek and to follow the Holy Breath's charismatic inspirations.

A theology of conversion attempts to probe the religious experiences that validate Christian doctrine. Let us then begin to explore those experiences that validate Vatican II's insistence on the charismatic character of the Church and of its ministry. As we shall see, the council's teaching on this point provides an important clue for understanding how the Church becomes a matrix of divine grace that nurtures its members to conversion and to mature holiness.

2. Charism, Sanctification, and Mission. The charisms of the Holy Breath transform human experience in ways that contrast with growth in the theological virtues. Christians share the same hope in Christ, profess the same faith, live united in a common love, and hunger and thirst after the same divine justice. One can lay no other foundation for Christian living than growth in the theological virtues and dedication to the establishment of God's just kingdom on earth as in heaven. Both constitute, then, the common patrimony of all Christians.

In the preceding chapter we examined the foundations of this common patrimony: namely, the fact that God calls all Christians to docility to the Holy Breath in putting on the mind of Jesus. As his moral and religious vision informs human affectivity, belief, moral judgment, and sociopolitical involvement, it endows them with a specifically Christian character that anchors the convert simultaneously in this world and in the next.

In a sense the charisms of service also belong to the common patrimony of all Christians, since God calls all believers to exercise some gift of service. Nevertheless, the charisms differ from the theological virtues and from the Christian search for social justice in at least one respect: for while God calls all believers to grow in the same hope, faith, love, and dedication to justice by serving the ideals of the kingdom, the Breath of God does not inspire every individual to the same kind of service. Different individuals receive different gifts. The particularity of the charisms, the fact that they come tailored to specific individuals, marks them, then, as graces inherently different from the grace of justification or from the three theological virtues. This fact will, as we shall see, assume enormous importance in understanding the purpose of the rite of confirmation.

The particularity of the charisms raises several interrelated theological questions. We need first of all to reflect on what makes the charisms shareable: particular gifts transform particular moments in the development of human experience. Second, we need to understand how the charisms transform natural gifts by examining the ways in which particular charisms can effect the gracing of particular human personalities. Finally, we need to understand how each particular gift contributes something distinctive to the shared faith consciousness of the Christian community as a whole and to its collective witness to Christ. As we shall see, the sharing of all the charisms creates the matrix of grace that nurtures individual believers to Christian maturity. Let us examine each of these questions in turn.

a. Some Charism Transforms Each Moment in the Growth of Human Experience. Paul the Apostle introduced the term "charism" into Christian vocabulary. As we have seen, by it he meant a particular, graced manifestation of the action of the Breath of Christ that builds up his body. We find in his writings several lists of charisms. The First Letter to the Corinthians includes two such lists. In one Paul speaks of preaching wisdom, preaching instruction, faith, healing, miracles, prophecy, discernment, tongues, and the interpretation of tongues (1 Cor 12:8-10). Later in the same chapter Paul ranks a number of charisms in their order of importance. Apostles head the list, followed by prophets, teachers, miracles, healing, helpers, leaders, and tongues (1 Cor 12:28-31). The Letter to the Romans names prophecy, administration, teaching, preaching, almsgiving, officials, and works of mercy (Rom 12:6-8). The Letter to the Ephesians, whose pauline authorship some exegetes dispute, lists apostles, prophets, evangelists, pastors, and teachers (Eph 4:9). Elsewhere Paul speaks of marriage and celibacy as charisms (1 Cor 7:6-7). Even a quick glance at these lists reveals that they do not match.

Interpreting the Pauline Charisms

The lists also overlap. Prophecy and gifts of teaching and preaching appear in all four lists. Other gifts appear in only two lists: healing, miracles, tongues, apostles, and pastoral leaders. Paul mentions the following gifts only once: faith, discernment, interpretation, helpers, administrators, almsgivers, officials, and works of mercy.

The texts of Paul's letters give us no valid reason to believe that he regarded these lists as exhaustive of the Breath's charismatic inspirations. Interestingly enough, Paul also neglected to describe in any detail most of the gifts he mentioned and seemed to presuppose that those he addressed already knew what he meant by them. Apparently, then, the Pauline lists enumerate typical graces, services, and ministries in the communities to which he wrote, graces and services that its members experienced as charismatically inspired.

Because Paul himself failed to explain in his letters the meaning of most of these gifts, exegetes have given them a variety of interpretations but have provided inadequate norms for choosing one possible interpretation over another. Faced with the failure of exegesis to provide an adequate account of the gifts, a contemporary theology of conversion may, then, hazard its own interpretation based on the experience of living Christians. Let us begin to explore the scope of Christian charismatic experience by considering the gift of faith.

The Charism of Faith

As we have seen, theologians use the term "faith" in three different senses. We have already reflected on the first two. In its first and broadest sense "faith" means a person's complete openness to the action of divine grace. In its first meaning faith encompasses and transforms the entire person: affectivity, intellect, conscience, social relationships. The first dynamic of Christian conversion, its mediation between affective and moral conversion, grounds this first meaning of faith and effects justification. In its second, more restricted sense, "faith" designates one of the three theological virtues and contrasts both with Christian hope, love, and commitment to a just social order. The second dynamic of Christian conversion, its transvaluation of the other forms of conversion, grounds the second meaning of faith by effecting the transvaluation of intuitive and inferential perceptions of reality. In its third and most restricted sense of all, "faith" denotes one of the charisms.

Why begin these reflections on the gifts of service with an obscure gift like faith? Paul mentioned this gift only once and then failed utterly to describe it. His inclusion of faith among the charisms certainly suggests, however, that in the Pauline communities some Christians displayed a certain quality of faith that distinguished them from others. At some point in our own lives we have all probably met such people. I think of a missionary who not long ago visited the place where I teach. He was returning to work among the poor in Central America after a brief visit to the United States. He expected that his apostolic involvement with the poor would probably lead eventually to his own violent death, but he faced that prospect with utter tranquility and trust in God. Others gifted with faith exhibit similar traits: trust in God's providential care for them that frees them to dedicate their lives selflessly to the service of others, a sense of their own human limits coupled with an absolute confidence that God will work through them to accomplish his own saving purposes, a peace and tranquility in the face of suffering for the sake of Christ, a childlike capacity to turn to God in their every need with the confidence that he will hear their prayers.

As I have pondered the lives of such people, I have come to look upon the gift of faith as a bridge between the theological virtues and the other charisms. By that I mean that as Christians grow in holiness, as they deepen in hope, faith, love, and a hunger for God's own justice, at some point the quality of their trust in God begins to distinguish them from the other members of the Christian community. Often without knowing or intending it, by the sheer depth and confidence of their trust in God they bear effective witness to those less advanced on the path to holiness. I regard such individuals as gifted with faith in a special way. By the very peace and confidence with which they look to God, they strengthen the wavering and give hope to the disconsolate and despairing.

I have come to regard the gift of faith as a bridge between the theological virtues and the other gifts for two reasons. First, I believe that growth in hope, faith, and love matures spontaneously into the charism of faith. Second, I expect those who exercise any other gift authentically to exhibit a quality of faith similar to that of those who possess faith as their special charismatic endowment. In other words, on the one hand, the gift of faith transforms the pursuit of personal holiness into a form of public witness; and, on the other hand, the other gifts endow that witness with a special ministerial purpose. For example, prophets, teachers, pastoral leaders, and others who serve others in a public manner all witness to Christ in ways that give them public visibility. At the same time, the specific gift they exercise has a particular pastoral focus—confrontation, instruction, guidance—absent from the more generic gift of faith. Accordingly, in such an interpretation of Christian charismatic development, one measures the authenticity of every charism by the extent to which it endows the faith witness of Christians with a special visibility even as it embodies the mind of Christ in some concrete act of service to the Christian and human community.

Let us, then, interpret the gift of faith as a bridge between the experience of ongoing sanctification and the other gifts of service. We shall then reflect on the other charismatic gifts in the light of a contemporary Christian experience of the Breath of Jesus. We can, interestingly enough, correlate each of the other Pauline gifts with a specific moment in the growth of human experience.

Experiencing Charisms of Prayer

As we have seen, human evaluative responses develop in predictable stages. Through sensation we become initially and vaguely present to our own bodies and to the world that surrounds them. Because our sensations display affective coloring, they reveal to us in an extremely vague and inchoate manner not only the efficacious impact of the physical forces that affect us but also a very vague, initial sense of the kinds of tendencies that generate those forces.

Gifts of prayer transform this first moment in the growth of human experience. We cannot, of course, sense God in exactly the same way that we sense physical objects. Nevertheless, God does touch us efficaciously; and we do feel it when he does. We feel it in shared worship. We feel it in private prayer.

All forms of shared worship engage the senses directly as the words and gestures of others inform one's own relationship to God in prayer. Moreover, the Fathers of the Church correctly spoke of spiritual sensibilities that result from faith. If one purifies the term "spiritual" of dualistic connotations, then it designates sensibilities born of faith through which we respond to the touch of God.

On occasion shared prayer can yield a vivid, palpable sense of the divine presence that goes beyond one's awareness of the other persons and things that inform and constitute the act of worship. We also sense the presence of God in solitary meditation. When we pray in solitude, we open our hearts to God. In prayer we often play an active role: we speak to God and place before him our many needs. The God-seeker who cultivates a habit of shared spontaneous prayer and of private meditation soon discovers, however, that prayer also involves learning how to listen to God, so that in the things we ourselves say and do we can more and more respond to him on his terms rather than on those we ourselves would dictate.

When, moreover, God touches us in solitary prayer, we quite literally feel it. We sense ourselves called, healed, moved to some form of action in God's name. Understandably, then, the literature of prayer abounds in sensory images. It encourages us to feel, to savor, to relish the movements of the Holy Breath in our hearts. Visionary and locutionary experiences can sometimes disclose the significance of God's gracious touches. Such experiences always need discernment: but, if authentic, they can lead us to closer union with God and can give religious direction to our lives.

Glossolalia

The gift of tongues numbers among the gifts of prayer. Paul described it as a way of speaking to God (1 Cor 14:2). Singing in tongues dramatizes the prayerful character of this charism: those who sing in tongues open their hearts to the Lord in praise. This gift also schools one to prayerful receptivity to the inspirations of the Holy Breath. I find that I myself cannot pray in tongues without centering in a special way upon God, and I have found that others who pray in tongues share that perception.

Moreover, glossolalic prayer itself exhibits a curious kind of passive activity. When one prays in tongues, one prays actively, forming sounds in an attitude of worship and praise; but the prayer itself lacks conceptual content. This absence of images and concepts stills the mind and prepares it to feel and respond to the Breath's further enlightenment. This dimension of glossolalic prayer might help explain why the Holy Breath bestowed it first upon the disciples assembled in the upper room on Pentecost.

The sharing of prayer always builds up a community of faith, but shared glossolalic prayer contributes something distinctive to the collective faith consciousness of the Christian community. Its presence in Christian assemblies reminds them of the Church's birth on the first Christian Pentecost and teaches believers to look upon Pentecost as an ongoing event in the life of the Christian community. It also reminds the community of the charismatic character of Christian prayer.

Gifts of prayer, including the gift of tongues, transvalue in faith the first moment in the growth of human experience: our sensory perception of the persons and forces that act upon us. Other charisms address later stages of human experiential development.

Discernment and Judgments of Feeling

As human experience develops beyond initial sensory contact with reality, it changes into an affective perception of the kinds of forces that give shape to one's world. Feelings of anger or of fear warn us of potential threats; the sympathetic emotions teach us to appreciate the goodness and beauty of the persons and things that surround us.

As we have seen, human affections perform a double function within human experience: not only do they yield an initial perception of the kinds of forces that impinge upon us, but they also pass judgment on our attempts to understand those same realities imaginatively.

We can distinguish two kinds of natural judgments of feeling: aesthetic judgments and prudential judgments. Aesthetic judgments express themselves in literature and art. Prudential judgments express themselves in judgments of conscience.

The gift of discernment transforms aesthetic judgment into the art and literature of faith. Fra Angelico once said that only those who live with Jesus can paint him. Moreover, great religious art and literature communicate a powerful passion for God as well as a discerning insight into how to express that passion.

The gift of discernment transforms prudential judgments too by teaching them docility to the Breath of Christ in the formation of one's conscience. Like judgments of natural prudence, judgments of discernment seek to understand the kinds of impulses that influence and motivate human behavior; but they do so prayerfully and not just prudently.

Discerning Spirits

Christian writers speak of the discernment of spirits. As I have already indicated, I myself prefer to avoid the term "spirit" when thinking theologically because its speculative history has endowed it with too many misleading connotations. I replace it therefore by the term "breath." The Old Testament associates the image of breath or breathing very early with the experience of a vitalizing religious illumination. The Hebrew prophets experienced their enlightenment as the breathing of God, as an empowering inrush of divine vitality. They discovered, however, that evil impulses could disguise themselves as piety. When that happened, one needed to discriminate between the different "breaths" that surged in one's own heart or in that of another.

Those who possess the charism of discernment read accurately the character of those different breaths and judge them intuitively according to the mind of Christ. The prudent mind deliberates, weighing alternative actions, their motives, and their consequences. It assesses the impulses of the heart by sound psychological, logical, and moral principles. The discerning heart forms its perception of the same realities prayerfully, not self-reliantly. It seeks from God an accurate, felt assessment of personal impulses and social movements. By thus teaching prudential judgments of feeling docility to the Breath of Christ, the gift of discernment graces the second, affective moment in the growth of human experience.

Prophecy and Intuition

The gift of prophecy transforms the third. As we have seen, the human mind perceives reality both intuitively and inferentially. Intuitive perceptions lend clarity to initial feelings about the benign or threatening character of our world. They do so by engaging the creative imagination. Inferential perceptions, by contrast, engage logical thought. An imaginative perception of reality through lyric and narrative marks, then, the third stage in the growth of human experience. Prophetic thinking engages the same kinds of intuitive perceptions.

Prophets speak a word from God: a word of hope to the discouraged and despairing, a word of repentance to the obstinate. Even a cursory perusal of prophetic literature will reveal that the prophetic mind thinks spontaneously in powerful images. The great Hebrew prophets wrote sublime poetry. They did not argue a position; they proclaimed their message in an oracular fashion. They addressed above all the human heart and called it to discern and respond to the saving deeds of God in human history. The prophetic mind sees visions and dreams dreams. It expresses itself in imaginative literary forms and in symbolic gestures: in lyric, in parable, in startling narratives, in powerful rhetorical images. In all of these ways, then, the gift of prophecy teaches the intuitive imagination docility to the inspirations of the Breath of Jesus. An interpreted message in tongues functions within shared charismatic prayer like a prophecy (1 Cor 14:1-33).

Teaching, Intuition, and Inference

As human experience develops naturally, intuitive thinking gives way to logical inference. Gifts of teaching engage the inferential as well as the intuitive mind. All authentic Christian teaching, even when carefully reasoned, however, always retains a prophetic character; for Christian teachers, like Christian prophets, serve the Word of God and attempt to relate it to human life in a transforming manner. Prophets declaim that word like oracles; teachers use arguments and explanations both rhetorically and rationally in an attempt to convince others of its truth. Think of Peter's Pentecost sermon or of the complex arguments constructed by theologians in their attempt to explain the meaning of revelation to others.

The Christian community has from the beginning needed two kinds of teachers. On the one hand, it has needed evangelists who proclaim the Word of God kerygmatically and summon others to initial and ongoing conversion to Christ. On the other hand, it has also needed those who instruct the community in an ongoing fashion concerning its history, identity, and destiny in Christ. The former proclaim the word of wisdom revealed in Christ; the latter teach instruction. By enabling the Christian community to retrieve its origins and history, Christian teachers endow it with a shared sense of identity. By explaining the consequences of a Christian faith commitment, teachers, like prophets, enable the Church to decide its future in faith.

Charisms of Healing

Teachers whose words effect healing in their hearers proclaim the Word of God in power. As a consequence, faith healing never occurs in a vacuum. It presupposes an expectant openness to God that prophecy and teaching create. Those who possess gifts of healing must, then, to some extent build their ministry upon the gift of teaching. Charismatic healers do not themselves effect healing in others. Instead, through prayer and through the proclamation of the Word, they dispose sick and sinful hearts and bodies to respond to God's own healing touch.

Needless to say, God's efficacious healing, like God's touch within prayer, also engages human sensory experience; for when God heals us, we experience it sensibly, sometimes physically. I think of a woman I knew in New Orleans who had a withered optic nerve in one of her eyes. The day after a friend of hers begged for the restoration of her sight, she awoke with a brief, intense pain in her blind eye. When she opened it, she could see. Miraculous healings have no natural explanation, and indeed the doctor who examined the woman with the restored optic nerve pronounced the cure miraculous.

Charisms of Action

We have till now been considering the charisms that transform human evaluative responses. Paul the Apostle, however, named a number of other gifts that transform one practically: helping, administration, almsgiving, performing works of mercy, apostolic and pastoral leadership. These gifts normally function outside the context of prayer. They function instead in either an ecclesial or a secular context.

In the growth of human experience decision, practical action, both terminates and expresses human evaluative responses. Our words and actions communicate that response: we speak or act lovingly, angrily, rationally, prudently, discerningly. The charismatically inspired activity of the Christian community ought, then, to express a faith consciousness nurtured by the gifts that grace all the different evaluative phases of human experience. Practical service to others in the name of Christ ought to proceed from a felt sense of the reality and transforming presence of God that gifts of prayer and of healing instill. Charismatic deeds of service ought to flow from hearts converted and inspired by prophecy and from minds informed by sound teaching. Charismatic acts of service should also obey the judgments of discernment.

Nevertheless, the action gifts make their own distinctive contribution to the gracing of human experience. They differ from the other gifts in the way that thinking about having a party differs from throwing it. The Christian community needs the action gifts in order to transform its shared hopes and beliefs into shared deeds of love and into the construction of a just social order.

Charism and Shared Ministry

We are reflecting on the ways in which the charisms of service differ from the theological virtues and from the Christian search for social justice. We have located that difference in the particularity of the charisms. God calls all Christians to grow in the same hope, faith, love, and longing for justice because the same ideal of the kingdom that Jesus proclaimed informs all of these graced growth experiences. God also calls all believers to exercise some kind of charismatic ministry. The particularity of the gifts lies, however, in the fact that God calls different people to different kinds of charismatic ministry. No one believer possesses all the charismatic gifts, with the probable exception of Jesus.

The charismatic gracing of personal experience produces, then, ministerial specialization. Christians minister to one another and to the world in ways that express their charismatic competence. One who shares with others a gift of prayer or of healing heightens the Christian community's felt sense of the efficacious presence of God to his people. Discerners help the community to make intuitive judgments and to form its conscience collectively in faith. Prophets encourage the community or call it to repentance. Teachers proclaim the wisdom of Christ kerygmatically or instruct others in the meaning of divine revelation. Those who exercise the action gifts coordinate the community's shared ministerial activity.

The charisms transvalue the different moments in the growth of experience by focusing them on divine realities and by ensuring that one respond to them experientially with a receptivity to the Holy Breath's guidance. In this sense, the charisms transvalue experience not only by shaping the realities that believers experience but also by changing the way they experience them.

Sharing the Charisms

The fact, moreover, that different gifts transform different moments in the growth of natural human experience, makes them shareable. I may not possess the specific gift that graces this or that kind of experience, but I can allow the gifts of others to transform that dimension of my life. Those schooled in speculative theology may lack the practical wisdom of pastors and administrators, just as pastors and administrators may lack the expertise of a trained theologian. Both, however, need one another. Nuts-and-bolts administrators and prophets may dislike dealing with one another, but each has an important contribution to make to the life of the community. Prophets dream dreams; nuts-and-bolts administrators make dreams realities. Everyone needs the wisdom of discerners in reaching sound judgments of conscience. All need healing, whether or not they exercise a ministry of healing.

The particularity of the gifts when combined with the fact that no single member of the Christian community has all the gifts has, then, important consequences for the shared life of faith. It means that Christians need one another's gifts in order to ensure that every dimension of their own personal experience develops under the inspiration of the Breath of Jesus. My gifts help others in areas in which they lack charismatic competence. Their gifts help me in other areas in which I lack graced competence. In other words, the Breath of Jesus graces us in ways that ensure that we cannot learn to experience God adequately alone. We can only do so in a community of faith that supports us in our need and that allows and encourages us to minister charismatically to one another's needs.

Through the mutual ministry of believers, the Breath of Jesus creates the social matrix of faith within which believers can advance to integral conversion and thus grow in holiness. In the two sections that follow we shall attempt to understand in greater detail how this occurs.

b. Particular personalities display an obediential susceptibility for certain kinds of charisms. In his study of different psychological types, C. G. Jung at two points suggested the possibility of correlating specific charismatic gifts with particular kinds of ego bias. He observed that the Hebrew prophets exemplify the intuitive introvert and that introverts focused on feeling could well develop a penchant for mysticism.[3]

As we soon shall see, one should avoid any rigid correlation between the charisms of the Holy Breath and specific human temperaments. Nevertheless, Jung's observations point to some fruitful insights into the natural gifts that help ground the Holy Breath's charis-

---

3. C. G. Jung, *Psychological Types; Collected Works,* Vol. 6, translated by H. G. Baynes (Princeton: Bollingen, 1974), 390, 400.

matic inspirations; for the charisms, like every other kind of created grace, heal, elevate, and perfect natural human endowments. Moreover, one can expand Jung's list of correlations between particular charisms and different psychological types. Let us, then, examine Jung's theory of personality types for the possible light it has to throw on the presence of an obediential potency within human nature for charismatic transformation in the Holy Breath of God.

Attitudes: Introversion and Extroversion

Jung's personality theory distinguishes personality attitudes from personality functions. Jung speaks of two kinds of attitudes: introversion and extroversion. He describes four personality functions: sensation, intuition, thinking, and feeling.

Personality attitudes characterize the way an individual responds to environmental stimuli. Extroverts exhibit considerable sensitivity to the world around them. They tend to conform to the social expectations of others. They value hard facts. They form their attitudes, intuitions, and beliefs through social interaction with others. As a consequence, extroverts run a double risk: they can either lose themselves completely in the world of things, or they can conform slavishly to the demands of others. When that happens, they can tragically lose touch with the personal motives and needs that govern their behavior.

Introverts exhibit very different personality traits. Introverts, like extroverts, acknowledge the presence of environmental stimuli and challenges but relate to them differently. Introverts organize their lives, not around the expectations of others, but around personal interest and preference. They value things, not for their own sake, but for their personal, idiosyncratic appeal, for the way one feels or thinks about them. Introverts tend to read meanings into things, meanings derived not from the things themselves but from the introvert's own complex and sometimes convoluted psychological processes. While extroverts run the risk of losing themselves in things, introverts run the risk of entrapment within the labyrinthine corridors of their own psyches.

Personality Functions

The personality functions that Jung described correspond to the four stages in the evaluative growth of human experience: sensation, feeling, intuitive imagination, and rational thought. In the course of putting together a personality, different individuals develop varying degrees of sensitivity to one or other stage of human evaluative response. Sensate individuals cultivate variety and intensity in their conscious sensory experiences. Individuals focused on feeling explore the whole spectrum of human emotions; they perceive and judge reality accurately with their affections. Intuitive individuals think imaginatively; they see visions and dream dreams. Thinking individuals perceive and judge reality rationally.

Empirical studies of the human personality disclose a notable degree of stability in personality attitudes but considerably more variation in personality functions. The latter seem to change with age and circumstance. If, however, we treat Jung's psychological types as real possibilities on a sliding scale of personality development, we can begin to discern within different kinds of personalities a natural obediential capacity for specific charismatic gifts.

Jung himself, as we have seen, correlated the charism of prophecy with the intuitive introvert. Intuitive introverts dwell within the realm of their own imaginations. Typically they become poets, artists, visionaries. They tend to develop highly imaginative but idiosyncratic views of reality, as did the Hebrew prophets, who voiced their perceptions of God and of human events in sublime religious poetry. One can, moreover, make other correlations between specific charisms and other personality types, as we shall see in the paragraphs that follow.

The charism of prophecy teaches the human imagination docility to the Breath of Christ. It frees intuitive perceptions from neurotic idiosyncrasy. It teaches imaginative thought to perceive the incarnation of divine grace in Jesus and in those inspired by his Breath. It attunes natural intuitions to God's own vision of the world and of its future.

Personalities who perceive and judge reality affectively, whether introverts or extroverts, display a natural susceptibility for the charism of discernment. As we have seen, the discerning mind, like the prudential, functions deliberatively. Though both natural prudence and the charism of discernment measure events and conduct in the light of hard facts and of abstract principles, neither judges reality finally on the basis of abstractions but by a felt sense of what suits a concrete person or situation. The gift of discernment ensures that such prudential judgments submit prayerfully to the Holy Breath's illumination and guidance.

The charism of discernment frees judgments of feeling from neurotic distortion and teaches them both docility to the Breath of Christ and sensitivity to his religious vision. It accustoms the heart to judge persons and things not only in the light of this world but also in the light of the next.

Extroverts, whether intuitive or sensate, display natural talent for different styles of leadership and administration. The sensate extrovert tends to develop into a nuts-and-bolts administrator who insists that community projects advance with adequate staff, funding, and resources. The intuitive extrovert, on the other hand, develops into the charismatic leader who cannot confront a situation without thinking of a dozen different ways of handling it.

The action gifts teach those temperamentally disposed to exercise administrative or leadership roles how to transform them into ministry to others in the name of Jesus. They place administrative competence and the exercise of leadership at the prayerful service of the kingdom of God. These gifts attune those in positions of authority to the voice of the Holy Breath speaking in others. They also free leaders and administrators from neurotic egocentrism.

Both thinking and intuitive personalities, whether introverted or extroverted, manifest a natural capacity for the charism of teaching, although they will probably develop different pedagogical styles. I sometimes team teach seminars with a colleague whose strong extroversion counterbalances my own extreme introversion. We make a good team. He thinks out loud and therefore engages the students immediately in dialogue, while I need to listen to them and mull over their comments before I can engage them in discussion. As a consequence, he usually dominates our seminars during the first half; I, during the second. Teachers biased toward thinking will tend to organize their materials logically. Intuitive teachers will probably run a more chaotic classroom but will make up for their lack of rational organization by their ability to inspire enthusiasm in their students.

The charism of teaching transforms naturally competent instruction into a faith-filled ministry to others and to the word of God. It accustoms teachers to approach the revealed word with humility and to serve it and other people rather than one's own academic ego. It trains teachers to balance personal study and scholarship with the prayerful cultivation of divine wisdom. This charism inspires both the kerygmatic proclamation of the word and the ongoing instruction of the Christian community in things it needs to know. The same gift enables those who teach more secular subjects to transform them prayerfully into genuine Christian ministry.

Ordinary and Extraordinary

We have been considering possible ways in which ideal personality types might display a natural, obediential susceptibility to receive this or that charism of the Holy Breath. She, however, graces, not ideal abstractions, but concrete human beings and does so with sovereign freedom. One should not, then, imagine that only those persons with a developed natural ability for this or that charism can receive it.

One's natural abilities do, of course, themselves develop and change over the course of a lifetime. Persons who have cultivated affective sensitivity can learn to balance felt judgments with rational ones, and vice versa. Sensate individuals can learn to cultivate their imaginations, just as intuitive individuals can learn to enjoy sensory satisfaction more. As a consequence, one's natural obediential capacity for this or that gift might shift as one's personality evolves.

Whatever charism one receives, one can, however, predict with high probability that one's ego bias will condition the way in which one exercises it. At the same time, the Breath of Christ can and does bestow her charisms on individuals who possess little or no natural talent for exercising the very gifts they receive from her. When that occurs, their charismatic ministry begins to take on an extraordinary character. One senses then the human limitations of the person through whom the divine Breath acts at the same time that one acknowledges the irrelevance of those limitations to the work she accomplishes in and through them. In the judgment of those who trained the Cure of Ars for ministry, he had little or no natural aptitude for it; and yet the Breath of Jesus transformed him into one of the greatest pastors of his day. Similarly, God chose an obscure peasant girl, Bernadette Soubirou, as his instrument for honoring his mother and effecting the healing of countless people. Moreover, in every age the Holy Breath chooses to pour out abundant charisms upon the weak and foolish in order to confound the strong and the wise of this world.

Nevertheless, the fact that the Breath's charisms can and do heal, elevate, and perfect naturally cultivated talents yields an important insight into their variety, which far exceeds the New Testament lists. Viewed psychologically, the charisms have as their purpose the gracing of a human ego. We can, then, number at least as many charisms as kinds of people who minister to one another prayerfully in the name and image of Jesus. Were Paul the Apostle alive today, he might well include the charisms of community organizers, lobbyists, and political activists in his list.

Popular Misunderstanding of the Charisms

Here, moreover, we need to correct two serious, popular mis-understandings unintentionally occasioned by the Catholic charis-matic renewal. This movement continues to rank as one of the im-portant developments in contemporary lay spirituality. At its debut in the late sixties, its leaders called themselves Catholic Pentecostals; but the North American bishops very soon changed that name. On investigating the movement, they found it basically sound, but they also expressed concern about a certain number of pastoral problems that needed facing. Among other things, the bishops suggested that the name Catholic Pentecostalism had a denominational ring that could create the false impression that the movement's leaders were seeking to found a new Church. The bishops, citing the teachings of Vatican II concerning the importance of the Holy Breath's charis-matic activity in the Church, suggested that the new movement call itself instead The Charismatic Renewal of the Church. Those involved in the movement cared little what name people gave it. They accepted the bishops' suggestion gladly.

The presence within the Church of a movement of limited membership officially called "The Charismatic Renewal of the Church" has, however, led many to restrict the term "charismatic" artificially to those who attend charismatic prayer meetings. Worse still one finds those who restrict the term "charismatic" even more sharply to those who speak in tongues. These and similar unfortunate linguistic abuses have created the false and spiritually destructive im-pression that those who do not attend charismatic prayer meetings can regard openness to the charisms as personally optional. In point of fact, the Breath of Jesus calls every believer to some form of charis-matic ministry within the Church.

A second popular misconception haunts the charismatic re-newal. In the early days of the Catholic charismatic renewal its leaders dreamed of the day when all Catholics would attend prayer meet-ings. We shall almost certainly never see that day. Charismatic piety blends elements of popular Catholic devotion and Classical Pente-costalism. It exhibits the strengths and limitations of both those tra-ditions and will probably never appeal to those who prefer a staider style of worship.

The Charismatic Renewal as a Leaven

Nevertheless, this movement has in point of fact contributed significantly to the charismatic renewal of the Church as a whole, but in ways that contrast with the original expectations of its leaders. Not long ago I met in Austin, Texas, a young man who ran a soup kitchen for the poor of that city. On discovering that I have been personally involved with charismatic prayer, he remarked, "I also came by the charismatic way." His participation in charismatic prayer had transformed his life. It had led him to a religious conversion and to his present ministry to the poor, even though he no longer attended prayer meetings. Countless others have walked a similar path. They have passed through an experience of charismatic prayer to other forms of charismatic ministry in the Church. Through such people the renewal, in addition to the specific gifts it especially cultivates, does function as a charismatic leaven in the rest of the community.

Nevertheless, the fact remains that the piety inculcated in large segments of the renewal lacks charismatic balance. The movement prizes some gifts to the neglect of others. For most of those actively involved in the renewal, shared charismatic prayer provides the focus of their piety. As a consequence, they tend to value most those charisms ordinarily exercised within the context of shared prayer: tongues, healing, ecstatic prophecy, certain forms of teaching. Unfortunately, however, the action gifts especially find little scope for exercise in a formal prayer context. That fact leaves some charismatic piety tinged with pietism and spiritual narcissism.

If the Church hopes to experience the kind of charismatic renewal to which the Second Vatican Council has called it, it will need to transcend both of the misunderstandings that popular charismatic piety has unwittingly engendered. Christians who attend charismatic prayer meetings, like those who do not, need to cultivate an openness to all the gifts. In addition, every Christian, not just those who go to charismatic prayer meetings, needs to cultivate personal openness to the charisms. Moreover, until that happens, the Christian community as a whole will fail to achieve the shared faith consciousness it needs in order to ensure the sanctification of its members. We shall reflect on this final point in the section that follows.

c. The mutual charismatic ministry of all Christians transforms their personal experience of faith into a shared, ecclesial experience and empowers the Church's ministry to non-Christians. We have thus far focused our attention on the contrast between the particular charisms that individuals receive and the common call of all believers to grow in hope, faith, love, and active longing for God's justice. The time has come to reflect on the dynamic relationship that unites these two kinds of created grace. In what does that relationship consist? It consists in this: that the sharing of all the charisms creates the Christian community's shared faith consciousness and in the process creates that matrix of grace within which individuals mature in hope, faith, love, and the Christian search for justice. How does this happen?

Personal and Shared Consciousness

Personal consciousness grows by distinguishing interrelated realities and by understanding their relationship to one another. I used to look on bird-watchers with tolerant condescension until I realized that only by learning how to distinguish one species of bird from another, could I begin to see for the first time each one's unique beauty. Discrimination, then, enhances personal consciousness. So too does the grasp of relationships. We interrelate word, concepts, and realities. Indeed, every time we cry, "Eureka!" we grasp some relationship that previously eluded us and in so doing expand our awareness of the shape of things.

The shared consciousness of a community grows out of the personal consciousness of its members, but it engages as well complex processes of interpretation and communication. History, the process by which reality evolves, defines the character of every created reality, not some fixed and immutable essence. I understand who I am personally when I grasp the events that have shaped my life and the ways in which I have chosen to respond to them. Communities need to go through an analogous process together: a large, enduring community comes to a shared sense of its specific identity by remembering collectively the events that brought it into existence together with the history that links it to those founding events.

Interpreting Christian Origins

The ministry, death, and resurrection of Jesus of Nazareth combine with his sending of the Holy Breath on Pentecost in order to found the Christian community. In remembering Jesus' own mission, the Church prolongs it. That memory binds his living disciples to incarnate and proclaim his vision of the kingdom. Christians remember Jesus practically by allowing his Breath to teach them to live in his image. They do so when they share freely the material supports of life with one another, especially with those in greatest need, and when such sharing expresses their mutual forgiveness in God.

The resurrection reveals Jesus' divinity, his vital identity with the Father and with the Breath. When, therefore, we remember the resurrection in faith and in the power of the Holy Breath, that memory orients the Christian community to the transcendent reality of God. It grounds Christian hope for risen life. It teaches Jesus' disciples to live and die not only for the things of this world but also for those of the next. The memory of the Church's roots thus opens it to its future in God.

The memory of Pentecost teaches the Church to order its life in accord with the Holy Breath's charismatic inspirations. It reminds Christians that she calls them to share not only the physical supports of life in community but also the very life of God through mutual charismatic ministry. That same memory also reminds the Church of its universal mission to prolong the ministry of Jesus by proclaiming the good news with charismatic power to every creature.

Interpreting the Christian Story

In addition to remembering the events that originally brought it into existence, the Christian community also needs to remember the history that links it to those events; for that history too defines the present reality of the Church. Church history tells the story of human sin and of the triumph of grace.

The New Testament sets the pattern. It portrays the disciples of Jesus with stark realism: their ambition, obtuseness, jealousy, complacency, treachery. The Gospels also tell, however, of their love for Jesus, of their fidelity to him despite their inability to comprehend fully his person and message, of their willingness, despite all their limitations, to share with him his life and ministry. The Acts of the Apostles describes the initial triumph of grace in the lives of Jesus' followers, but it tells too of tensions and factions within the early Church.

Sin, division, and grace also combine to shape the history of the post-biblical Church. As a consequence, living Christians come to collective self-understanding as a community as much by recalling their failure to live the gospel as by remembering their fidelity to it.

Any community, the Church included, grasps the events that define its character by understanding their significance. It achieves such understanding through complex, though fallible, processes of evaluation that endow its history with present meaning. Theologians, scholars, and Church historians devote their lives to trying to help the Christian community comprehend itself by understanding its own tradition.

Achieving a Shared Sense of Christian Identity

Because the retrieval of its history defines a living community's present understanding of its character, that community needs to reach a consensus concerning the significance of those events. Every generation of Christians seeks such a consensus, not always successfully. The emergence of contradictory accounts of the Church's foundation and history can subvert an existing consensus of faith and demand the patient reconstruction of a new consensus.

Consensus within a community concerning its historical origins endows it with a present sense of identity. Every community needs such a shared sense of identity if it expects to aspire to a shared future, for disagreement about the very nature of a community inevitably breeds dissent concerning its purpose and therefore concerning its common destiny. The Christian community needs, then, to achieve two kinds of consensus in faith: consensus concerning the kind of community that historical events have made it and consensus concerning the kind of community that God is calling it to become.

Shaping a Common Future

Moreover, the Church needs to face its shared future at three levels. First, the paschal mystery orients Christian hope to union with God in a life beyond this one. As it deals more proximately with this life, Christian hope must, in the second place derive from reflection on its history a shared insight into the kind of community into which the Holy Breath seeks to transform it. Finally, it must translate its ideal self-image into shared projects, policies, and strategies for immediate group action; for a community needs more than shared memories and shared hopes in order to achieve full self-awareness as a community. In other words the Church needs to transform both its shared memories and shared hopes into shared lives.

Each member of the Christian community has something distinctive to contribute to the work of the Church. The successful realization of the Christian community's common hopes demands, therefore, the successful orchestration of the gifts and talents of each member of the community toward the achievement of its divinely decreed purpose.

Orchestrating the Charisms

The successful orchestration of the community's gifts requires in turn certain kinds of ordained leaders, those for which the Second Vatican Council called. It requires that the ordained renounce the temptation to monopolize the task of leadership and that they encourage others with the needed charismatic competence to lead the community as well. Authentic Christian leadership seeks, moreover, to open each member of the community in faith and in prayer to the Pentecostal Breath of Christ, so that she may teach them by her charisms how to contribute to the shared life of the Church. Since, moreover, not only individual Christians but the Church's institutional structures need constant purification from the effects of human sinfulness, the ordained leader cannot assume automatically that the Holy Breath's charismatic inspirations will conform automatically to the institutional Church's bureaucratic expectations.

The collaboration of all Christians in the work of the Church must advance in an atmosphere of freedom that only the integral conversion of all its members can guarantee. The absence of conversion breeds both individual acts of oppression and oppressive institutional structures. Integral conversion teaches both individuals and communities to advance beyond elementary human freedom to the responsible reordering of interpersonal relationships and to the responsible search for a just social, economic, and political order both within the Church and within secular society.

To what great enterprise does God summon the Church? The Our Father supplies the Christian community with its most fundamental mission: the establishment of God's kingdom on earth as in heaven through perfect obedience to the divine will. As we have seen, God's will came to normative historical revelation in the Son of God's moral teaching. His vision of a community of faith-sharing, mutual service, and mutual forgiveness gives concrete shape to Christian hope, faith, and love and to the Christian search for social justice. The Christian community needs, however, to translate that vision into concrete programs of activity. Vatican II set itself the enormous task of doing precisely that, of relating Jesus' vision of the kingdom to contemporary human society.

If, then, we consult the documents of Vatican II, we find there the Church's most recent consensus concerning the future to which Christ calls it. The council speaks of two major enterprises confronting the contemporary Church: the conversion of all people to Christ and the Christianization of secular society. Let us reflect on each of these enterprises in turn.

The Church As Mission

The council quite correctly rooted the Church's missionary activity in Jesus' own driving sense of mission. The Father sent his Son into the world to share with all people his own divine life and to make one family of a fragmented, sinful humanity. In proclaiming the kingdom Jesus did not act as an isolated individual but summoned his disciples to collaborate in his own ministry. Moreover, in sending the Holy Breath to effect among his followers the enduring Pentecost of the Church, the risen Christ reversed the effects of the tower of Babel. At Babel God had confounded the tongues of a sinful humanity, dividing the human race into alien and warring nations. On Pentecost the Holy Breath confounded human tongues anew in glossolalic prayer and praise as a foreshadowing of the reconciliation of all nations and peoples in Christ (*Ad gentes,* 1–6).

Despite the spread of the Church to every nation on earth, an immense missionary work still remains to do. The command of Christ to preach the gospel embraces every person: members of other religions, those estranged from God, those who deny him. The process of evangelization should reflect the message that the Church proclaims. Evangelists must, therefore, approach all people with esteem and love. They should understand and value the traditions of those to whom they preach. They should show universal charity and should reach out especially to the poor and afflicted (*Ad gentes,* 10–12).

Evangelizing Communities

The proclamation of the gospel gathers in the people of God. It expands the Church. The responsibility for bringing the good news to unbelievers and to those of different faiths flows from the mission of the Church as a whole and therefore engages every Christian in its fulfillment. In addition, then, to seeking personally to win others to Christ, each member of every local church needs also to take responsibility for its catechumens; for the catechumenate gives institutional expression to the Church's most fundamental mission (*Ad gentes,* 13–14, 23). Moreover, those who presume to summon others to an integral, fivefold conversion need to have experienced such a conversion themselves and to understand its dynamics. Otherwise, they will never nurture it authentically and successfully in others.

Christian evangelization seeks, then, to bring into existence thoroughly converted communities whose inculturated living of the gospel gives credibility to its formal proclamation of the word to unbelievers. Evangelization should engage the gifts of every member of the believing community: laity, clergy, religious. Through the charismatic service of its members local churches should seek to become self-supporting and self-ministering (*Ad gentes,* 15–18).

The Foreign Missions

Those called to proclaim to gospel to those who do not know Christ deserve the support of the rest of the community whom they represent. The foreign missionary responds in a special way to the universal call of Christ to herald the good news to unbelievers. Missionary vocations also need cultivation. The entire Church should, therefore, see to it that its missionaries have adequate preparation in Christian doctrine, in missiology, and in the pastoral and catechetical skills they will need in order to carry on the work of world evangelization (*Ad gentes,* 23–26).

Christianizing the Secular

In addition to converting every individual to Christ, a second enormous task confronts the living Church: the Christianization of contemporary society. In its search for a just social order, Catholic theology has traditionally distinguished four kinds of justice. Legal justice regulates the relationship of individuals to society as a whole. It seeks to ensure that individuals respect the common good. Distributive justice regulates the relationship of society to the individual. It too seeks the common good by trying to ensure that all share equitably in available goods and services. Commutative justice seeks to ensure that individuals deal justly with one another. Contributive, or social, justice seeks to defend the right of every individual to contribute to and benefit from the common good.

A Christian search for a just social order needs to take into account all four forms of justice; but, as we have seen, it measures the justice or injustice of existing institutions, whether ecclesial or secular, not merely by rational human standards but also and especially by God's own justice. God's justice justifies. It includes compassion, mercy, and a patient determination to save us despite our sinfulness. The incarnate Word reveals to us the full sense of divine justice in his vision of the kingdom and through his death, resurrection, and sending of the Holy Breath. His vision of the kingdom holds up God's own ideal of a just social order. His death and resurrection reveal the full extent of God's determination to save us. He sends the Holy Breath in order to establish God's just reign in his disciples' hearts and shared lives and in order to empower them to extend the reign of God to the ends of the earth.

Vatican II attempted to translate Jesus' vision of the kingdom into specific apostolic goals that claim the active, collaborative support of all Christians and of persons of good will. The council rests its assessment of the contemporary human condition on a certain number of fundamental truths: the solidarity of the human race, whom God calls to live as a single family reconciled in Christ; the interdependence of persons and of social institutions that shape human lives; the responsibility incumbent on every individual and institution to seek the common good of society and of the human race as a whole by seeing to it that all have the opportunity to contribute to and share in the benefits of the body politic and of the Church; the need to ground social freedom and equality in a just social order; the dignity of persons and of human labor; the simultaneous autonomy and interpenetration of the Church and of secular society (*Gaudium et spes,* 1–45).

The Family

In a world in which divorce, abortion, sexual irresponsibility, and exploding populations threaten the very survival of the most basic unit of human society, the family, Vatican II reminds the Christians of their responsibility to reaffirm the sanctity of both marriage and the family and to defend both against the forces that subvert them (*Gaudium et spes,* 46–52).

Modern Communications

In a world of technology in which expanding communications are creating for the first time the possibility of a worldwide culture, Christians need to foster inculturated evangelization, defend the right of every individual to education for a humane life, oppose the totalitarian suppression of truth, and ensure that political and economic ends not dominate, destroy, and impoverish cultural development (*Gaudium et spes,* 46–52).

The Economy

In a world divided between rich and poor, Christians need to see to it that everyone enjoys a just share in the blessings of this life without at the same time making an idol of worldly advancement. Christians must protect both the dignity of labor and the right and duty of individuals to work and to unionize. Christians must defend the opportunity of all able individuals to participate in economic life. Christians must also seek to ensure that economic institutions genuinely promote financial security, employment, and sufficient income for all people everywhere. They must see to it that the right to private property takes second place to the more fundamental right of all people to share in the goods of the earth. The more economically advantaged nations must come to the aid of the economically developing nations (*Gaudium et spes*, 63–66).

Politics

In a world in which politicians trample upon fundamental human rights, Christians must see to it that governments promote the common good of all their citizens and of the human race as a whole. Governments must serve human needs, not the private interests of power elites. Christians must defend human and religious freedom against the encroachments of political oppressors. They must defend the right of every citizen to participate in the political process (*Gaudium et spes*, 73–76).

Disarmament

In a world that has known total war and that faces the threat of a nuclear annihilation, Christians must labor to ground peace in a just social order. They must oppose violent solutions to economic and political conflicts. They must oppose the arms race, which not only increases the possibility of nuclear holocaust but diverts billions of dollars into the creation of weapons of destruction, dollars that might have alleviated the suffering and misery of the poor. Christians must oppose aggressive war, total war, and the indiscriminate use of nuclear weapons as immoral. They must seek to effect international agreements that would bar war altogether and seek negotiated solutions to international conflicts (*Gaudium et spes*, 77–82).

The Common Good

Finally, in a world shrinking under the impact of modern technology and communications, Christians must labor to see to it that the actions of nations respect the universal common good of the human race as a whole. Christians should foster a just international economic order in which economically developing nations promote the good of all their citizens rather than feed the affluence of the First World. Christians of all three worlds need to right the injustices that greed for profit, nationalistic ambition, militarism, and political oppression foment. In the interests of justice they need to promote the international coordination of the world's economy (*Gaudium et spes*, 83–93).

The high ideals that Vatican II held up to the Church and to the world will remain only ideals until they find embodiment in concrete policies and strategies for achieving the kind of just social order to which God summons us. In reflecting on the apostolic responsibilities that flow from the rites of Christian initiation, we shall begin to reflect on the way in which contemporary Christians can not only derive from Jesus' vision of the kingdom general principles for personal conduct and for the transformation of human society but can also translate those principles into specific policies and strategies that advance the Christianization of human society.

The Charisms and Shared Faith Consciousness

We have been examining the social processes through which the Christian community achieves the shared faith consciousness that nurtures its individual members to mature sanctity and mutual service. In a sense, the Church must go through the same human processes as any other large, historical community in order to achieve communal awareness. Its shared memories endow it with a sense of identity that grounds its shared hopes. Its shared hopes motivate its members to share their lives in a coordinated effort to realize a common future. The Church, however, differs from a merely natural human community in that it must come to shared self-awareness in faith.

The Church can achieve communal self-awareness in faith only through the mutual charismatic ministry of all its members. It needs gifts of prayer and of healing to endow it with a conscious sense of God's effective presence to it and to a sinful world. It needs the gift of tongues to remind it of the first Pentecost and of the ongoing Pentecost of the Christian community. It needs prophets and evangelists to summon it to repentance, ongoing conversion, and hope if it expects to effect conversion in others and to respond vigorously to the challenges of life in the contemporary world. It needs teachers to retrieve its history and to help it to clarify its identity and its shared ideals. It needs all the action gifts to translate its shared aspirations into actuality. Two perennial hopes challenge the living Church: the conversion of the entire world to Christ and the Christianization of human society. Their realization translates Jesus' vision of the kingdom into an actuality.

The sharing of all the charisms of God's Holy Breath ensures that the Christian community comes to shared consciousness in faith. It does so through a global commitment to Christ and to the moral demands to discipleship, through a sound understanding of the meaning and consequences of divine revelation, and through an expectant faith in God's saving action in the Church and in the world. As we have seen, the charisms teach the human ego docility to the Breath of Christ. Without charismatic inspiration, the Church's recall of its origins, its sense of its shared identity, its common hopes, and its attempt to incarnate those hopes in practice would express at best human self-reliance, at worst human sinfulness. The Christian community will therefore successfully achieve shared faith consciousness only to the extent that the mutual ministry of its members embodies the Holy Breath's charismatic inspirations. Moreover, unless the Church achieves shared faith consciousness, it cannot provide the matrix of divine grace its members need in order to advance to mature adult sanctity.

Charismatic Apathy and the Diminishment of Shared Faith

The reflections of this chapter also point to another fundamental spiritual challenge facing the Christian community. Because different charisms grace different moments in the development of human experience, the absence of specific gifts from the community diminishes specific kinds of shared faith awareness as well.

The absence of gifts of prayer and of healing diminishes the Church's sense of presence to the God it worships and to the Breath that guides it. Presence to God and to the action of his Breath bears fruit in docility to the movement of divine grace. In the absence of such docility sin and egocentrism don the robes of piety. Worship becomes hollow. God seems absent. Rationalism together with the legalism that it tends to inspire begins to infect the shared life of the Christian community. The absence of tongues from a community of worship diminishes its shared consciousness of its Pentecostal origins.

The community of faith that lacks prophets will display serious symptoms of lack of conversion, for the prophetic word summons believers to repentance and to both initial and ongoing conversion.

That word also summons believers to hope. Communities in which no prophets proclaim God's Word will, as a consequence, tend to measure their future in terms of human potential and of their own complacent expectations rather than in terms of God's omnipotence. Diminished hopes breed narcissism, despair, and oblivion of God's promises. Prophecy speaks directly to the human heart. Faith communities without prophets will, then, very likely also suffer from the absence of affective conversion. As a consequence, they will know the oppression born of personal and institutionalized neurosis. The members of such communities will exhibit little conscious sense of God's guidance of their personal lives and common destiny.

Communities of faith that lack adequate teachers profess a faith infected by fundamentalism and distorted by the absence of intellectual conversion. In the absence of critical reflection on the meaning of revelation, piety will tend to degenerate into a mindless emotionalism, often tinged with neurotic rigidity. Since teachers help communities retrieve their history, the absence of teaching bears bitter fruit in the lack of a shared sense of ecclesial identity. Individualistic visions of Jesus and of the Church claim divine inspiration, and the community of faith fragments into warring sects. A community deprived of adequate teaching will also lack a solid basis for planning its future, for common hopes spring from a community's shared sense of identity. Sound teaching also elaborates the intellectual criteria that inform sound judgments of discernment. In the absence of sound teaching, therefore, the pastoral judgments that direct the shared life of a faith community will tend to oppose head and heart in ways that encourage either mindless pietism or shallow rationalism. Finally, pastoral decisions that express false beliefs and false hopes create institutional structures that oppress rather than liberate the people of God. Think, for example, of the suffering that has resulted from the Christian community's acquiescence in clericalism, racism, and sexism.

A community that lacks adequate gifts of discernment will find itself swept to and fro by every wind of doctrine that blows its way. It will lack the means to judge the religious authenticity of the movements that surface within it. Rudderless, it will founder in indecision for lack of a clear sense of pastoral direction. The conflicting movements that surface within such a community will leave it internally divided or may cause it to fragment into warring denominations.

A faith community that lacks the action gifts will tend to divorce shared faith from shared practice. Its prayer will fail to find communal embodiment in deeds of love. Its privatized professions of belief will degenerate into polite academic discussions and empty manifestos devoid of practical or institutional consequences. Its hope will degenerate into pious sentimentality. Individualistic, privatized piety will probably ambition the institutional reform of neither the Church nor secular society. In such communities one tends to find the complacency of the rich and middle class, on the one hand, or the fatalism of the poor, on the other. Practical Christian longing for justice with its preferential option for the poor languishes and dies for want of pastoral leaders to mobilize the community in concerted social action.

Restoring Diminished Shared Faith

The opposite occurs, however, in a Church in which all the charisms of the Holy Breath flourish. By sharing the gifts, the Christian community reappropriates the memory of Jesus, of his vision of the kingdom, and of his saving death and glorification. Christian teachers bear a large part of the responsibility for retrieving that memory and for proclaiming it to the community. Prophets summon the Church to welcome that memory with transforming repentance and with hope in the fidelity of God. Evangelists proclaim Christ to those who do not know him. Gifts of prayer deepen in the heart of each believer and in the community as a whole the memory of Jesus, of his proclamation of the kingdom, of his death and glorification, of his sending the Pentecostal Breath. Gifts of prayer also help ensure that that memory bears fruit in practical faith and in deeds of love. Prayer and healing together yield a sense of God's presence to those who seek him. Gifts of discernment enable the community to distinguish between sound and unsound interpretations of Jesus, of the kingdom, of the paschal mystery, and of the claims that all three make upon the Christian conscience. The action gifts mobilize the Christian community to shared deeds of love and to the shared search for a social order that reflects God's own justice.

Individual Christians can, then, grow effectively in personal hope, faith, love, and longing for justice only by active participation in a community of faith whose every member seeks in prayer the power and enlightenment of the gift-giving, Pentecostal Breath of Christ. Without the charisms the shared life of the Christian community expresses not the action of divine grace but natural impulses, egotism, and sin. Natural human hopes, beliefs, and prudential insight become sinful when they seek through human self-reliance to supplant the Word of God. Sin and egocentrism blind and confuse the Church, transforming it from a matrix of grace into a stumbling block and a scandal that stifles personal holiness in its members instead of nurturing it.

The Charisms and the Local Church

These reflections make important practical demands on local Christian communities and on the Church as a whole. Every local community's shared faith consciousness will wax or wane to the extent that it cultivates all the charisms of the Holy Breath. If such a community hopes to provide its members with a matrix of grace capable of nurturing them to adult holiness, it must either do so directly through the mutual charismatic ministry of its own members or else supply for its lack of specific gifts by drawing on the charismatic resources of the diocese or of the Church as a whole. Even local communities abundantly supplied with charismatic leaders need to attend to the action of the Holy Breath in the rest of the Christian community. Otherwise charismatic inbreeding will betray such communities into sectarianism as they choose arbitrarily and needlessly between the alleged action of the Breath among their members and her action in the Church as a whole.

Every Christian community needs to cultivate gifts of prayer and of healing. Those, however, that lack for local prophets need to listen carefully to the prophetic voices that arise in the rest of the Christian community. Those that lack for local teachers need to nourish their faith by reading and studying the works of acknowledged Christian teachers both living and dead. When the local community's own discernment fails, local communities need to rely on the resources of the larger Church to resolve their conflicts and to plot the path for the future. Similarly, every local community needs to enter into collaboration with leaders at a diocesan, regional, national, and international level in order to translate the shared hope and faith of all believers into deeds of love that minister to the needy and change the shape of human society.

3. Conclusion. We have been trying to understand the social dynamics of sanctification in the Church of Jesus Christ. We began by examining the ecclesial vision of the Second Vatican Council. We focused especially on its insistence that all authentic Christian ministry derives its inspirations from the charismatic activity of the Holy Breath of Jesus. We then began to probe the experiences that validate this facet of the council's teaching. In examining the charisms we found that they differ by their particularity from the hope, faith, love, and longing for justice common to all Christians; for, while the Breath of God calls all Christians to some form of charismatic ministry, she calls particular individuals to minister differently. We found that the particularity of the gifts of service manifests itself in two ways. First, different gifts transform different moments in the growth of human experience. Second, particular personalities exhibit a natural, obediential potential for specific charisms.

Despite their particularity, however, the charisms enter into the common spiritual patrimony of the Church by being shared. Indeed, the sharing of the charisms creates the shared faith consciousness of the Church. It creates that matrix of divine grace that nurtures the individual members of the Christian community to mature holiness by enabling them to put on the mind of Christ.

In the chapter that follows we will begin to probe the sacramental significance of adult Christian conversion. We shall focus on the symbolic character of the event of conversion itself. As we shall see, Christian conversion culminates in incorporation into God's human family, the Church. That fact, however, expresses an even deeper mystery. Christians worship a triune God. As a consequence, the very reality of God can be legitimately understood on an analogy with human social experience. In addition, however, we can also imagine the social reality of the Trinity on an analogy with the human family. As a consequence, incorporation into the Church, God's human family, begins the process by which converts enter into familial communion with the members of the divine family, a communion that culminates in total personal and social transformation in God. To these considerations we turn in the chapter that follows.

CHAPTER IV
Socialization into the Family of God

In the preceding chapters we have examined both the personal and the social dynamics of Christian conversion. We have focused first on the person of the convert and then on the social matrix of divine grace in which adult conversion transpires. Our reflections have, moreover, endowed the scholastic notion of "created grace" with practical meaning; for through an understanding of the structure and dynamics of conversion we have begun to grasp the kinds of practical commitments that graced transformation in Christ demands of converts.

Uncreated Grace

In the present chapter our attention shifts from created to uncreated grace, from the change that grace makes in human experience to the divine reality that graces us. I regard such a shift in perspective as speculatively inevitable, for a theology of conversion must concern itself not only with converts but with the realities they encounter by converting. A complete and adequate theology of conversion needs to explain how converts ought to perceive the reality of God, of Jesus Christ, of the Church, of the sacraments, and of any other reality to which faith opens access, for a false or inadequate perception of such realities can exert negative, even disastrous influences on the process of conversion itself. Think of converts or believers trapped in the distorted belief that God responds to sin vindictively; or think of ambitious clerics who misunderstand their role in the Church as the exercise of coercive power rather than as the humble service of God's people; or think of lay Christians who avoid their religious responsibilities by equating the Church with the hierarchy. Such distorted perceptions of the realities of faith either prevent or undermine conversion by suffusing it with debilitating and, on occasion, even with a sinful inauthenticity.

One might object, however, that most sacramental theologies proceed without troubling the reader with discussions of Trinitarian doctrine. I would concede that a thorough treatment of the speculative issues raised by Trinitarian belief lies beyond the scope of a book on the sacraments. Although Christianity offers a coherent vision of life and of reality, a single focused study can after all deal only with limited aspects of divine revelation. Nevertheless, I would deem any sacramental theology incomplete that fails to relate sacramental worship in any way to Trinitarian faith for the simple reason that the doctrine of the Trinity ultimately grounds the sacramental character of Christian faith.

Trinity and Sacrament

I realize, of course, that such a contention needs arguing. Most Catholic theologians would, I expect, spontaneously associate sacramentality and the incarnation. Edward Schillebeeckx's portrayal of Jesus Christ and the sacrament of the encounter with God enjoys widespread acceptance in the Church. However, I would suspect that fewer theologians would associate Trinity and sacramentality, even though Karl Rahner's theology of symbol opens the way to such an association.

In the present chapter I shall attempt to provide experiential foundations for linking Trinity and sacraments. The limits of time and space prevent a detailed discussion of Trinitarian doctrine. Those who would like to explore in greater depth the approach to the Trinity which I will suggest in the pages which follow will find it in my book *The Divine Mother: A Trinitarian Theology of the Holy Spirit.* Here I can only allude to some of the conclusions of that study.

My argument focuses not on the sacramentality of the rituals that seal conversion but on the sacramental character of the experience of conversion itself. More specifically, I shall attempt to show that we should interpret the experience of adult conversion as socialization into the family of God: first into God's human family, which we call the Church, but also and ultimately into the family of the Trinity itself.

I shall argue for the truth of six interrelated theses: (1) Converts ought to look upon adult conversion as socialization into God's human family, the Church. (2) Incorporation into God's human family unites converts to the triune God. (3) Converts should perceive the relationship among the divine persons as social. (4) Converts should perceive the character of the social relationships among the

divine persons as familial and progressive union with God as socialization into the divine family. (5) The social structure of the divine
experience makes it symbolic and therefore revealable. (6) The historical revelation of the divine family endows graced social relationships
with a sacramental character.

1. **The Church: God's Human Family.** In this section I shall
attempt to argue the first of the above theses: namely, that *converts
ought to look upon adult conversion as socialization into God's human
family, the Church.*

Abba and His Children

The first Christians thought of themselves as belonging to the
family of God. The tendency to portray the Christian community as
a family traces itself to Jesus' *Abba* experience. Jesus experienced God
intimately as "Papa" and invited his disciples to share that intimacy.
Drawing on his own sense of relating to God as Son, he tried to teach
his followers to live in his own image as God's sons and daughters
(Matt 17:26). He seems to have spoken of his disciples as brothers
and sisters (Matt 25:40).

It comes as no great surprise, then, that the first Christians experienced baptism as adoption into the family of God (Gal 3:27–4:11;
Rom 8:1-17; Eph 1:5; John 1:12). Baptism guaranteed the baptized
a share in the inheritance of God's own Son: a present participation
in his glory and hope for eternal life with him in God (Rom 8:17,
29; Col 1:18). It gave them access to the Holy Breath of Jesus, who
taught them to pray to *Abba* as Jesus did (Gal 4:6; Rom 8:14-17, 29).
In this context, the use of the Our Father as a preparation for Eucharistic Communion takes on familial connotations. When Christians
gather to share in the Body and Blood of Christ, they do so as the
family of the Father from whom every human family takes its name
(Eph 3:15). Membership in God's family binds Christians together
in mutual affection and love; for, as the First Letter of John observes,
whoever loves God loves those whom God has begotten (1 John 5:1).

Creating God's Human Family

The Christian community becomes the family of God through
conversion, sanctification, and sharing the gifts of the Holy Breath.
Conversion and sanctification unite believers by teaching them all
to put on the mind of Christ. As faith in Jesus and in his vision of

the kingdom transvalues human aspirations for the future, it engenders the Church's shared hope. As it transforms rational and intuitive perceptions of reality, it gives birth to the Church's shared faith. As the vision of faith informs the consciences of Christians, it motivates the deeds of love and the shared search for social justice on the terms set by the triune God. As they grow in faith and mutual charismatic service, Christians learn to treat one another as brothers and sisters in the Lord; for their lives imitate the faithful obedience of God's incarnate Son.

Sharing the gifts of service also cements the bonds that unite believers into a single family. Not only do the charisms of the Holy Breath teach the members of the Christian community to minister to one another's needs, but they also empower the evangelization of nonbelievers and the Christianization of secular society. As the Church expands, the family of God grows. As that family confronts the forces of antichrist, the very struggle that ensues deepens the solidarity that unites its members.

For all these reasons, therefore, converts ought to perceive the Church as the human family of God. Conversion, however, does more than introduce one into the Church. It also unites one to God. To this point we turn in the section that follows.

2. Union with the Triune God. In this section I shall attempt to argue the second thesis enunciated at the beginning of this chapter: *incorporation into God's human family unites converts to the triune God.*

Mutual Consent and Social Union

Dissent fragments experience. Fear, rage, hatred, violence, war, conflict, economic and political oppression; indeed, every humanly destructive event, whether deliberately caused or not, shatters the unity and integrity of experience even to the point of sometimes annihilating human life itself.

Consent unifies experience and creates the bonds of social union. We experience consent as love, affection, friendship, romance, support, nurture. The consent of persons to one another unites them socially. Affection bonds families. Friendship blends hearts, minds, and lives and unites people in common enterprises. Nations that advance life instead of oppressing it grow through the mutual consent of the governing and the governed.

Divine Consent

Christian conversion embodies the consent of Christlike love. In consenting to Jesus as the normative historical revelation of God, one also consents to his vision of the kingdom. The vision of the kingdom holds up an ideal of a specific kind of community of faith: a community in which trust in God's providential care frees its members to share with one another the physical supports of life; an open community that welcomes especially the poor, the marginal, and the outcast; a community whose worship expresses the mutual forgiveness of its members. Inevitably, then, Christian conversion culminates in the rites of initiation that incorporate one into the community Jesus founded.

Conversion, however, does more than unite us to the Church. It also unites us to God himself. Throughout the process of conversion the God who loves us even in our sinfulness holds the initiative. God holds the historical initiative because, without our deserving it, he sent his Son into the world to reveal by dying for us the unconditioned character of his love for us and commitment to us. In the experience of conversion God holds the personal initiative as well, because every Christian convert consents to God in the divine Mother's empowering illumination.

Because conversion expresses consent to a personal offer of divine love, it unites the convert to God in friendship. Christians express their friendship for God by befriending one another (John 15:13-15). Incorporation into the Church, therefore, embodies at one and the same time love of God and love of neighbor.

Love grows through deeds that express it. Moreover, as the love of God deepens through ongoing conversion, friendship with God matures into mystical betrothal and mystical marriage. When that occurs, knowing God and loving God coincide. When they coincide, one lives united to God with an ever deepening intimacy that longs for fulfillment in that perfect union that only the direct vision of God can bring. Conversion, therefore, begins a process of loving transformation in God that aspires finally to perfect union with God in love.

Christian conversion unites us to the God historically revealed in Jesus and in his Holy Breath. The historical missions of God's Son and of his Holy Breath reveal to us a plurality of persons in God, for mission implies distinction: the sender differs from the one sent. Christian conversion, therefore, not only unites us to the one God but to a God who is three persons in one deity.

In other words, in their longing for God Christians do not desire to dwell alone with the Alone, as Neoplatonic mystics did. Instead, they seek integration into the social life of the Godhead. In the section that follows we shall begin to explore the meaning of such an aspiration.

3. The Divine Society. In this third section, I shall attempt to argue the third thesis enunciated at the beginning of this chapter: *converts should perceive the relationship among the divine persons as social in character.*

Toward a Social Construct of the Trinity

The Christian God stands historically revealed as triune: as three divine persons in one. In human societies persons enjoy social relationships with one another. Can we, then, conceive the way the divine persons relate to one another within the Trinity on an analogy with human social relationships? I think we can.

Here, of course, we must avoid all literalness of mind. The infinite, all-encompassing, transcendent reality of God differs from finite, human realities. If, then, we can discover similarities between the social relationships that unite human and divine persons, we may anticipate that we will also find enormous differences between them as well. If God stands historically revealed as a social reality, then the divine society will differ in significant ways from human societies.

The Forms of Experienced Relationship

As we have already seen in chapter one, three kinds of relationship give dynamic shape to human experience: conceptual, factual, and habitual. Each kind of relationship structures a distinguishable dimension of experience.

Human evaluative responses form a continuum of conceptual relationships that begin in sensation but also encompass affections, images, and abstract concepts. Sensations give rise to the images that illumine our emotions. Our emotions pass judgment on the truth or falsity, adequacy or inadequacy of our imaginative perceptions of reality. Imaginative thought provides in turn the models that empower hypothetical inference. Moreover, not only do inferential abstractions imply one another, but despite our attempts to render them conceptually precise through definition, they nevertheless retain affective and irrational connotations. The conceptual relations unify and structure the way we perceive reality.

Action and reaction, collaboration and coercion endow experience with concrete factual relationships. Things bump into us, and we bump back. Persons speak to us, touch us, and we respond. Interaction links one autonomous experience to another.

Within the dynamic flow of experience we must also speak of the selves who interact and respond evaluatively to one another. Every finite self consists of an autonomous complex of habitual tendencies that react or respond either decisively or evaluatively. We call selves capable of acting with self-conscious responsibility "persons." When persons interact or collaborate, social bonding results.

The persons and things with whom we interact or collaborate help shape us experientially into the kinds of persons we eventually choose to become. The events of our lives mold us happily or tragically, as the things we experience become quite literally a part of us. Through social interaction and collaboration human lives also blend. People who share themselves with one another become part of one another. We experience that fact most poignantly through the separation and loss of loved ones.

The Social Sharing of Life

Moreover, through social interaction and collaboration human persons come to share vital similarity. We imitate those we love and admire. Friends share similar hopes and dreams. Teachers by their insight and enthusiasm mold the experience of their students. Spouses blend their lives, their very selves.

Nevertheless, the embodied character of human experience, the fact that each human person originates at a particular moment in space and time and develops with physical autonomy, means that human persons can share only a similarity, never an identity, of life. We cannot share identically the same life as another human person because we can never possess identically the same body as that individual. The infant nestling in its mother's womb comes, perhaps, as close as humans do to sharing physical life with another. Even then, however, the mother's body provides the physically autonomous child with the temporary environment it needs for physical survival prior to birth. Nevertheless, the mutual loving consent of two human persons to one another does endow them with vital similarity.

The Divine Experience

We can conceive the reality of the triune God on an analogy with human experience. The same generic variables we discover in human social experience, we find analogously present in God. Humans respond evaluatively; so does God. God knows, loves, judges, comprehends the world he has made. In Jesus he has revealed to us his saving intentions. Humans respond concretely and decisively to the efficacious intrusions of the world. God acts decisively and efficaciously by creating the world from nothing and by intervening in the course of human history. By gracing us God also enters into a collaborative relationship with his creatures which Christians call the new covenant.

Efficacy also shapes the immanent life of the triune God. Within the Trinity the Father generates the Son efficaciously from all eternity; and both Father and Son give rise to the Holy Breath who proceeds from them with eternal efficacy. We find the eternal processions of the Son and Breath historically revealed in their missions. The Son's efficacious mission into the world by the Father reveals his eternal procession from the Father. The Breath's efficacious mission into the world by both Son and Father reveals her eternal procession from them. The relationships of the divine persons that spring from procession, therefore, not only imply efficacy but also ground the distinction of the divine persons from one another within God.

Finally, we discover within the triune God three distinct selves, or persons. As the source of the other two divine persons, the Father, who proceeds from no one, stands historically revealed as the source of creative efficacy within the Godhead. Because the incarnate Word understood his relationship to the Father through the inspiration of the divine Breath, the Breath of God stands historically revealed as the cognitive link between the Father and the Son, as the source and origin of divine evaluative responses, as the mind and wisdom of God. The Son confronts us historically as standing in a relationship of perfect obedience to the Father who sends him and to the Breath who inspires him. That obediential relationship does not make him inferior to the Father and to the Breath, but it does constitute him the one through whom the other two divine persons speak and act, the one through whom they create the world, the one through whom they redeem it (John 1:1-18; 1 Cor 8:6; Col 1:15-20).

The fact, then, that we can discover in God the same generic kinds of variables that constitute human experience means that we can legitimately speak of the triune God as a divine experience.

The Supremacy of the Divine Experience

If, however, we can legitimately interpret the reality of the tri-une God as an experience, we must also understand it as the supreme exemplification of experience, as that experience whose greater we cannot conceive. We must conceive the divine experience as supreme for the simple reason that, if it lacked supremacy, some other su-premely perfect reality would surpass it in perfection and would there-fore enjoy divinity in its stead.

As the supreme exemplification of experience, God must ex-perience everything capable of being experienced. Nothing, there-fore, lies outside the scope of the divine experience. God knows himself, all past and present actuality, all future possibility.

If God experiences all things, then all things exist within the divine experience; for what one experiences stands within experience. Ever since the Apostle Paul proclaimed on the Areopagus that in God all things live, move, and have their being (Acts 17:28), Christians have known and taught that all created reality subsists in God. The New Testament asserts this truth in a variety of ways (Eph 1:23; Col 1:15-20), and Christian teachers have taught it from the first to the twentieth century.

Not only may we look upon God as the supreme exemplifica-tion of experience, but we must also look upon the divine experience as inherently social in character. Here, we need to distinguish two kinds of activity in the social life of the Godhead: the efficacious procession of the divine persons from one another, which grounds their distinction, and their mutual self-gift to one another in pure love, which grounds their unity. Let us reflect first on the divine processions.

As we have just seen, the historical missions of the divine per-sons reveal the way they relate to one another. They therefore re-veal their eternal processions. The Son's historical mission by the Father reveals not only his distinction from the Father but also the fact that within the Godhead he proceeds from the Father. The fact that both Father and risen Son send the Holy Breath into the Church reveals both Her distinction from them and the fact that she proceeds eternally from both of them as from a single efficacious principle.

Not only does salvation history tell us something about the way the divine persons originate within God, but it also tells us some-thing important about the way they relate to one another as distinct persons within the Godhead. We find those relationships most clearly revealed in Jesus, the Word of God incarnate.

The Self-Donation of the Divine Persons

The incarnate Son of God obeyed the Father's commands and the Breath's inspirations perfectly, to the point of submitting to an unjust death on the cross (Phil 2:1-11). In dying the Son gave himself totally to the Father in loving obedience (Luke 23:44-46). Moreover, in obeying the Father he also obeyed the divine Breath whose inspirations taught him the Father's will (Mark 1:9-11; Matt 3:13-17; Luke 3:21-22). Hence, in giving himself to the Father, he also gave himself to the Breath.

Mutual self-donation in love constitutes, then, the second kind of activity that shapes the inner social life of God. Not only do the Son and Breath proceed from all eternity, but all three divine persons give themselves to one another with an absolute and unconditioned totality of love.

The Unity of the Trinity

As we have seen, in human societies, the embodied character of human experience prevents human persons from ever sharing an identity of life. Our histories begin and end at different points in space and time. Our lives touch and divide as we move in separate directions over the face of the earth. We organize our bodies into personal life-support systems, into the environment that sustains us as persons and from which we emerge individually. No two human persons share the same physical life support system, the same body, although in the case of Siamese twins, the shutdown of one system produces the shutdown of the other.

The physical distinction of their bodies prevents human persons from ever sharing an identity of life. The divine persons, however, labor under no such limitation. The divine experience transcends space and time; it contains them both and therefore transcends them. We therefore call God infinite, because he contains everything and is contained by nothing.

Because the divine persons have no physical bodies, they do not experience that same kind of vital separation from one another that human persons do. By giving themselves to one another freely in love, human persons can, as we have seen, come to share a similarity of life. They dwell lovingly in one another and nurture one another in life-giving ways. Untrammeled by the limitations of physical life, the divine persons enjoy the capacity to give themselves to one another with such a totality and perfection of love that they share, not a similarity, but an identity of divine life.

That the divine persons share an identity of life we find historically revealed in the paschal mystery. In dying Jesus gave himself totally to the Father in loving obedience to his will (Luke 23:44-46). He also gave himself totally to the divine Breath in loving obedience to her illumination. In his resurrection he stands historically revealed as the recipient of their free gift of themselves to him. The risen Christ confronts us as Lord, as one who bears the Father's divine name and shares his very life (Phil 2:9-11); and we know him too as a life-giving Breath, as one so perfectly united to the divine Breath that he shares with the third person of the Trinity, as with the Father, identically the same life (2 Cor 3:18).

The coequality of the divine persons demands that the same kind of relationship which defines the Son's relationship to Father and Breath characterize their relationship to him and to one another. In addition, therefore, to the relations of distinction within God which flow from the divine procession, we also need to speak of unitive relations that create their perfect identity of life.

Moreover, each divine person contributes something distinctive to the shared life of the Godhead. The Father, the aboriginal source of creative efficacy in God, in giving himself totally to the Son and Breath endows them with the capacity to create. The Breath, the mind and wisdom of God, in giving herself totally to the Father and Son, acts interpretatively rather than efficaciously: She illumines them. She endows the Father with creative wisdom. She conceives the word of wisdom that the Son embodies. The Son, the source of obediential efficacy within the Godhead, in giving himself totally to the Father and to the Breath becomes their symbolic expression, the one through whom the Father creates, the one through whom the divine Breath communicates to her creatures.

The Analogy of Social Experience

We may, then, conceive the inner life of the Trinity on an analogy with human social experience. We need, however, to insist on the term "analogy." The divine experience resembles human social experience, but the two kinds of experience also differ radically. Human experience grows within the limits of space and time; the divine experience transcends them both. Indeed, the divine experience transcends all created limitation. By the same token, the divine society enjoys a vital unity that transcends anything we encounter in human social relationships. That unity results from a mutual self-gift so total that it utterly transcends the self-gift of human persons to one another. As a consequence, through faith in Christ we experience the unity of the divine persons as a limit which human societies can approach but can never perfectly attain; for the lives of the divine persons blend with a vital perfection unavailable to physically embodied persons.

The spontaneous egocentrism of our minds betrays us into imagining that human persons exemplify most perfectly what the term "person" signifies. Divine revelation, however, gives the lie to our self-preoccupied perceptions of personhood. The divine persons exemplify most perfectly the meaning of the term "person." They do so in the perfection of their interpersonal, social relationships, in the supreme totality and perfection of the love with which they give themselves to one another. Natural human love ranks as a partial and poor second by comparison.

We can, then, understand God as an experience. We can conceive the divine reality on an analogy with human social experience. Can we also understand the divine society on an analogy with a human family? To this question we turn in the section that follows.

4. The Divine Family. In this fourth section I shall attempt to argue the fourth thesis enunciated at the beginning of this chapter: *converts should perceive the character of the social relationships among the divine persons as familial and progressive union with God as socialization into the divine family.*

As we have just seen, we can legitimately imagine adult conversion as socialization into God's human family, the Church; and we can legitimately understand the reality of the triune God on an analogy with human social experience. Can we also legitimately imagine the divine society as a family? If we can, then socialization into God's human family symbolizes sacramentally a much deeper reality than natural incorporation into a human organization. In entering the Church we embark on a lifelong relationship with the triune God, a relationship that culminates in perfect union with God in the life to come. Hence, if we can imagine the divine social relationships on an analogy with a human family, then incorporation into the family of the Church symbolizes sacramentally the beginning of our graced assimilation into the divine family itself. Let us examine this last point in greater detail.

Graced transformation in the family of the Church, as we have seen, teaches Christians to call God their Father and Jesus their brother. It teaches sinful humans to live reconciled to one another as brothers and sisters in Christ.

Every human family, however, includes a mother. If we can legitimately imagine God as our Father and Jesus as God's Son and our brother, can we also imagine God as our mother as well?

In Search of the Divine Mother

The Hebrew Scriptures certainly apply maternal imagery to God. God's merciful compassion resembles the tender love of a mother for her child (Pss 25:6; 116:5). God consoles us as a mother comforts her children (Isa 66:13). God's love for us outlasts a mother's love for the fruit of her womb (Isa 49:15).

The Hebrew sages also imagined the wisdom of God as feminine. Divine wisdom mothers the children of God (Prov 8–9). She nourishes them with the bread of understanding and slakes their thirst for enlightenment (Sir 15:1-10). Moreover, the Book of Wisdom identifies the divine wisdom that descends from on high with the Holy Breath of God (Wis 1:6). It therefore gives biblical sanction to imagining the Breath of God as both feminine and maternal.

Moreover, a much neglected strain in Christian theology develops this insight in some depth. It suggests that we can legitimately imagine the third person of the Trinity as the divine Mother of God's only-begotten Son. In order, however, to understand the issues at stake in this particular theological strain within Christian pneumatology, we need to reflect both on the way imagination functions within faith and on the way theological reflection on the Holy Breath has evolved over the centuries. To each of these questions we turn in the paragraphs which follow.

How, then, does the imagination function within faith? As we have seen, we perceive reality in two ways: (a) intuitively and affectively with our hearts and (b) logically and rationally with our heads. The way we imagine the Holy Breath engages our imaginative, intuitive perceptions of God. In order to reach an integrated perception of the divine reality, we need to coordinate our intuitive and rational perceptions of the Godhead. In this task a Christian theology of the Holy Breath has failed significantly.

If we consult the development of Christian doctrine, we will find that Christian theologians failed at two important points to integrate adequately their perceptions of the third person of the Trinity. In the first place, they failed to coordinate their rational explanation of the Holy Breath's saving activity with the intuitive perceptions of that same activity canonized in the Old and New Testaments. In the second place, while they developed logical justifications for calling the Holy Breath a divine person, they as well as Christian artists failed to create images that would allow Christians to imagine the third member of the Trinity as personal.

Let us examine each of these theological failures in turn, for they hold the key to reaching an integrated perception in faith of the reality of the God we worship.

Logos Christology and the Eclipse of God's Breath

It took centuries to write the Bible, but even though its composition engaged the religious experience of different people living in different ages and in different social and cultural circumstances, a remarkable consistency attends biblical portrayals of the divine Breath's saving activity. The Breath of God makes the transcendent reality of God present in history by inspiring every form of genuine religious enlightenment: faith, prayer, prophecy, teaching, discernment, charismatic leadership.

In the second century A. D., however, an important shift occurred in patristic theological thinking. Justin Martyr began the shift. He portrayed the Breath of God as the source of graced enlightenment, but he attributed all rational enlightenment to the second person of the Trinity, to the *Logos*. The Fourth Gospel had called Jesus the incarnate Word (*Logos*) of God (John 1:1). By that John the evangelist meant that God speaks to us, touches us in the person of Jesus and reveals to us his face. Justin, however, drawing on Neoplatonic philosophy, interpreted the *Logos* as a divine intelligence and as the source of all rational (*logikos*) enlightenment (*First Apology*, 5, 13-33, 39; *Second Apology*, 10, 13; *Dialogue with the Jew Trypho*, 7, 19, 34, 36, 38, 43, 63).

The New Testament had, of course, referred to Jesus as the Word (John 1:1) and Wisdom of God (1 Cor 1:24). The New Testament, however, had failed to clarify two important theological points: in speaking of the incarnate Son of God, should we interpret the term "Word" as the conceived or as the spoken word of God? Similarly, in calling Jesus Christ the wisdom of God, do we mean the conceived wisdom of God; or do we mean the one who reveals that wisdom definitively in human history? Justin's Platonism led him in Christological discourse to identify the Word and Wisdom of God with the conceived word and wisdom.

In the third century, moreover, Clement of Alexandria went beyond Justin. He taught that the *Logos* effects not only rational but gracious enlightenment as well. Clement's student, Origen, held a similar position. So did Athanasius, Augustine, and a host of the Fathers of the Church. These patristic writers interpreted the *Logos* philosophically as the conceived word of God rather than biblically as God's spoken word.

Unfortunately, however, such an interpretation of the saving role of the *Logos* appropriates to the second person of the Trinity those very activities that the Bible consistently appropriates to the third. This strain in patristic theology inhibited the development of pneumatology and eventually culminated in the Arian heresy which denied the divinity of both Son and Breath. We cannot rehearse here all the details of this important controversy. Suffice it to say, that the truth or falsity of any postbiblical theological theory lies in its ability to interpret correctly the biblical witness. A *Logos* Christology which appropriates to the *Logos* saving activities which the Bible attributes to the Breath of God replaces the biblical witness to the Breath with a misleading philosophical and theological theory. Christian converts ought, therefore, to reject this particular strain in patristic theology as false and misleading because it prevents them from relating as they ought to the second and third persons of the Trinity.

The Logos as Spoken Word and God's Feminine Wisdom

Another strain in patristic thought, however, stayed closer to the biblical witness. We find this theological strain represented in the writings of Irenaeus of Lyons in the second century and in those of Basil of Caesarea and of Victorinus in the fourth. This second, healthier strain in patristic Trinitarian thinking interpreted the *Logos* of the Fourth Gospel as the spoken word of God, as the one through whom the Godhead speaks and acts. Not only did this second account of the *Logos* interpret more accurately the intent of the Fourth Gospel, but it also agreed better with the biblical witness to the Holy Breath. Irenaeus, Basil, and Victorinus all looked upon the divine Breath as the source of every kind of gracious enlightenment and as the feminine wisdom of God (Irenaeus, *Against the Heresies*, IV, xx, 4; V, viii, 1, xiii, 4, *Demonstration of the Apostolic Preaching*, V, VII; Basil of Caesarea, *On the Holy Spirit*, IX, XVI; Gaius Marius Victorinus, *Against Arius*, II, 1. 57. 28-29).

Imagining the Holy Breath as the feminine wisdom of God, as the source of divine enlightenment within the Godhead and within salvation history, provides us with a personal image for the third person of the Trinity. It took twelve centuries for Christian theologians to produce a systematic theology of the divine persons, but Christian theology and iconography failed in the process to develop an adequate personal image of the third person of the Trinity. With rare exceptions Christian iconography portrayed the Breath instead as fire, as a descending dove.

In other words, a return to the *Logos* doctrine of Irenaeus, Basil, and Victorinus offers five important theological advantages to contemporary converts: (1) It allows them to interpret the *Logos* of the Fourth Gospel correctly. (2) It allows them to conceive the saving action of the incarnate Son of God in such a way that it does not encroach on the Breath's saving activity. (3) It supplies them with a personal image for the third person of the Trinity. (4) It allows converts to coordinate their intuitive and rational perceptions of the third person of the Trinity. (5) It allows them to imagine the third person of the Trinity as the maternal wisdom of God, as the divine Mother. Moreover, if we can imagine the Holy Breath as the divine Mother, then we can also imagine the Trinity as a whole on an analogy with a human family. Let us probe a bit more deeply into this fifth and final insight.

The Spoken Word of God Reveals both Father and the Breath

Jesus reveals the Father to us by the perfection of his obedience. He says and does whatever the Father tells him to do. His words and deeds express to us perfectly, then, the Father's saving commitment to us. As incarnate Son of God, however, Jesus knows the Father's will through the enlightenment of the divine Breath. As a consequence, the incarnation reveals to us that the Holy Breath functions within the Godhead as the cognitive link between the Father and the Son, as the mind of God and of Christ (1 Cor 2:4-16). The mind of God conceives the wisdom of God. The mind of God also conceives the Word of wisdom that God speaks to us in Jesus.

Mothers conceive their children. If, then, the Holy Breath of God through her unitive relationship with the Son and in her function as divine wisdom conceives from all eternity the Word of grace the Father spoke in sending his Son into the world, then we may also legitimately imagine her as the mother of God the Son from all eternity. When we identify the Breath of God with the divine wisdom and speak of her maternal conception of the person of the divine Word, we pun, of course, on the meaning of the term "conception."

The intuitive imagination, however, finds puns a congenial way of dealing with reality; for the intuitive mind grasps analogy metaphorically.[1]

Imagining Jesus as the spoken Word of God and the Holy Breath as the mind, or wisdom, of God offers other theological advantages as well, for it allows us to discover in the incarnate Son of God the simultaneous revelation of both the Father and the divine Breath. Jesus reveals the Father to us through the perfection of his obedience to the Father's missioning will. He reveals the Holy Breath to us by his mind, his vision, his understanding of God's intentions toward us. His human mind grew and developed in perfect docility to the inspirations of God's Breath. It therefore embodies more perfectly than any other human mind how the divine Mother perceives reality. For that reason we can measure the extent to which human conceptions conform to her inspirations by their conformity or disconformity to the mind of Christ.

The Divine Family

The fact that we can legitimately extend maternal imagery to the third person of the Trinity means then that we can perceive the social life of the triune God on an analogy with a human family. We find a maternal, a paternal, and a filial dimension within divine social experience. As we have seen, the fact that Jesus called God "Papa" and was revealed in his resurrection as the only-begotten Son of God justifies in an initial way the application of familial imagery to the triune God. When we call the Holy Breath our Mother, we extend our image of God beyond those invoked explicitly in the New Testament; but we do so legitimately by drawing upon both Scripture and tradition.

Moreover, in calling God "Papa," Jesus invited us to relate to the deity with a new kind of intimacy. When we imagine the Breath of God as maternal and begin to call her "Mama," we draw her into the same circle of divine, personal intimacy.

Needless to say, however, all such images function only analogously. They both reveal and conceal the divine reality to which they

1. Here we need to recognize that in saying that the divine Mother conceives the Word of God, I in no way intend to assert that he proceeds from her. On the contrary, her historical mission by the Father and Son reveals that she proceeds from both of them as from a single principle. The term conception, then, does not imply a relationship of procession, which grounds the distinction of the divine persons, but a unitive relationship, which grounds their vital identity.

refer. When I call the first person of the Trinity "Father," I assert that something in my relationship to that divine person resembles my relationship to my human father, even though God the Father did not beget me biologically as my human father did. I also assert that those perfections in my human father that remind me of my relationship to the first person of the Trinity, like compassion, steadfast love, and the origination of life, exist in my divine Father in a supremely perfect manner.

When I call Jesus my brother, I make a similar analogous assertion concerning my relationship to him. I assert that I discover in my relationship to God the Son something like the solidarity I experience with my natural brothers and sisters, a solidarity founded not on human familial relationships but on the incarnation of the second person of the Trinity, on his gracious willingness to share my human condition so that I might share his divine life. He became my brother by taking on human flesh, by dying for me and for all sinners, and by sending the divine Mother to conceive the human family of God, the Church, through her saving inspirations. As a consequence, the graced bonds of solidarity that unite me to Jesus as my brother transcend utterly natural sibling relations.

When we imagine the Holy Breath as the divine Mother, we include her imaginatively in the family of God, where she surely belongs. When I call the divine Breath "Mama," I look to her to conceive within me divine life and wisdom, to nurture me with the milk of divine compassion and love, to encompass me with her love as our human mothers do. At the same time, I recognize that the divine nurture that she accomplishes in me utterly transcends anything my human mother ever did for me.

So far, we have argued four points: (1) We may legitimately perceive the Church as God's human family. (2) Joining God's human family also unites one to God himself. (3) Within the Christian God we discover social relationships that resemble and transcend human social relationships. (4) We can legitimately imagine the triune God as a divine family and therefore progressive union with God as incorporation into the divine family.

We need now to show the relationship between these Trinitarian insights and Christian sacramental worship. To this task we turn in the sections that follow.

5. The Divine Symbol. In this section I shall argue the fifth thesis enunciated at the beginning of this chapter: *the social structure of the divine experience makes it symbolic and therefore historically revealable.*

Experience Both Social and Symbolic

In reflecting on the social structure of the divine experience, I distinguished three interrelated dimensions of both human and divine experience: a realm of evaluations, a realm of concrete actions, and a realm of habitual tendencies peopled by interacting, collaborating selves.

As we have seen, the dynamic interplay of these three realms of experience endows it with a social structure. That same interplay makes every experience inherently symbolic. By a symbol I mean a reality that mediates the evaluative grasp of significance.

Realities signify something when they possess a relational structure capable of evaluative perception. The evaluative perception of significant realities endows them with meaning.

Let us try to put some flesh on these abstract definitions by examining the three kinds of symbols that structure human experience. We need to distinguish expressive symbols, interpretative symbols, and communications.

Expressive Symbols

Expressive symbols engage the realms of fact and of law. By an expressive symbol I mean an event, something that happens: physical, chemical, and biological reactions; storms; earthquakes; shifting weather patterns; the eruption of volcanoes; continental drift; the progress and cure of diseases; indeed, anything the physical sciences study. Events such as these signify something. In trying to understand events we first need to gather the facts that make them up, for the facts of an event hold the key to its significance. We grasp the significance of an event when we understand the laws, or tendencies, that generate the facts that reveal it. We test our grasp of those laws by our ability to predict how things will act in the future.

Weather forecasters, for example, spend their lives trying to predict the behavior of fronts, storms, and other weather patterns by a sound insight into the laws that govern their behavior. Similarly, when the United States was trying to build the Panama Canal, the outbreak of an epidemic of yellow fever among the canal's builders threatened the project's ultimate success. Scientists investigating the cause of yellow fever eventually traced it to the bite of a mosquito of the species *aedes.* Once investigators had isolated the source of the disease, those directing the construction of the canal could begin to take measures to eliminate it. Work on the locks advanced.

We do not always think of events as symbols, but we should. Events symbolize by signifying something. In occurring, they express something significant. In order to grasp evaluatively what events signify, we need to employ interpretative symbols. Interpretative symbols engage two realms of human experience simultaneously: the realm of quality and the realm of law. When we use interpretative symbols we characterize events and the tendencies that generate them.

Interpretative Symbols

We cannot characterize anything without evaluating it in some way. Even our most basic sensory responses evaluate things; for, when we sense things, we experience them in a vague, initial way as emotionally charged. When we respond affectively, imaginatively, or rationally to events, we endow our evaluations with greater and greater conceptual complexity. As we learn to evaluate the complex character of events, we develop habitual ways of interpreting them. By an interpretative symbol, then, I mean an habitual way of responding evaluatively to oneself and to one's world. Because interpretative symbols involve evaluations they engage the realm of quality; because they involve habitual ways of doing so, they involve the realm of law. Interpretative symbols, then, make human experience meaningful by revealing through the processes of evaluation the significant structure of events.

Communications

Ordinarily, however, human evaluative responses involve more than just interpretative symbols. They also involve communications. Communications transform human evaluations into social dialogue. We communicate with one another when through words and gestures we attempt to express in an intelligible fashion our evaluative interpretation of events.

Expressive and interpretative symbols each engage only two realms of experience. Communications engage all three. Because they require some kind of physical activity like gesturing, creating an art object, or speaking, communications qualify as events, as human social events capable of being interpreted in turn by others. The event of communication like every event expresses something; but unlike events of a purely physical character, communications attempt to express human evaluations. They signify habitual ways of perceiving reality and of expressing those perceptions in some kind of language. Because they involve simultaneously habits, evaluations, and physical acts, communications engage all three realms of experience.

Moreover, the way people communicate socially radically conditions the way they respond evaluatively to reality. Not every human evaluative response uses communications. I can experience things emotionally or perceive things that I never express or for which I have no adequate words. Similarly, our unconscious evaluations lack symbolic expression until we raise them to consciousness and name them. The vast majority of conscious human evaluations have, however, been conditioned in some way by language and by other forms of symbolic behavior, for we learn through dialogue with others to clarify our evaluative perceptions of ourselves and of our world.

The Symbolic Structure of the Divine Experience

We have concluded to the legitimacy of understanding the Trinity on an analogy with human social experience; we have also just seen that human experience contains expressive symbols, interpretative symbols, and communications. The same symbols function analogously within the divine experience and shape the way the divine persons relate to one another.

We should not, of course, imagine the divine persons speaking to one another in the way that human persons do. Human communication requires bodily acts that establish social bonds between individuals physically distinct from one another. The divine experience transcends space and time. Moreover, as we have seen, unlike human persons, the divine persons share an identity, not a mere similarity of life. As a consequence, the divine persons labor under none of the same social limitations as human persons. We find no breakdown of communication among them. We do not even find human conversation among them. They all share the same, identical mind, the same, identical will, the same, identical life.

Nevertheless, we can discern within the Godhead the presence of evaluative symbols. As we have seen, the incarnate Word comes to personal self-awareness as the Son and grasps the Father's missioning commands through the enlightenment of the Holy Breath. As a consequence, she stands historically revealed as the mind of God, as the source of divine wisdom and enlightenment, as the principle of the divine evaluative responses within God (1 Cor 2:1-16).

We can also discover within the Trinity something like eternal events. From all eternity the Father generates the Son efficaciously.

From all eternity the Father and Son efficaciously spirate the divine Mother. The three divine persons also give themselves eternally to one another in the supreme unity and perfection of love.

As we have also seen, we can distinguish two principles of efficacy within the Godhead. The Christian creeds attribute creative efficacy to the Father who proceeds from no one because as the source of both Son and Breath he originates absolutely everything. The Son, however, as we have seen, exercises obediential efficacy within the Godhead. That fact has been historically revealed in his perfect loving obedience to the Father's will and to the divine Mother's enlightenment. The Son's obediential relation to the divine Father and Mother does not imply his inferiority to them, for he enjoys coequality and coeternity with the other two divine persons. It does, however, transform him into the person within the Godhead through whom the divine Father and Mother speak and act. Through the Son they communicate with us.

We can, then, discern a symbolic structure of the divine experience analogous to the symbolic structure of human experience. It contains events (or expressive symbols), evaluations (or interpretative symbols), and the expression of divine evaluations in and through the eternal Word of God (or communication).

Revealing the Divine in History

Moreover, God's ability to reveal himself in space and time results directly from the symbolic structure of the divine experience, for the symbolic structure of the divine experience endows it with a relational structure that can come to symbolic expression and that the finite human mind can in some measure understand though never fully comprehend or exhaust.

The symbolic structure of the divine experience also shapes the social relationships within the Godhead in such a way as to make it necessary for the divine family to communicate with humanity through the Son, provided of course the divine persons should freely and graciously decide to communicate at all with their creatures. The symbolic structure of the divine experience requires this because within the family of the Trinity, the Son's obediential relationship to the divine Father and Mother constitutes him from all eternity as the one through whom they speak and act, the one through whom they create the world, the one through whom they save it.

The symbolic, social structure of the divine experience also dictates the content of divine revelation, should that revelation ever take place historically. The symbolic structure of the divine experience makes it revealable, graspable by a created intelligence, even though no finite mind can ever comprehend an infinite divine experience.

The social structure of the divine experience also determines the content of revelation, because revelation discloses the very reality of the triune God. A triune God can only stand historically self-revealed as a social reality, indeed as the supreme exemplification of interpersonal social relationships. The free self-communication of the triune God in history must, therefore, by revealing the social life of the Trinity, simultaneously disclose to humans a new way of relating to one another as persons that transcends anything that human persons can accomplish left to their own natural resources.

The historical revelation of the mystery of divine love, of the eternal procession and mutual self-donation of the divine persons in the perfection of love, invites human persons into a new kind of social communion with God and with one another. It does so by inviting and empowering the members of God's human family to love one another in a way that approximates the love that binds together the members of the divine family.

In the section that follows we shall reflect on how the symbolic revelation of God happens historically.

6. The Sacramental Character of Graced Experience. In this final section I shall argue the sixth thesis enunciated at the beginning this chapter: *the historical revelation of the divine family endows graced social relationship with a sacramental character.*

Sacrament and Symbol

All experience, both human and divine, has, as we have seen, a symbolic structure. God's free and gratuitous self-revelation through an act of self-communication effects the gracing of human experience. Human experience acquires a graced character when it undergoes transformation in faith. Through God's historical self-revelation and through the faith that perceives it, God and those to whom he reveals himself experience one another in new ways. They therefore exist in one another in new ways as well. When, therefore, the historical self-revelation of God in human history occurs, one symbolic reality, human experience, is transformed in another symbolic reality, divine experience. Through that symbolic transformation God communicates with his creatures.

In every gracing of human experience God enters into a collaborative relationship with his creatures. Moreover, that collaboration endows human experience with a sacramental character. The term "sacrament" designates an event that both conceals and reveals the reality of God.

Graced Experience as Sacrament

When a human experience undergoes gracious transformation in God, the very process of transformation reveals in some way the God in whom and through whom it occurs. When, for example, God spoke to the heart of Isaiah and he responded, his prophetic oracles revealed to us God's saving action in him and in his chosen people. Something analogous holds true for every graced transformation of human experience. As a consequence, every human conversion reveals God's presence and action in this world.

The incarnation too reveals God to us by effecting the graced transformation of a human experience in the divine experience. Jesus' human experience, however, reveals God with a perfection that no other graced human experience does; for in Jesus Christ we encounter a human experience efficaciously transformed in God in such a way that it became the human experience of being a divine person. When Jesus speaks, we hear God's human words. When Jesus thinks, he thinks God's human thoughts. When Jesus acts, the Son of God makes human decisions. When Jesus suffers, a divine person suffers.

Moreover, in Jesus we encounter a totally graced human experience. Sin mars our own experience of human life. It divides us from ourselves and from one another. It dehumanizes us. Only in Jesus do we encounter a human experience transformed in the person of the Son with perfect obediential efficacy. Hence, only in the sinless Christ do we encounter not only the perfection of humanity but the one supremely approachable and accessible human being (Heb 4:14–5:10).

Through the perfection of his obedience Jesus reveals to us the inner life of the divine family, hidden in God from all eternity. By the perfection of his obedience he reveals to us the Father's saving will. By his vision of divine truth he reveals to us the divine Mother's eternal wisdom. His mission by the Father and his sending of the Pentecostal Breath reveal the social character of the divine experience, the presence in God of a plurality of persons. By his perfect and total self-gift to both Father and Mother, he reveals the perfect self-donation of the divine persons to one another in love.

Jesus: Human Icon of the Divine

We encounter Jesus, therefore, as a human icon of the immanent, social life of the triune God. Some symbols, like arrows or
weathervanes, designate the realities they signify by pointing at them.
Other symbols, like descriptions or explanations, designate the realities to which they refer by discoursing about them. Iconic symbols,
like realistic paintings and photographs, designate the realities to
which they refer by resembling them. In addition, religious icons
negate themselves. By that I mean that in the very act of resembling
transcendent realities, they make it clear that they themselves are not
those same realities.

In Jesus we see the human face of a divine person. His mission,
death, and resurrection disclose to us the inner life of the Godhead.
No other created icon reveals God to us as perfectly as he. At the same
time, his humanity points beyond itself to the transcendent reality
of the Father, to the inner life of the Trinity.

The perfection of Jesus' obedience to the Father and to the
Breath also reveals him historically as the normative paradigm of
graced transformation in God. In Jesus we encounter a perfectly
graced human experience, one transformed efficaciously and obedien-
tially in the person of the Son. All other humans experience gracious
transformation, not in the Son, in the Breath of God. She transforms
us not efficaciously but persuasively, by disclosing to our hearts the
divine beauty incarnate in Jesus and inviting us to consent to it in
loving faith.

The incarnate Son of God invites all humanity into the intimacy
of the divine family. Through him we learn to call the first person
of the Trinity "Papa," the third person "Mama," and the Son himself "brother" and "friend." Inclusion in the intimacy of the divine
family requires of God's adopted children, however, that they call
one another brother and sister as well. It also requires that they take
the love of Jesus as the norm and model of love in God's family.

Consent to Jesus in faith as the normative revelation of God
in obedience to the divine Mother's gracious enlightenment transforms the human family of God into a corporate social icon of God's
incarnate Word, an imperfect icon, to be sure, but an icon nevertheless. Paul the Apostle expressed this truth by calling the human family of God the body of Christ, and correctly so. For to the extent that
the Christian community allows the divine Mother to transform it
through shared sanctification and mutual service in Jesus' image, to
that extent it resembles the Word made flesh and prolongs his mission in space and time.

The Church: The Social Icon of God

To the extent that it embodies the love of Christ, the Christian community also symbolizes sacramentally and iconically the social reality of God, the inner life of the Trinity; for by loving in the name and image of Jesus, Christian love approaches asymptotically but never perfectly reproduces the mutual self-gift of the divine persons to one another in perfect love.

The iconic character of graced experience endows it with a sacramental character. An event takes on a sacramental character when it both conceals and reveals the reality of God. The Son of God incarnate reveals the reality of God more perfectly than any other human individual, even though the limitations of his humanity prevented him from revealing God exhaustively. The Christian community reveals the incarnate Son to the world to the extent that it lives corporately in his image through faith. The love of its members for one another and for all those in need imitates the saving love of God. The Christian community conceals God from the world by its limitations and sinfulness.

Ritual sacraments celebrate sacramental events and acquire their sacramental significance from that of the events they celebrate at the same time that they endow the events in question with sacramental meaning and communicate their significance. All of the experiences we have been describing in the preceding chapters—initial conversion, sanctification, and the social dynamics of grace—all enjoy an iconic, revelatory sacramentality that the rites of Christian initiation attempt to interpret. To the ritual interpretation of these same iconic, sacramental events we turn in the chapters that follow.

PART II

Sacramental Initiation

CHAPTER V

The Challenge of the Restored Catechumenate

We have been examining the dynamics of an adult Christian conversion as a foundation for understanding the significance of sacramental worship. We have considered five forms of conversion and the ways they mutually condition one another. We have reflected on the specific contribution that commitment to Christ makes to the total process of conversion; and we have described the social dynamics of sanctification. We have seen that the sharing of the divine Mother's charisms in community creates a matrix of divine grace that nurtures new members to mature hope, faith, love, and longing for justice. Finally we have reflected on the ultimate foundation of Christian sacramentalism: the revealable, symbolic structure of the divine experience.

Adult conversion culminates in sacramental incorporation into the Christian community. The ritual incorporation of adults into the Church advances in a series of interrelated stages. It begins with the precatechumenate, a period of initial contact and inquiry. The catechumenate itself follows and culminates in a period of intensive preparation for the rites of initiation. After sacramental initiation there follows a period of postbaptismal catechesis, or mystagogy, that seeks both to consolidate the work of the preceding stages of initiation and to accustom the new converts to life among the people of God.

In the present chapter we begin to examine the rites of Christian initiation themselves and to probe their significance. The chapter divides into four sections. The first sketches briefly the history of the catechumenate. The second examines the structure of the restored catechumenate. The third draws on the theology of conversion developed in the preceding four chapters in order to cast light on the kinds of growth that the precatechumenate and catechumenate seek to instill. The fourth section probes the challenge that the restored catechumenate poses to the rest of the Church.

1. The Ups and Downs of the Catechumenate. When the Fathers of the Church discussed the initiation of converts, they spoke of catechumens rather than of the catechumenate. Today theologians speak differently. They publish scholarly and pastoral treatises on the history and institutional restoration of the catechumenate. Contemporary discussion of the catechumenate expresses, of course, genuine concern for the new converts to Christianity; but in a symbolic sense this shift in theological diction tells the catechumenate's story. Pastoral concern motivated Christians during the first three centuries to evolve responsible social processes for incorporating new members into the Church. Their pastoral and theological attention focused, then, on the converts themselves and secondarily on the institutions they were in process of creating. Today, in obedience to the Second Vatican Council, the Church is attempting to restore the institution of the catechumenate after fifteen centuries of its eclipse. The challenge of reshaping the institutional structures of the living Church to make place for this ancient institution has, then, understandably focused the attention of contemporary theologians and pastors on the catechumenate as such.

The Rise of the Catechumenate

The first five centuries of the Christian era saw the development and decline of the catechumenate. During the first two centuries we find flexible processes for welcoming new members into the Church. From the beginning, adult converts were, of course, expected to profess faith in Christ in ways that transformed their lives; but the Christian community employed a variety of methods for verifying conversion in candidates for baptism. They relied on the testimony of witnesses and on other tests of the candidate's sincerity. The actual preparation of converts lasted for a more or less prolonged period of time and seems to have been conducted largely by lay Christians (Justin, *1 Apology*, 61.2; Tertullian, *De Praescriptionibus Adversus Haereticos*, 41; Eusebius, *History of the Church*, 6.3).

By the third century the process of initiation had begun to take on greater institutional definition. Before admission to the catechumenate as such, candidates for baptism were expected to have experienced an initial conversion to Christ that committed them to living in accord with the demands of Christian discipleship. Before becoming catechumens they received preliminary instruction in the faith. The catechumenate itself lasted for an average of three years and included frequent communal instruction. The three years of indoctrination culminated in the rites of sacramental initiation. The ritual incorporation of new candidates lasted for an entire week and engaged the rest of the Christian community with considerable intensity (Tertullian, *On Baptism,* 20; Athanasius, *Epistola Festalis,* 39; *Apostolic Tradition,* 20; Augustine, *In Johannem,* 44.2; *De Catechezandis Rudibus;* Eusebius, *Vita Constantini,* 4.61; Leo the Great, *Letter,* 16.6).

The Decline of the Catechumenate

The fourth and fifth centuries saw the gradual deterioration of the catechumenate. In 313 the pagan emperor Constantine declared Christianity one of the official religions of the Roman empire. As imperial patronage evolved into caesaropapism, Christianity acquired greater and greater social respectability. Increasing numbers of people seeking baptism for the social advantages it brought led to a relaxation of the criteria for admission into the catechumenate. Unconverted catechumens found the rigors of the original catechumenate too taxing and absented themselves from religious instructions in greater and greater numbers. Some postponed baptism indefinitely.

Church leaders recognized a growing pastoral problem in the decline of the catechumenate and made some attempt to remedy the situation. They instituted an intense period of catechetical and religious formation for adult baptismal candidates during the season of Lent. Nevertheless, forty days of fasting and intense religious exercises offered an inadequate substitute for the three years of catechesis that had in the past formed candidates patiently in gospel living. Even the seven weeks of intense preparation proved too demanding for the "new" catechumens, and Church authorities reduced the period of intense catechesis to four or even three weeks. As the Church continued to baptize candidates whose lives manifested at best minimal signs of converted commitment, even the Lenten catechumenate deteriorated into a relatively empty formality.

After the fifth century the catechumenate for all practical purposes ceased to exist. Infant baptism became the accepted pastoral practice in places where the Church had already established itself institutionally. We even find a kind of "catechumenate" for infants in sixth-century France. On weekdays during Lent parents brought their babies to preparatory scrutinies. The custom probably represented the vestigial survival of including babies in the ceremonies that advanced adult catechumens toward ritual baptism, but it also probably provided a pastoral opportunity to catechize parents in their Christian responsibilities (*Ordo Romanus,* 11).

Feeble Efforts to Restore the Catechumenate

In mission areas, however, the common practice of mass baptisms after perfunctory preparation periodically motivated insufficient efforts at reform. The Council of Braga (A.D. 572) required adult candidates for baptism to submit to three weeks of preparation. In the eighth century, St. Boniface, the apostle of Germany, required at least two months of adult preparation prior to baptism. During the same century mass conversions under Charlemagne motivated Alquin to press for an adult baptismal preparation that lasted from seven to forty days. Even these timid efforts at reform, however, soon faded from memory.

The explosion of missionary activity in the Church during the sixteenth century refocused pastoral attention on the need for adequate adult preparation prior to sacramental initiation. In 1534 Augustinian missionaries to Latin America petitioned to restrict the celebration of baptism to only four times a year: on Easter, Pentecost, the feast of St. Augustine, and the Epiphany. In 1538 a Latin American bishops' synod required that adult converts undergo prior to baptism a forty-day catechumenate that included fasting, instruction, and the scrutiny and exorcism of candidates. In practice, such legislation seems to have had little pastoral impact.

In the early days of missionary activity in Asia and Africa, little was required of Christian neophytes prior to baptism. In 1552, however, St. Ignatius Loyola required his Jesuit missionaries in India to establish houses in which candidates for baptism would be gathered for three months of preparation prior to initiation. The Indian bishops eventually endorsed his recommendation.

The Catechumenate Restored

The seventeenth century saw the beginning of more serious pastoral efforts to retrieve the catechumenate. Missionary bishops in Asia instituted a catechumenal preparation that unfortunately lacked a liturgical dimension and failed to advance in clearly defined stages.

From the eighteenth century on, the Holy Ghost missionaries in Africa intensified their efforts to ensure a thorough program of catechesis prior to adult baptism. Largely through the efforts of Cardinal Lavigerie, the African Church successfully established a catechumenate that not only advanced in stages but also lasted long enough to ensure the likelihood of perseverance in the faith. The African catechumenate required a postulancy of two years, a two-year catechumenate, and a prebaptismal retreat.

The African catechumenate caught the attention of the European Church. In 1962 before the convocation of Vatican II, the Sacred Congregation of Rites issued a decree restoring ritual stages of preparation for adult initiation. The decree left the existing rite of baptism untouched and the implementation of the ritual stages to the discretion of the local bishops [*Acta Apostolicae Sedis* 54 (1962) 310–338].

Vatican II went, of course, much further. It called for the revision of all the sacraments and allowed their celebration in the vernacular. The council also legislated a universal restoration of the ancient catechumenate (*Sacrosanctum Concilium,* 64).

2. The Shape of the Restored Catechumenate. The restored catechumenate develops in four stages punctuated by rituals of advancement: the precatechumenate, the rite of acceptance into the catechumenate, the catechumenate itself, the rite of election (or enrollment of names), the Lenten period of purification and enlightenment prior to initiation, the rites of Christian initiation, and a period of postbaptismal catechesis (or mystagogy) after initiation.

a. The Precatechumenate. During the precatechumenate prospective converts establish initial contact with the Christian community, which welcomes them, responds to their questions about the faith, and proclaims the gospel to them. The precatechumenate lasts for an unspecified period of time. It envisages especially non-Christians who have never been evangelized; but the conferences of bishops have accommodated it to the needs of non-Catholic Christians interested in joining the Catholic communion. At this early stage of contact evangelists should establish an atmosphere of warmth, interest, and hospitality. Those making inquiries (or "sympathizers") need at this stage to learn to identify in a preliminary fashion with the community of faith they are contemplating joining, and that community needs to begin the process of actively incorporating the candidate into its life. They should at this preliminary stage manifest rectitude and sincerity of intention.

Welcoming Inquirers

Those welcoming the precatechumens need to get to know them personally. Evangelists should treat each inquirer as unique and should adapt early evangelization to each individual's personal journey of faith. Evangelist and precatechumen should relate to one another in an atmosphere of ease, friendship, and mutual hospitality. Even at this early stage the local community, too, needs to find ways to welcome the inquirers actively and warmly.

Initial Evangelization

The precatechumenate welcomes inquirers in order to evangelize them. Once the pastoral team has certified rectitude of intention, the reception into the precatechumenate may take place at some informal gathering of the local community in which the sympathizers can converse with its members. The occasion, though informal, should include some ceremony of formal reception in which a friend introduces each sympathizer to the community and the pastor or some other local representative of the community welcomes the individual.

Early evangelization should focus on the paschal mystery: on Jesus' death and glorification and on his sending the divine Mother. It should invite inquirers to let the story of Jesus illumine their own personal journey. Preliminary evangelization should teach prospective catechumens to pray the gospel. The entire process should culminate in conversion: in a purification of the inquirer's motives for seeking admission into the Church, in the renunciation of sinful habits, in a solid commitment to follow Christ even in suffering, and in the determination to seek sacramental incorporation into the body of the Church (Rite of Christian Initiation of Adults, 36-40; hereafter I shall abbreviate all references to this ritual as RCIA).

Preparation for Admission to the Catechumenate

Once both the pastoral team and the sympathizer have satisfied themselves concerning the latter's readiness to enter the catechumenate, a suitable period should elapse before celebrating the rites of admission themselves. During this period pastors should interview the prospective catechumen, who should also be instructed in the significance of the rite of admission.

Those who scrutinize candidates for the catechumenate should seek to discover in them signs of the foundations of a personal spirituality. Candidates should grasp the fundamentals of Christian belief and practice. They should show initial signs of repentance and conversion. They should want to cultivate a habit of prayer and should have experienced shared prayer with other Christians. They should have contacted personally some priest or other official representative of the Christian community. They should understand the Rite of Becoming a Catechumen (RCIA, 41–43).

The Rite of Admission to the Catechumenate

This rite finds appropriate celebration in a communal setting, preferably at a regular Sunday Eucharist, as a symbol of the entire Eucharistic community's active commitment to the preparation of the new candidates for baptism. The ritual advances in three stages: the presentation of candidates and the Liturgy of the Word. The Eucharist may follow.

At the start of the ritual of presentation, the candidates, their sponsors, and a group of the faithful assemble at the entrance of the church (RCIA, 48). The celebrant greets the candidates in a warm and personal manner and gives voice to the joy of the occasion. The celebrant asks each of the candidates to state his or her name and asks them what they seek from the Church. The candidates respond that they seek the faith that leads to eternal life (RCIA, 50). With proper preparation the celebrant can personalize this dialogue to fit each candidate. Those who plan the ceremony should take care that the congregation see the candidates clearly and hear what they say. In the case of non-Christians an exorcism and renunciation of non-Christian worship may follow when it seems pastorally advisable (RCIA, 51). In presenting candidates from a Christian background the ceremony should omit all references to forswearing paganism.

The candidates then accept the gospel publicly with the affirmation of both their sponsors and the community (RCIA, 52–53). First the sponsors and then the celebrant sign the candidates on the forehead. The celebrant may expand the rite to include the signing of all five senses (RCIA, 54–57). The candidates may at this point also receive a new name (RCIA, 73).

The rite of presentation then welcomes the candidates into the church and to the table of God's Word. They may at this point receive a crucifix (RCIA, 74). A Liturgy of the Word comprised of suitable readings taken from the lectionary then follows. After the homily the new catechumens may receive a Bible. Prayers of intercession for the catechumens follow together with a concluding prayer over the catechumens by the celebrant (RCIA, 60–66).

The celebrant then concludes the liturgy of acceptance by dismissing the catechumens. They may depart at this point accompanied by their sponsors and by friends and gather immediately to share their experiences during the ceremony of acceptance. If a Eucharist follows and the catechumens remain for it, the celebrant instructs them not to receive communion but welcomes them to remain for the rest of the ceremony (RCIA, 67).

b. The Catechumenate. The catechumenate itself seeks to deepen the conversion that has already occurred during the precatechumenate. Its length varies according to the needs of individual catechumens. During this period the Church encourages the catechumens with prayer, instruction, personal support, appropriate liturgical rituals, and involvement in Church ministries (RCIA, 75–77).

Catechetical Instruction

Catechesis should seek to ensure a personal internalization of the Word of God. It should engage the catechumens personally and experientially. The entire parish should take part in the formation of the catechumens, although sponsors bear special responsibility for monitoring each catechumen's progress and for providing needed example, encouragement, and support. Communal celebrations of the Word should introduce catechumens to the liturgical cycle. They may also terminate catechetical sessions (RCIA, 78–89).

Exorcism, Blessing, Anointing

The celebration of the minor exorcisms seeks to encourage repentance and the renunciation of anything incompatible with gospel living (RCIA, 90–93). Blessings should occur whenever appropriate, but they should especially conclude celebrations of the Word of God. Such blessings seek to encourage, support, and inspire the catechumens to advance in faith and commitment to Christ (RCIA, 95–96). Anointings with the oil of catechumens during the course of the catechumenate also remind the catechumens of their need for God's help and strength (RCIA, 98–101).

During this period of formation catechumens need to engage actively in Church ministry of various kinds. This involvement provides them with an opportunity to witness personally to their maturing faith and teaches them to serve others in the name of Jesus (RCIA, 75).

The Aims of the Catechumenate

During the catechumenate catechumens face four fundamental tasks. They need to mature in conversion and in the life of faith. They need to allow their commitment to Christ to penetrate and transform their way of living. They need to integrate themselves into the life of the worshipping, ministering community. Finally, they need to decide when they are ready for sacramental incorporation into the body of Christ (RCIA, 75).

As catechumens advance in holiness and practical service of others in Jesus' name, they will need the ministry, support, and guidance of discerning spiritual mentors. The responsibility for helping and supporting them falls especially on their sponsors, catechists, and pastors; but other charismatically gifted members of the community should stand ready to nurture the faith of the catechumens when their services are required (RCIA, 76).

As the catechumens advance toward sacramental baptism, they need to select their godparents. The pastor, sponsor, and catechists can all assist in the selection process; but catechumens should make their final choice with the pastor's assistance. A close bond of affection and friendship should unite catechumens to the godparents they choose. The latter should have a sound understanding of the demands of gospel living and manifest a willingness to share that understanding with their godchildren. As ecclesial ministers, godparents need to be designated by the local community with the approval of the pastor (RCIA, 80, 123).

Assessing Readiness for Adult Baptism

In assessing a catechumen's readiness to receive the sacraments of Christian initiation, pastor, sponsors, catechists, godparents, community leaders, and the community as a whole need to consider the candidate's degree of conversion, maturity of faith, advancement in charity, understanding of Christian doctrine and practice, and personal sense of readiness for the rites of initiation themselves (RCIA, 118–120).

More should be expected of the candidate than mere theological insight. Candidates need to have appropriated in a personal and practical way the Church's living tradition. They need to experience concretely and personally their own identification with Jesus and with the worshipping Christian community. They should manifest earnest longing for sacramental incorporation into the body of Christ (RCIA, 121).

The Rite of Election

The decision to accept a candidate for sacramental initiation culminates in the rite of election. Normally this ritual occurs on the first Sunday of Lent. Either the bishop or one publicly designated by him must preside at the election of candidates for sacramental initiation as a sign that the entire Church actively chooses each candidate (RCIA, 121–122, 125).

The bishop or his presiding delegate should explain to the candidates and to all those present the meaning of the rite of election. He should ratify the apostolic work of the parish in successfully bringing the catechumens to this point of spiritual readiness (RCIA, 125).

The rite of election itself occurs during the Eucharistic liturgy after the homily. The candidates are presented to the bishop together with their godparents. The bishop questions the godparents concerning each candidate's suitability for baptism. Then the congregation is asked to ratify the candidates' election. The candidates' names are inscribed in the Book of the Elect. They cease thereafter to be known as catechumens and go instead by the title of "the elect," "those to be enlightened (*illuminandi*)," or "the co-petitioners (*competentes*)." These titles derive from the ancient catechumenate and have an odd ring in contemporary American ears. The rite of initiation allows, therefore, that they may be replaced by some other title that indicates that the candidates have advanced to the final, intensive stage of preparation: the period of purification and enlightenment (RCIA, 124). After the enrollment of names the rite of election takes place, followed by prayers of intercession for the elect. These close with a prayer over the elect said by the celebrant, who then dismisses them (RCIA, 129–137).

c. Purification and Enlightenment. Two liturgical rituals give public expression to the growth processes expected of candidates during the final preparatory period of purification and enlightenment. The scrutinies assist the elect in the work of final purification. The presentations celebrate the degree of enlightenment they have reached and encourage them to further progress along that path.

The Scrutinies

The scrutinies are celebrated with proper singing and solemnity on the third, fourth, and fifth Sundays of Lent. The scrutinies do not seek to determine the worthiness of the candidates for sacramental initiation, since that has already been decided in the final stages of the catechumenate and ratified in the rite of election. Instead, the scrutinies give ritual expression to the candidates' own self-examination and efforts at final self-purification in preparation for the sacraments of initiation themselves (RCIA, 141–146). The rituals themselves consist of prayers for the elect, intercessions, and exorcisms (RCIA, 150–177).

The Presentations

The presentation of the creed to the elect is celebrated after the first scrutiny. This ritual seals and celebrates the work of the catechumenate and entrusts to the elect the profession of faith that they will make at the time of their baptism (RCIA, 157–163). The presentation of the Our Father follows the third scrutiny. The celebrant explains its meaning in a homily. The rite closes with prayer over the elect and their dismissal (RCIA, 178–184). The presentations seek to complement the scrutinies liturgically. The scrutinies encourage the final purification of the elect; the presentations celebrate their enlightenment (RCIA, 138–140, 147).

On the Holy Saturday preceding their sacramental initiation into the Church, the elect spend the day in prayer and fasting. During the day preparatory rituals ready the candidate for the sacraments themselves. These preparatory rituals include the recitation of the creed, the opening of the ears of the elect, and anointing with the oil of catechumens (RCIA, 1, 2, 26).

d. Mystagogy. A period of postbaptismal catechesis, or mystagogy, follows the rites of initiation themselves. During this final phase of initiation the neophytes are instructed more intensely in prayer and meditation, participate in special Eucharistic liturgies, and receive further instruction in the Scriptures. These exercises seek to deepen their commitment of faith. The neophytes also participate in various kinds of shared prayer and in shared reflection on the entire process of initiation. Normally, the period of mystagogy ends with a formal celebration on or near Pentecost Sunday (RCIA, 244–251).

We have examined the shape of the restored catechumenate. Does the theology of conversion developed in the preceding four chapters help us to understand better the growth processes through which adult converts ought to pass in the course of their incorporation into the body of Christ? To this question we turn in the section that follows.

3. The Maturing Convert. To date, commentary on the restored catechumenate has focused primarily, though not exclusively, on the rituals through which converts must pass. The theology of conversion developed in the preceding chapters, however, explores in considerable detail the growth processes through which adult converts may be expected to advance in the course of their incorporation into the body of Christ.

The Precatechumenate and the
First Dynamic of Christian Conversion

One must, of course, in dealing with candidates for Christian initiation accept people at whatever stage of faith development they happen to stand. At the same time, however, one needs to explain to them honestly the demands of integral conversion to Christ.

In the new rite of adult initiation, an initial Christian conversion signals the candidate's readiness to pass from the precatechumenate to the catechumenate. At this point only an initial conversion to Christ suffices for advancement. Nevertheless, before acceptance into the catechumenate candidates also need to understand clearly that Christian conversion claims them totally as persons: heart, mind, and conscience. They must also recognize that gospel living consecrates them as Christians to the search for a just social order. They need not at this point understand in detail the consequences of these commitments, but they do need to express a willingness to explore those consequences practically in the course of the catechumenate itself.

In other words, in the course of the precatechumenate candidates need to have experienced the first and most fundamental dynamic of Christian conversion: its mediation between affective and moral conversion. One should not, however, underestimate the claims that this first dynamic makes on the converts. It requires of them an initial repentance, in which they face and renounce in a preliminary way attitudes, beliefs, commitments, and social entanglements that stand in the way of their consenting in faith to the God revealed in Jesus and in the divine Mother whom he sends. It demands a preliminary healing of the resentment, fear, and guilt that prevent the candidate from responding to the beauty of God incarnate in Jesus and in people who resemble him. It entails a commitment to Christ that opens every facet of the candidate's personality to the divine Mother's healing touch. Finally, the experience of the first, fundamental dynamic of Christian conversion demands that candidates express a willingness to accept the moral consequences of conversion to Christ by allowing a global faith in the triune God to transform every facet of their lives. Candidates who have advanced this far in the process of Christian conversion show openness to the other four forms of conversion and a preliminary readiness to explore the other six dynamics of the conversion process. To this complex task they turn during the catechumenate itself.

The Six Dynamics of Conversion During the Catechumenate

The theology of faith sketched in the preceding chapters also helps clarify the aims and goals of the catechetical instruction undertaken during the catechumenate. This second, crucial period of preparation for sacramental incorporation into the body of Christ makes more strenuous demands of the candidates than does the precatechumenate. The second stage seeks to lead catechumens to a fivefold conversion in which the interplay of all seven dynamics of conversion ensures the candidates' integral development in Christian faith.

The Affectively Converting Catechumen

In other words, during the catechumenate candidates need to experience an ongoing, affective conversion that gives zest and enthusiasm to their religious progress. Repentance, as we have seen, presupposes an initial affective conversion; for it demands that candidates face and renounce the rage, fear, and guilt that separate them from God. Emotional healing demands of candidates the willingness to acknowledge and to forgive past hurts. It also requires the renunciation of every form of social bigotry: racism, sexism, classism, *machismo,* militarism, chauvinism, elitism. As repressed negative feelings are brought to healing in faith, candidates need to learn to own and express their positive, sympathetic affections: love, friendship, compassion, sensitivity, enthusiasm. In order to grow affectively, catechumens will need sound spiritual direction and, when necessary or helpful, therapy of some sort.

In addition, during the course of the catechumenate, candidates need to allow their commitment to Christ to transform their healed affective perceptions of the future into Christian hope. They should learn to resonate emotionally to Christian symbols and stories. They need to transcend imaginative perceptions of reality that express only personal ego-bias. They must learn instead to imagine the world in incarnational terms: to perceive the reality of God in concrete, sensible realities; to respond with enthusiasm to the vision of the kingdom; and to translate that enthusiasm into concrete strategies for embodying God's will on earth. By sharing their possessions and lives with those in greatest need, catechumens need to learn to live not simply for the things of this world but also for those of the next.

The Intellectually Converting Catechumen

In the course of the catechumenate candidates need to advance to an intellectual conversion informed by Christian faith. Here evangelists and pastors need to attend not only to the candidates' degree of conversion but also to their level of faith. The catechumenate seeks to lead candidates to an adult faith. As we have seen, an adult Christian conversion presupposes that one has advanced beyond conventional to individuating faith. Individuating faith demands the willingness to appropriate divine revelation in personally meaningful terms. The personal appropriation of religious belief presupposes in turn some measure of intellectual conversion.

Hence, a complex challenge faces those who undertake the doctrinal instruction of Christian catechumens. That instruction must ensure that the candidates have not only passed through the stage of conventional faith but have also begun to appropriate the shared faith of the Church in a personally meaningful way. The early stages of doctrinal instruction should, then, seek to ensure that candidates have mastered the skills of conventional belief; for without mastering the attitudes and skills of conventional faith, one cannot personally appropriate its meaning in a responsible manner. Christians appropriate the meaning of the gospel responsibly when they do so in dialogue with other Christians, with the Christian tradition, and with the pastoral leaders of the Church. Responsible participation in such dialogue presupposes a solid insight into doctrinal development and a clear grasp of official Church teaching.

Early instruction should, then, root catechumens solidly in a Catholic approach to Scripture and tradition. The Christian tradition itself contains, however, abundant resources for advancing candidates beyond conventional belief to personalized faith. The Bible, for example, contains a variety of theological viewpoints. Catechists can use the pluralism present in sacred Scripture in order to challenge new converts to advance beyond a fundamentalistic reading of Scripture to a personally integrated perception of the meaning of divine revelation.

Moreover, while in the course of its development theological debate over Christian doctrine has produced broad areas of consensus, it has also left numerous questions unanswered. A study of theological controversies should challenge converts either to opt among the available solutions to disputed questions or to formulate an answer of their own. Conflict and contradiction within the Christian tradition should pose an even more serious intellectual challenge, for here even expert opinion often fails to reconcile entrenched theological positions. In presenting each of the Christian sacraments in the chapters that follow I have tried to sketch briefly the major controversies that surround it as an illustration of the kind of doctrinal confrontations I mean.

Besides ensuring that candidates appropriate the Christian tradition with adult responsibility, those charged with the training of catechumens need to see to it that their intellectual conversion informs every other aspect of their Christian growth and development. Catechumens need to understand something about the dynamics of ongoing repentance and of sound emotional growth in faith. They require some insight into possible methods for interpreting and reflecting on the meaning of divine revelation. They need to examine critically the processes of prudential reasoning and to acquire techniques for forming their faith in Christ. They need to anatomize the causes of institutional injustice and to judge them in the light of Jesus' moral teaching and Catholic social doctrine.

The Morally Converting Catechumen

A balanced program of catechetical instruction will also teach candidates how to form their consciences as Christians. It will ensure that both moral and Christian conversion orient their choices toward natural and divine realities that make absolute and ultimate claims upon them. Instruction should ready the candidates to deal with the moral dilemmas that confront them personally, but it should also educate them to the fact of institutional injustice and exploitation. A conscientizing program of moral instruction will also supply candidates with principles and methods for dealing responsibly with injustice within the Church and with the moral challenges that will face them as members of the Christian community.

Moral catechetical instruction must ensure that candidates understand the meaning and consequences of the ethics of discipleship that Jesus lived and preached. Catechumens must understand the meaning of a Christian preferential option for the poor, the marginal, and the oppressed. They must grasp clearly and practically the consequences of dedication to the common good of humanity and of the Church. They must learn to criticize the false value systems that corrupt the Christian conscience and turn it away from the work of the kingdom.

The Sociopolitically Converting Catechumen

A sound program for catechetical instruction will, then, also ensure that candidates' sociopolitical conversion bears fruit in a Christian activism that deprivatizes their commitment to Christ. Candidates need to learn to hunger and thirst for God's own justice and to dedicate themselves in Christ's name to some specific sociopolitical cause. They need to understand the Church's divine mission to convert the world to Christ and her program for the Christianization of secular society. Catechumens must ponder prayerfully the contribution that they can make personally to that complex enterprise.

The Charismatic Catechumen

In the course of the catechumenate, the interplay of the seven dynamics of conversion ensures that catechumens grow in hope, faith, love, and Christian dedication to the cause of justice; but the mutual charismatic ministry of baptized Christians must also create the matrix of grace that nurtures catechumens to adult holiness. An adequate program of catechumenal instruction ought, then, to nurture candidates for adult initiation to respond with sensitivity to the charismatic inspirations of the divine Mother. The catechumens need not only to experience the gifts operative in their local Christian community but also to ponder the divine Mother's charismatic action in the Church as a whole. Candidates need to study the way in which her charisms have shaped the lives of the great saints and prophets of the past. They need to reverence the great teachers and doctors of the Church, both living and dead. They need to value the gift of discernment and sound pastoral leadership. They need to learn concretely how they themselves might serve others in Jesus' name. They need to nurture gifts of prayer and seek personal healing in faith.

Discerning the Catechumen's Charisms

Catechumens also need to begin to discern the ways in which they have been charismatically anointed to serve the Church and humanity. They need to understand that ordinarily the divine Mother's charisms heal, elevate, and perfect natural, human skills and temperaments. In discerning the ways in which they might enjoy charismatic competence to minister, catechumens should, then, ponder the strengths and weaknesses of their own personalities. In addition they should meditate on the needs of the Church and of society at large. They should also take into account that the divine Mother may in fact be calling them to an extraordinary ministry, to one for which they have few natural endowments and little natural inclination; for on occasion she can indeed call her children to tasks for which they feel initial repugnance.

Catechumens need to pray their way to an insight into their charismatic call to ministry. In discerning that call they need first of all to understand clearly the demands of discipleship. They follow a suffering Messiah who expects them to take up their Cross in his image. Any authentic charism consecrates Jesus' disciples to the work of the kingdom and to the obedience of faith. Any ministry to which the divine Mother calls incarnates the mind of Christ. It embodies the ethics of discipleship that Jesus lived and preached.

Having understood the moral demands of charismatic ministry in Jesus' name, those attempting to discern their personal call to service need to commit themselves in prayer to undertake anything the divine Mother may summon them to do. As they ponder the possible ways in which they might serve others in Jesus' name, catechumens will almost certainly find some forms of charismatic ministry more personally attractive than others.

Candidates will not, then, possess the emotional freedom to hear the divine Mother's call until they deal with any repugnance they might experience toward any form of ministry to which she might summon them. A particular individual may, for example, have the capacity to labor among the poor or in foreign lands but recoil at the prospect.

Until, however, one can ask God with complete serenity that he choose one for the kind of service one finds most repugnant and least attractive, one has good reason to suspect one's emotional preparedness to hear and respond to the divine Mother's charismatic summons. When God's call comes, it may lead one to choose the more attractive option. Nevertheless, until one experiences an emotional readiness to do *whatever* God asks, one lacks the necessary affective freedom to respond to God on God's own terms.

Catechumens need to situate their personal call to service in the context of the mission of the Church as a whole. They need to ask themselves how they might extend the kingdom by summoning unbelievers to faith in Christ. They need to ponder the ways in which they might advance the Christianization of secular society. They should weigh different vocational options: the lay apostolate, ordained ministry, religious life. If they have already made a vocational option they will need to deepen in their understanding of its Christian responsibilities.

Finally, as catechumens approach the moment of sacramental incorporation into the Church they need to manifest genuine love for the human family of God. They should view the Church realistically with all its limitations and sinfulness and should love it nevertheless with the atoning love of Christ. They should also experience an ever more intimate relationship in prayer with each of the divine persons. The divine Mother's nurturing wisdom should free them to trust confidently in the Father's providential care and in Jesus' atoning and fraternal love.

4. The Challenge of the Restored Catechumenate. In restoring the catechumenate the bishops at Vatican II passed judgment on the pastoral practice of fifteen centuries and found it wanting. Missionary experience in India and especially in Africa provided the grass-roots experience from which the restored catechumenate has emerged. As a consequence, its restoration has taken the rest of the Church by surprise as much as Vatican II's liturgical reforms took those parts of the Christian community that had never experienced the liturgical movement.

The restoration of the catechumenate comes, moreover, at the end of a series of liturgical reforms whose implementation has inspired mixed feelings even among the new liturgy's most enthusiastic supporters. We have as a Church moved beyond the initial euphoria that greeted liturgy in the vernacular, the revised lectionary, and the streamlined rituals legislated by the council. We have entered into very ordinary liturgical time in which through our experience of day-to-day worship we have come to realize that liturgical renewal requires more than the revision of rites. It demands finally integral conversion before God.

Apprehensions about the Restored Catechumenate

Some commentators on the restored catechumenate fear that it will only intensify disillusionment with Vatican II's liturgical revolution. These commentators point out that the first catechumenate grew out of an historical experience very different from our own. It took shape in a small, persecuted Church imbued with an intense sense of divine election. The architects of the first catechumenate shared a sense of communal identity as a worshipping community that transcends anything we ordinarily encounter in most contemporary parishes. The first catechumenate succeeded because the entire Christian community took responsibility for it. The gloomier commentators on the restored catechumenate fear, then, that the conditions that will ensure its successful restoration have simply ceased to exist in the contemporary Church. They therefore predict that this latest liturgical innovation inspired by Vatican II will only augment by its failure the malaise that surrounds the council's other liturgical reforms.

We need to listen carefully to these prophecies of doom, for their predictions flow from a sense of the enormity of the challenge that the catechumenate's restoration poses for the Church as a whole. The very decision to restore the catechumenate tacitly affirms that for fifteen centuries the Church has sacramentalized adult converts without evangelizing them adequately. That fact raises questions about the quality of evangelization in the Church as a whole.

The Church Sacramentalized but not Evangelized

Ever since the first Pentecost the Christian community has experienced internal tensions; nevertheless, the extreme polarizations that trouble the contemporary Church give evidence of a widespread lack of conversion among living Christians. These tensions have deep historical roots; for, to tell the truth, Catholic theologians and preachers have not concerned themselves in any notable way with the dynamics of conversion for centuries. Moreover, as we have seen, shared faith consciousness results from sharing the divine Mother's charisms in community; but for centuries the piety of the mainline Christian Churches has manifested little popular concern for the third person of the Trinity and even less for her charismatic inspirations. Hierarchicalism, clericalism, and authoritarianism have combined with religious individualism, pietism, and apathy to school even sacramentally active Christians to religious passivity.

The theology of conversion sketched in the preceding chapters helps pinpoint with greater accuracy the terms of the challenge that the restored catechumenate poses to converted Christians. The catechumenate seeks to lead adult converts to an integral, fivefold conversion. The dynamics of that conversion should nurture catechumens to adult holiness and to charismatic ministry within the Church. Pastoral honesty demands, however, that we ask frankly: how many members of the Eucharistic communities our new converts are joining have themselves experienced such a conversion? How many baptized Christians take seriously their own call to charismatic ministry?

Beyond Conventional Faith

The researches of James Fowler indicate that many people fail to advance beyond conventional faith. Until they do, we have reason to question whether they have taken full adult responsibility for their personal response to God. In other words, we have reason to question whether such individuals have themselves experienced that kind of conversion we ought to require of catechumens. These insights should give pause to pastoral leaders in all the mainline Christian Churches. How many baptized, sacramentally active Christians live nevertheless content with conventional belief? How many of those who have experienced religious conversion still lack conversion in some other important realm of experience? How many live a privatized piety?

Moreover, one can pass from conventional faith to reflective faith without simultaneously experiencing conversion. When that occurs, the transition to a higher level of faith consciousness can breed personal religious aberrations; for then one's formulation of a personal religious creed will express the limitations and sinfulness of one's biased ego rather than the divine Mother's wisdom and charismatic anointing. In our own day, the reforms of Vatican II have challenged the presuppositions of popular, conventional Catholicism. In the process those reforms have nudged many contemporary Catholics from conventional to reflective faith. How many of them, however, have in the process also experienced an integral, fivefold conversion? How many of them have instead passed to an individualistic, idiosyncratic, and inadequate personal religious creed?

The Needed but Often Missing Matrix of Grace

Similarly, in order to mature in faith, holiness, and service, new Christians need an environment of faith consciousness that flows from the sharing of all the divine Mother's charisms. When specific gifts fail, shared faith consciousness falters in predictable ways. In the absence of gifts of healing and of prayer, the Church loses a sense of God's presence. Lack of prophecy results in a faltering sense of divine guidance, in a religious complacency, and in an institutional rigidity that testifies to the lack of religious and affective conversion. Without teachers the Church loses its collective sense of identity as well as the shared sense of purpose that a consciously shared identity grounds. Without discernment the Christian community sways with every wind of false doctrine and succumbs to the scheming of fundamentalistic evangelists and religious charlatans. Without the action gifts the Church lacks the pastoral leaders it needs to transform its shared hopes and faith into shared action, while ordained pastoral ministry degenerates into autocratic clericalism.

The restored catechumenate challenges existing Eucharistic communities to transcend these sinful aberrations by providing the charismatic matrix of grace that will nurture converts to mature Christian ministry. The charisms inspire the Church's witness to Christ. They transform it into a missionary community burning with zeal to preach Christ to every creature. Not only do the charisms create the community of faith and mutual service that attracts converts, but they also empower the gospel's effective proclamation to unbelievers. As a consequence, without the gifts of evangelization and mutual service, the Church's missionary zeal falters and with it the number of adult converts that seek to join it. In very concrete ways, then, the restored catechumenate reminds the Christian community as a whole of its missionary vocation and of the demands that that vocation makes.

In addition, the new catechumenate presupposes a Church in which at least the majority of Christians enjoy charismatic competence to engage in active ministry. Charismatic competence to minister to others in Jesus' name and image presupposes not only an integral fivefold conversion but also considerable maturation in holiness; for, as we have seen, authentic charismatic ministry flows from hearts, minds, and consciences conformed to the mind of Christ rather than to the spirit of this world.

The Catechumenate and Church Conversion

In other words, the success or failure of the restored catechumenate rides upon the integral conversion and charismatic transformation of the Church as a whole. I use the term "charismatic transformation" rather than "charismatic renewal" lest I be misunderstood. I am not equating the Church's charismatic transformation with active participation in some charismatic prayer group, even though in my own opinion participation in a group with adequate teaching and pastoral leadership would probably benefit most Christians, especially those who resist it with greatest vigor. By a charismatically transformed Church I mean one in which the majority of its members have not only experienced integral conversion but have heard and responded to the divine Mother's call to serve the Church and the world in Jesus' name and image.

I am, therefore, also suggesting that the Church as a whole needs to do much more than "own" the catechumenate if that institution and the people it serves are to thrive. In addition, the Church itself must experience the kind of conversion and dedicated charismatic ministry that the restored catechumenate seeks to inculcate in neophytes.

These reflections suggest that far from expressing a liturgical afterthought or scholarly anachronism, the decision to restore the catechumenate taken at Vatican II forms an integral part of the council's overall program for Church reform. Contemporary Christians who labor to train the new catechumens should not, then, expect easy or overnight success to crown their efforts. The restoration of the catechumenate will succeed to the extent that Church renewal as a whole succeeds. Pastoral leaders, both lay and ordained, need, then, to renew their efforts to communicate the vision of Vatican II effectively not only to converts but also to the people of God as a whole.

As in the case of any human educational effort, we may also anticipate that some catechumens will succeed better than others in achieving the aims and goals of their baptismal preparation. Those who fail to experience an integral conversion by the time they are baptized will swell the ranks of Christians in serious need of radical evangelization. The successful product of the restored catechumenate could, however, develop into precisely the kinds of leaders the church needs if it is to advance further the reforms for which the Second Vatican Council called.

Finally, we note in conclusion that the theology of conversion developed in the preceding chapters serves the pastoral needs of the catechumenate better than a more traditional Catholic approach to conversion. A traditional Catholic theology of conversion addresses the needs of the precatechumenate since it describes for all practical purposes an experience of initial conversion, but it leaves one largely in the dark concerning the aims and goals of the catechumenate itself. Anyone, however, who espouses a theory in which conversion contains five forms and seven dynamics knows that an initial Christian conversion engages only one dynamic of the conversion process. It therefore leaves the major work of conversion yet to be accomplished. The precatechumenate culminates in an initial Christian conversion. The catechumenate itself seeks to inculcate an integrated, fivefold conversion.

In this chapter we have reflected on the history of the catechumenate, on the scope and dynamics of the restored catechumenate, and on the challenges that its restoration poses to the Church as a whole. The time has come, then, to turn our attention to the rites of Christian initiation themselves. We shall examine their history, structure, and significance in the chapter that follows.

CHAPTER VI

The Development of the Rites of Initiation

We are attempting to understand the rites that incorporate adult converts into the Christian community. In the preceding chapter we reflected on those rituals that advance converts to the threshold of sacramental inclusion in the body of Christ. In the present chapter and in the one that follows we shall reflect on the sacramental rites of initiation themselves. This chapter focuses on the way in which the rites of initiation evolved. The chapter that follows ponders their significance.

This chapter divides into three parts. The first examines biblical foundations for a theology of Christian initiation. The second section traces the ritual development of Christian initiation. The third part examines the controversies occasioned by each stage in the process of initiation.

1. Biblical Foundations for a Theology of Christian Initiation. The rites of Christian initiation seek to introduce converts into Jesus' own baptismal experience. John the Baptizer's baptism resembled Jewish rites of purification and Jewish proselyte baptism. It differed from both, however, in that it marked its recipients as John's disciples.

Early Christian Baptism

The Synoptic Gospels nowhere describe Jesus engaging in a baptismal ministry of his own. John's Gospel suggests, however, that he did do so for a time but abandoned it, even though his disciples continued to baptize (John 3:26-27; 4:2). Certainly, after the resurrection converts entered the Christian community through baptism (Acts 2:38-41).

All the Gospels agree, however, that Christian baptism differs from Johannine in its power to confer the Holy Breath of Jesus upon those who receive it (Mark 1:1-8; Matt 3:1-12; Luke 3:1-18; John 3:1-8). The first Christians also associated the Breath's reception with the laying on of hands (Acts 8:15-17; 19:5-6; Heb 6:2).

As we shall see, very early Christian initiation followed the baptismal washing with a ritual invocation of the Holy Breath. This second ritual came to be called "confirmation." The New Testament offers no clear evidence, however, of a rite of confirmation distinct from Christian baptism. The Letter to the Hebrews does allude to an instruction about "ablutions (*baptismoi*) and the laying on of hands" (Heb 6:2). Presumably the instruction in question contrasted Christian baptism with other rituals of washing, but the laying on of hands need not have followed the rite of baptism itself.

The Pentecost of the Samaritans

Luke, of course, does narrate the mission of Peter and John to lay their hands on the Samaritans whom the deacon Philip had baptized in order that the latter might receive the Holy Breath (Acts 8:4-24). Instead of describing standard ritual practice in the apostolic Church, however, Luke treats the incident as a pastoral anomaly. Despite their baptism by the deacon Philip the Samaritans surprisingly give no visible, charismatic evidence of having received the Holy Breath. The Jerusalem community therefore sends Peter and John to pray over the converts and to remedy the situation. Perhaps the apostles came in order to ratify the baptisms officially, since apparently in the heat of persecution the Jerusalem community had not commissioned Philip's mission to the Samaritans. In any case, the incident offers no clear evidence that initiation during the first century ordinarily included in addition to the baptismal washing a second invocation of the divine Breath through the laying on of hands.

Baptism in Paul

Indeed, the New Testament has much to say about the significance of Christian initiation but offers little information concerning the rituals that effected it. The Apostle Paul insists repeatedly on baptism's transforming consequences: the baptized have put off the old Adam and put on the new. They have abandoned the sinful ways that marked them as children of our first parents in order to obey the sanctifying Breath of the risen Christ that baptism imparts. She teaches them to live in Jesus' image (Rom 5:12-20; 6:12–7:6; 1 Cor 6:9-11;

15:20ff). The baptized have renounced the sins of the flesh and live instead sanctified by Christ's Breath (Gal 5:16-25).

For Paul baptism also marks the frontier between two worlds: the new age that Jesus' resurrection begins and the present age of this passing world. It divides those doomed to die from those destined to live forever with Christ (Rom 10:9).

Paul speaks of baptism as burial with Christ. He writes to the Romans:

> Do you not know that all of us who have been baptized into Christ Jesus were baptized into his death? We were buried therefore with him by baptism into death, so that as Christ was raised from the dead by the glory of the Father, we too might walk in newness of life. For if we have been united with him in a death like his, we shall certainly be united with him in a resurrection like his (Rom 6:3-5).

Baptism into Christ incorporates one into his body, the Church (1 Cor 12:12-13) and joins one in solidarity to the innocent savior, who died on the cross once and for all to sin. In rising he became "a life-giving Breath" (1 Cor 15:45). The death to sin that the Breath of Jesus effects in the baptized unites them to the risen Christ in a vital solidarity that guarantees their own share in his risen glory (2 Cor 1:21-22).

Through Breath-inspired faith the baptized "put on Christ" (Gal 3:27). In possessing his Breath they share his very mind—his attitudes, beliefs, hopes, and aspirations—and serve one another humbly in his image (Col 3:9-17; 1 Cor 2:6-16). The baptismal Breath incorporates believers into the new covenant (2 Cor 3:1-6). Initiation seals those who believe, marking them for resurrection on the last day (Eph 1:13; 4:30). The baptismal bath effects rebirth, regeneration, and renewal in the Breath of Jesus (Eph 5:25-27; Titus 3:3-8).

I Peter: A Baptismal Homily

One may or may not regard the First Letter of Peter as a baptismal homily, though some Scripture scholars certainly do. The epistle does allude more than once to the graced transformation made possible by Jesus' redemption and effected by Christian baptism. Like "newborn babes" (1 Pet 2:2) Christians experience rebirth (1 Pet 1:3, 23). Only once, however, does the First Letter of Peter make explicit mention of baptism. Like the waters of the flood that scoured the world of sin, the waters of baptism beseech God to cleanse the conscience of the baptized in the power of the risen Christ (1 Pet 3:21).

Baptism in John

John the evangelist refers more than once to the "living water" that Jesus will give to slake human thirst for everlasting life. The Gospel also identifies that water with the holy Breath of Jesus (John 4:14; 7:37-39; 19:34).

The cure of the paralytic at the pool of Bethsaida (John 5:1-9) and the healing of the blind man at the pool of Siloam (which means "one who has been sent" [John 9:7]) could also contain baptismal allusions (John 9:1-9). If they do, these two narratives suggest that baptism heals the paralysis of sin and commissions the enlightened believer to witness to Jesus with the courage of the man born blind. Nevertheless, scholars debate whether these passages do indeed allude to baptism.

The fourth evangelist, however, certainly regarded rebirth in water and the Holy Breath as a condition for entry into the kingdom of God (John 3:5). He also consistently linked water and Breath as the agents of heavenly rebirth. It seems likely, therefore, given the highly symbolic character of John's Gospel, that in his references to the living water and to healing baths he also intended to allude to Christian baptism.

2. The Development of the Rites of Christian Initiation. One may divide the history of Christian liturgical development roughly into eight periods: (1) The first four centuries exhibited considerable liturgical improvisation as different ritual traditions started to take shape. (2) Between the fourth and the seventh centuries Christian ritual began to employ fixed liturgical texts and standard readings. (3) Between the eighth and twelfth centuries liturgists gathered these standard texts into lectionaries and sacramentaries. (4) The thirteenth and fourteenth centuries witnessed the canonization of the major liturgies in the East and West. (5) The fifteenth century marked a period of liturgical decline, especially in the West. (6) In the sixteenth century Catholics and Protestants undertook the reform of worship in the Latin Church. (7) From the seventeenth to the nineteenth centuries the printing press encouraged the standardization and rubricization of worship. (8) While the roots of the liturgical movement extended back into the nineteenth century, it came to full flower in the twentieth century and culminated in the liturgical reforms of Vatican II.

Christian Initiation in the First Four Centuries

How, then, did the rites of initiation evolve in the course of the centuries? The New Testament, as we have seen, offers us little detailed evidence concerning the rites that the first Christians used to initiate converts. We know that in the apostolic Church the baptized were plunged into water or washed with it as the minister invoked either the name of Jesus or the triune name (Acts 2:38; Matt 28:19). The rite may have been followed by anointing or, in some Churches, by the laying on of hands. Very early, however, probably by the second century, baptism in the triune name had gained universal acceptance.

By the second century, moreover, we know that baptismal preparation had acquired greater institutional definition. Instruction had become more organized and insisted on the moral transformation that conversion requires. Fasting and prayer preceded ritual incorporation into the Church. Before candidates submitted to the bath of baptism itself they professed their faith in response to a threefold interrogation by the rite's minister. Because baptism gave neophytes access to the Eucharist, the rite of initiation now culminated in a Eucharistic celebration during which the newly baptized communicated in the Body and Blood of Christ for the first time (*Didache*, 1–10).

By the third century Christian initiation seems to have advanced in the following stages: (1) As we saw in the preceding chapter, the catechumenate, which culminated in an intensive period of preparation prior to the rites of initiation themselves, marked the first stage. (2) The baptismal ceremony itself opened with the blessing of the baptismal water (Tertullian, *De Bapt.*, 3 and 4; *Apostolic Tradition*, 21.1). (3) The candidates then repudiated Satan, his pomp, and his works in a threefold formula of renunciation (Tertullian, *De Corona*, 3, *De Spectaculis*, 4; *Apostolic Tradition*, 21.9). (4) The celebrant plunged the candidates three times into the water, inviting them to profess faith first in the Father, then in the Son, then in the Holy Breath. Each time the candidate replied, "I believe" (Tertullian, *Against Praxeas*, 26, *De Corona*, 3; *Apostolic Tradition*, 21.9). (5) The candidates, who after baptism would refrain from bathing for a week, now had their bodies anointed, probably from head to toe (Tertullian, *De Bapt.*, 7; *Apostolic Tradition*, 21.9). (6) The bishop then signed the candidates with the cross (Tertullian, *On the Resurrection of the Body*, 8).

(7) In the third century, Tertullian speaks of an episcopal imposition of hands and invocation of the Holy Breath in the course of the rite of initiation, although we have no way of knowing the extent to which such a ritual may have occurred in the African Church (Tertullian, *De Bapt.*, 7). Some have even questioned whether Tertullian is speaking of a distinct rite of confirmation like that which emerged later in the Roman liturgy. (8) The ceremony culminated in the Eucharist, where the newly baptized partook for the first time of the Body and Blood of Christ.

Christian Initiation from the Fourth to the Seventh Century

During the fourth century the Church emerged from the catacombs. Public celebration of the liturgy encouraged the symbolic elaboration of all the rites, including initiation. By the fifth century the ritual had developed the following stages: (1) The rite of baptism itself now began with the ritual introduction of the candidates into the baptistry (Cyril of Jerusalem, *Mystagogic Catechesis*, 1.2, 11, 2.2; Ambrose of Milan, *On the Sacraments*, 1.4, 10). (2) In the West the ceremony of the "opening" followed. In it the bishop repeated Jesus' gesture described in Mark 7:34. He touched the candidates' ears and nostrils with spittle saying in Aramaic and in Latin: "Be opened." The ritual prepared the candidates to hear the word of God and to respond to the good odor of Christ (Ambrose, *On the Sacraments*, 1.2). (3) The candidates were then stripped in preparation for bodily anointing and baptism by immersion. Putting off their garments reminded the candidates of their naked entry into life and of their naked departure from it (Job 1:21). It also symbolized casting off the old Adam in order to put on the new (Cyril, *Mystagogic Catechesis*, 2.2; Ambrose, *On Psalm 61*, 32). (4) The anointing of the whole body which followed had by now acquired the character of an exorcism embellished by other associations: for example, like the athletes of the Roman arena (who also rubbed down with oil), the candidates were anointed in order to prepare them in their fight against the devil or in order that they might shed all the traces of sin and share in Christ (Ambrose, *On the Sacraments*, 1.4; Cyril, *Mystagogic Catechesis*, 2.3). (5) The renunciation of Satan followed the exorcising anointing (Tertullian, *De Spectaculis*, 4; Cyril, *Mystagogic Catechesis*, 1.4, 7; John Chrysostom, *The Institution of Baptism*, 2.20). (6) In some rituals after renouncing Satan the candidates formally professed their determination to follow Christ (John Chrysostom, *The Institution of Baptism*, 2.21; Cyril, *Mystagogic Catechesis*, 1.8-9). (7) The blessing of the baptismal water followed

(Ambrose, *On the Sacraments,* 1.15, 18; Cyril, *Mystagogic Catechesis,* 5.7; Tertullian, *On Baptism,* 4). (8) Then came the triple immersion of the candidates accompanied by some mention of each person of the Trinity (Theodore of Mopsuestia, *Hom. Cat.,* 14). (9) After immersion, the candidates were anointed on the head with the sign of the cross (Ambrose, *On the Sacraments,* 2.24, 3.1; Theodore of Mopsuestia, *Hom. Cat.,* 13. 17-20). (10) In many churches the bishop and clergy would thereupon imitate Jesus' humble act of service at the Last Supper and wash the feet of the newly baptized (Ambrose, *On the Sacraments,* 3.7; *On the Mysteries,* 32). (11) As a symbol of their newly acquired innocence, the newly baptized were next clothed in a white garment (Cyril, *Mystagogic Catechesis,* 4.8; John Chrysostom, *On the Institution of Baptism,* 4.3; Theodore of Mopsuestia, *Hom. Cat.,* 14). (12) In the Roman Rite of the fifth century, the bishop would then invoke the Holy Breath upon the candidates, a rite that would spread by the ninth century to the Hispano-Gallican churches. In the Eastern baptismal liturgies, the post-baptismal anointing, by either presbyters or by the bishop, took on enhanced pneumatological significance (Ambrose, *On the Sacraments,* 3.8-10, 6.6-7; Cyril, *Mystagogic Catechesis,* 3.4; Theodore of Mopsuestia, *Hom. Cat.,* 13.20). (13) In some places the newly baptized were afterwards given candles to symbolize their new faith (Pseudo-Ambrose, *De Lapsu Virginis,* 5.19; Gregory of Nazianzus, *Orat.,* 40.46). These they carried as they (14) processed into the church, where they (15) joined in the celebration of the Eucharist and communicated for the first time (Tertullian, *Against Marcion,* 1.14.3; John the Deacon, *Ad Senarium,* 12).

Christian Initiation from the Eighth to the Thirteenth Century

As the number of Christians grew in the major urban centers of the Roman Empire, the frequency of infant baptism forced the adaptation and simplification of the rites of initiation. In the Roman liturgy of the sixth century, for example, initiation began with the blessing of the baptismal font. The infants were then immersed three times, though not until the eighth century did the custom develop of invoking the triune name at the time of their immersion. The babies were subsequently anointed on the head by a presbyter, vested, and prayed over by the bishop for the forgiveness of sins and for the sevenfold graces of the Holy Breath. The chrismation of the newly baptized also symbolized the gift of the Breath. The rite culminated in the Mass of the Paschal Vigil in which the newly baptized also communicated in the Eucharist for the first time (*Gelasian Sacramentary* [Mohlenberg edition] , 32–97).

The rites of adult initiation during the third and fourth centuries enjoyed a certain ritual integrity. The ceremony moved, with different degrees of symbolic elaboration from baptism, to the episcopal invocation of the Holy Breath, to first Eucharistic Communion. Oriental liturgy preserved this ritual integrity. In the West, however, as Europe evolved into Christendom, the ritual integrity of the ceremony of initiation first cracked and then fragmented.

Roman ritual reserved the second moment in the rite of initiation, the solemn invocation of the Holy Breath, to the bishop. As this practice spread to other Western liturgies, this particular ritual evolved into the sacrament of confirmation as it became temporally separated from the other rites of initiation. We discover signs of this development in early medieval sacramentaries, which in France and Holland omit the postbaptismal consignation and invocation of the Holy Breath. These abbreviated baptismal rituals were intended for the use of priests who had the liturgical right to baptize and distribute Holy Communion but lacked episcopal authority to call down the Holy Breath on the baptized. These abbreviated rites also anticipated that the bishop at the time of his next visitation would supply the omitted portion of the ceremony. In the ninth century Charlemagne's legal imposition of the Roman ritual on his entire kingdom transformed these liturgical innovations into the universal practice of the Gallican Church. Charlemagne's act also canonized Latin as the official liturgical language of the Church. Eventually, both innovations found acceptance wherever the Roman Rite prevailed.

The change had two important consequences: (1) It transformed the pattern of Christian initiation from (a) baptism, (b) invocation of the Breath, and (c) first Holy Communion to (a) baptism, (b) first Communion, and (c) invocation of the Breath. (2) With the postponement of the Breath's invocation for longer and longer periods of time, this ritual evolved in the Latin Church into a separate sacrament called "confirmation."

Christian Initiation in the Protestant Reformation

We shall reflect on Reformation debates over the sacraments in the section that follows. Here we focus instead on the way the rites of initiation themselves evolved. The Protestant reformers called for the simplification of Church ritual. Since they found the New Testament sanctioning only water baptism in the name of the Trinity, they regarded all the other rites of initiation—the blessing of the baptismal font, anointing, candles, spittle, etc.—as mere human inventions that often fostered superstition. Most of the Protestant reformers, however, retained the practice of infant baptism. All celebrated the rites of the Church in the vernacular.

Martin Luther's rite of baptism published in 1526 opened with an exorcism and signing of the child's forehead and breast. After several prayers, the celebrant again exorcised the child in the name of the Trinity. After a gospel reading all present recited the Our Father. The child was then carried to the font for baptism through immersion accompanied by the Trinitarian formula for baptism. The triple renunciation of Satan preceded baptism. The vesting with a white garment followed baptism and was accompanied by a prayer (Luther, *Works*, 53:106-109).

Ulrich Zwingli and Martin Bucer simplified the rite even more radically; John Calvin adapted their reforms in Geneva, where the ceremony began with a long sermon on the meaning of baptism. A reading of Matthew's account of Jesus blessing the children followed. A charge to the godparents culminated in the recitation of the Apostles' Creed. Then the child was baptized in the triune name (*Corpus Reformatorum*, 34: cols. 185-92).

Catholic Reform of Christian Initiation

The Council of Trent, in response to Protestant criticisms of late medieval sacramental abuses, undertook to defend and reform medieval sacramental practice. Its decrees ensured the rubrical celebration of medieval baptismal ritual in Latin, until the liturgical reforms of Vatican II. From Trent to Vatican II we find little change in Catholic baptismal practice.

We shall reflect in the next chapter on the revised rite of baptism promulgated by the Second Vatican Council. In order to do so intelligently, however, we first need to recall some of the theological controversies that Christian initiation has occasioned over the centuries. To these controversies we turn in the section that follows.

3. Controversies Concerning Christian Initiation. Each stage in the rite of Christian initiation—baptism, the invocation of the Holy Breath, and first Holy Communion—has occasioned theological controversy. Let us consider each stage in turn and ponder briefly the debates that have surrounded it.

a. Controversies About Baptism. The earliest debate over baptism concerned its minister. As heresy and schism fragmented the Church, the question inevitably arose, should orthodox Christians recognize a baptism celebrated by heretical or schismatic clergy? One strain in early patristic theology held that the minister of the sacrament must possess the Holy Breath in order to pass her on to others. Since schismatics and especially heretics had in the eyes of the rest of the Church sinned grievously, how could they pass on to others a reality that they themselves had forfeited?

Following this line of reasoning, Churches in Africa and some Eastern Churches required rebaptism of those baptized by heretical or schismatic ministers. The Roman and Alexandrian sees, however, took a more tolerant view of the matter and did not rebaptize. These differences in liturgical discipline eventually led to open disagreement in the third century between Cyprian of Carthage and Pope Stephen I (Cyprian of Carthage, *Epistles,* 71 and 73). The martyrdom of both antagonists terminated the debate but left it unresolved.

The Donatist Controversy

In the fourth century Donatus, the bishop of Carthage, refused to accept the laxer position on rebaptism. In addition, controversy over succession to his see split the African Church for over eighty years. In his anti-Donatist writings Augustine of Hippo countered the Donatist position in a series of polemic tracts. He distinguished between the grace that baptism confers and its permanence. Moreover, in defending the permanence of baptism he compared it to the indelible tattoo (in Latin, *character*) that soldiers received on joining the imperial army (Augustine, *On Baptism Against the Donatists,* I, iv, II, iv).

In his assault on the Donatists Augustine made two important contributions to the theology of Christian baptism. First, he made it clear that within sacramental worship, the relationship of the worshipper to God cannot depend on the state of conscience of the one who administers the sacrament (Augustine, *Answer to the Letters of Petilian the Donatist,* II, vii). Second, in invoking the metaphor of a tattoo, or brand on the soul, in order to account for the paradoxical permanence of baptism even in the absence of the grace it confers, Augustine contributed a new term to sacramental theology and bequeathed a perplexing problem to medieval theologians, who were left with the task of explaining the nature of this mysterious "mark on the soul."

Debate Over the Baptismal Character

In 1201 Pope Innocent III in the course of responding to a letter from Umbertus, the archbishop of Arles, took the position that the administration of baptism imposes a character on the baptized who do not deliberately place an obstacle to its reception (D 411).

The great medieval scholastic theologians developed the theology of the character in various ways. In general, however, they sharpened the distinction between it and the grace that the sacrament confers; and, with help from Augustine who argued that ordination too confers a character, they taught that any sacrament that can be administered only once confers a character. Since by the late Middle Ages, theologians had come to regard the unrepeatable rite of confirmation as a distinct sacrament, they held that it too conferred a mysterious character, even though they found it hard to agree on its nature.

Bonaventure, for example, in the thirteenth century described the baptismal character as a habit that disposes the soul to receive the grace of baptism. The character of confirmation, he held, disposes it to resist cowardice in testifying to the Christian faith. He believed that the character of orders functions as a sign of the spiritual power to perform priestly functions (Bonaventure, *Commentary on the Book of Sentences*, IV, d.iv, p. 1, art.un., qq1 and 2; d.vii, a.ii, q.2; d.14, p.ii, a.i, qq.1-3). Albert the Great, the mentor of Thomas Aquinas, held that the character of baptism marks one as a member of the people of God. The character of confirmation marks one as a defender of the faith. The character of orders marks one as a prelate of the Church (Albert the Great, *On the Sacraments*, Tr.III, q.i, a.5; Tr.IV, a.7; Tr. VIII, q.4., a.3).

Eventually, however, Thomas Aquinas's account of the different characters imposed by unrepeatable sacraments had the greatest impact on the development of Catholic sacramental theology. He linked the character closely to cult. He described the character as an indelible mark on the soul that empowers one to active involvement in Christian cultic worship by conforming one to Christ, the high priest. Baptism empowers one to receive the other sacraments. Confirmation empowers one to witness publicly to Christ, especially by participation in public Eucharistic worship. Ordination empowers one to administer the sacraments in accord with Church discipline (Thomas Aquinas, *Summa Theologiae*, III, lxiii, 1-6, lxxii, 5-7).

Catholic conciliar teaching affirmed the reality of the three sacramental characters but failed to endorse any of the interpretations with which the medieval scholastics explained the term (DS 1316, 1514, 1672, 1767, 1774).

The Protestant reformers, however, rejected the idea of an indelible sacramental character as problematic and biblically unfounded (Ulrich Zwingli, *Commentary on True and False Religion*, 20; Luther, *Works*, 36:110-111).

The controversy over rebaptism has, then, reshaped sacramental theology in two important ways. It eventually produced a consensus that God's ability to grace people through the sacraments should not depend upon the worthiness of the ritual's minister. Disagreement over the existence and significance of the sacramental character continues, however, to challenge contemporary theologians either to make sense of this notion or to abandon it.

The Pelagian Controversy

A second controversy flared over the first stage in Christian initiation: infant baptism. The debate over infant baptism first raged in the fourth and early fifth centuries and pitted Augustine of Hippo against the British monk Pelagius. The two men differed radically in their understanding of the human condition and of the action of divine grace. In sacramental theology they differed over the need for infant baptism.

As we have seen, expanded Church membership from the fourth century onward caused the number of adult baptisms to decline and the number of infant baptisms to wax, especially in urban centers. Children, however, like adults were baptized "for the forgiveness of sins (*in remissionem peccatorum*)." Pelagius challenged the legitimacy of this practice on the basis of the fact that the baptized children had never sinned personally. Augustine conceded to Pelagius that the infants had committed no personal sin; but he argued to the legitimacy of baptizing them for the remission of sins on the basis of the fact that Christian initiation remits two kinds of sin: personal sin in adults and original sin in both adults and children (Augustine, *On the Grace of Christ and on Original Sin, On the Spirit and the Letter, On Marriage and Concupiscence, Concerning Nature and Grace*).

Infant Baptism and Original Sin in Official Church Teaching

Augustine's own understanding of original sin was colored by his pessimistic view of human nature and by his ambivalence toward human sexuality. He believed that the sin of Adam and Eve had so corrupted human nature that one could perform no virtuous act without the help of supernatural grace. He regarded concupiscence, the war of the flesh against the spirit as one of the chief consequences of human fallenness. He believed that human parents communicated both original sin and concupiscence to their children in the act of procreation.

On the whole official Church teaching tended to side with Augustine rather than with Pelagius. With Augustine, conciliar teaching asserted the absolute primacy of divine grace in the work of human salvation. It vindicated the legitimacy of baptizing infants "for the remission of sins." It asserted the reality of original sin and of concupiscence.

Nevertheless, official Church teaching refrained from endorsing every theological strain in Augustine's anti-Pelagian diatribes. The conciliar tradition did not subscribe to his pessimistic assessment of human nature, his theory of the transmission of original sin, or his sexually colored interpretation of both original sin and concupiscence (DS 222-231, 370-397).

Indeed, at the time of the Reformation, the Council of Trent would counter the Augustinian pessimism of the Protestant reformers by endorsing the Thomistic doctrine that fallen human nature can perform naturally good acts, even though it needs divine grace in whatever concerns human salvation. Trent would also reaffirm the fact of human fallenness, but it would offer no clear definition of original sin. Moreover, its definition of concupiscence differed notably from that of Augustine. By "concupiscence" Trent meant, not personal sin, but anything in the experience of baptized Christians that comes from sin and leads to sin (DS 1510–1516, 1557).

At the time of the Reformation Luther, Zwingli, and Calvin all defended the practice of infant baptism (Luther, *Works,* 36:73ff.; Calvin, *Institutes,* IV, xvi; Zwingli, *Works,* 3:357-437); but the Anabaptists did not (Melchior Hofman, *The Ordinance of God*).

We shall deal with the question of infant baptism in discussing the responsibilities of Christian parents for the rearing of their children. For the moment we focus our attention on adult baptism. The debate over infant baptism, however, forced a reinterpretation of adult baptism as well; for it led orthodox sacramental theologians to assert that adult baptism removes two kinds of sin: personal and original. After baptism, moreover, Christians must still deal with concupiscence. A contemporary theology of adult baptism needs, as a consequence to make sense both of the distinction between personal and original sin and of the idea of concupiscence. We shall return to these questions in the chapter that follows.

b. Controversies About Confirmation. The second moment in the rite of adult initiation has occasioned three principal controversies. First, theologians have offered contrasting accounts of the ritual's significance. Second, they have disputed its sacramentality. Third, they have questioned the existence and significance of the "character" that this sacrament allegedly impresses on the soul.

Patristic Teaching about Confirmation

We find contrasting explanations of the meaning of the chrismation that followed baptism in the writings of the Fathers of the Church. Cyril of Jerusalem interpreted the invocation as purifying Christian neophytes from sin or as conferring upon them strength to resist the devil's wiles (*Mystagogic Catechesis*, 3.4). Theodore of Mopsuestia interpreted the rite eschatologically, as an anticipation of heavenly bliss (*Catechetical Homilies*, 14.27) or, more vaguely, as the completion of the rite of water baptism (14.19). In the West, Ambrose of Milan saw the ritual as conferring the seven gifts of the Holy Breath[1] (*De Sacramentis*, 3.8).

The doctrinal disarray of the Fathers on this point, their inability to come up with a consistent account of the ritual, points to the fundamental question that any theological explanation of Christian initiation must answer: since the rite of water baptism had already invoked the name of the Holy Breath upon Christian neophytes, why did the Church add a second invocation of the Breath immediately after the rite of baptism? The Greek Fathers offer no clear answer to this question.

---

1. Patristic teaching on the seven gifts of the Holy Breath derives from Isaiah's prophecy of the coming of a Breath-filled king who would act like a compendium of all the great charismatic leaders of Israel. The Fathers read this text with Greek eyes and often concerned themselves with defining the precise difference between the different "breaths" of which Isaiah spoke: wisdom, understanding, counsel, fortitude, knowledge, piety, and fear of the Lord. Since the Holy Breath had descended on Jesus at his baptism in order to empower him to fulfill this prophecy and since Christian initiation draws the baptized into Jesus' own baptismal experience, when the rite of confirmation took shape in the West, patristic writers and liturgical texts associated the ritual invocation of the Breath that followed baptism as a prayer for these seven "gifts" or "breaths."

Medieval Debate Over Confirmation

In the Latin Church the historical transformation of the second moment in the rite of initiation into a distinct sacrament, the sacrament of confirmation led medieval theologians to wrestle with the question, what special grace, if any, does this ritual confer? What, if anything, does it add to the rite of baptism?

Once again, however, theological opinion faltered. All agreed that the rite of baptism itself confers the gift of the Holy Breath. How then could she be given anew in confirmation? As we saw in reflecting on the baptismal character, theologians commonly held that confirmation strengthens in some way the graces of baptism, but how it did so remained obscure.

Moreover, for obvious biblical and historical reasons, medieval theologians also found themselves hard pressed to prove that Jesus had instituted confirmation as a sacrament distinct from baptism; for not until the early Middle Ages did the ritual evolve into a separate sacrament, and then only in the West.

Finally, since one could receive this rite of initiation only once, theologians agreed that it had to confer a character like baptism and orders; but because the ritual's purpose itself lay shrouded in obscurity, so too did the purpose of confirmation's sacramental character (Hugh of St. Victor, *On the Sacraments*, II, vii; Peter Lombard, *Book of Sentences*, IV, d. vii, ch.3; Bonaventure, *Commentary on the Book of Sentences*, IV, d. vii, ch.3, q.2; Albert the Great, *On the Sacraments*, IV, a.iv; Thomas Aquinas, *Summa Theologiae*, III, lxii, 1-6, lxxi, 5-7; John Duns Scotus, *Oxford Commentary on the Book of Sentences*, IV, d.vii, q.1).

Reformation Controveries Over Confirmation

Granted the theological disarray surrounding this sacrament at the close of the Middle Ages, it comes as no great surprise that the Protestant reformers rejected it as neither Christian nor scripturally justified (Zwingli, *Commentary on True and False Religion*, 15, 20; Luther, *Works*, 36:91-92; Calvin, *Institutes*, IV, 4-13). In response the Council of Trent insisted on confirmation's sacramentality and efficacy, but the three brief statements concerning confirmation that this council promulgated did little to clarify its saving consequences (DS 1628–1630).

Contemporary Confusion Concerning Confirmation

Contemporary theology has also failed to reach a consensus concerning the significance and effect of this ritual. Recent research into the origins of confirmation discovers its ritual seed in a blessing and dismissal that concluded the rite of water baptism and ushered the neophytes into the Eucharist, the second stage of initiation as it unfolded in the first centuries of Christian worship (*Apostolic Tradition,* 21). Such rites of dismissal seem to have abounded in early Christian liturgy until after the sixth century, when their popularity waned. In fifth century Roman ritual a solemn invocation of the Holy Breath replaced the earlier prayer of blessing that had concluded the baptismal rite. This transformation of Roman baptismal ritual had a number of historical motives. In 381 the Council of Constantinople's condemnation of those who denied the Holy Breath's divinity focused attention on the third person of the Trinity and helped motivate the enhancement of her liturgical status within the rite of initiation. The reservation of this ritual to the bishop also served to shore up episcopal authority in the face the growing liturgical activity of the presbyters, who by this time had evolved into Eucharistic celebrants. As we have seen, this reservation of the second moment of the rite of initiation to the bishop eventually transformed it in time into a separate sacrament in the medieval Church.[2]

Liturgists and liturgical theologians tend to deplore confirmation's temporal separation from the other rites of initiation; and some push for restoring the ancient order of baptism, confirmation, and first Holy Communion even in the baptism of infants. A second group of theologians pushes for a pastoral rather than for a purely scholarly approach to the effects of confirmation. This second group finds the first group's scholarly demand that we need to return in the twentieth century to fourth-century liturgical practice unconvincing either theologically or pastorally. These theologians, therefore, tend to argue for pastoral flexibility in ordering the stages of Christian initiation and urge that pastors postpone the confirmation of those baptized as infants until they have attained to Christian maturity. Those who urge a pastoral approach to confirmation have, however, failed to provide a convincing theological rationale for the pastoral practice they espouse.

2. See Aiden Kavanagh, *Confirmation: Origins and Reform* (New York: Pueblo Publishing Co., 1988).

A third group of theologians denies that confirmation confers any grace distinct from baptism itself. Those who espouse this position interpret the second stage in the rite of initiation as nothing more than episcopal confirmation of the first stage. A fourth and final group of theologians discovers in confimation graces distinct from those conferred by baptism. Unfortunately, however, those who make such a claim cannot agree on the nature of the graces in question.

Vatican II on Confirmation

Vatican II spoke of confirmation as strengthening Christians for the work of the lay apostolate and grounded that apostolate in the charismatic inspirations of the Holy Breath (*Apostolicam actuosiatatem*, 3; *Ad gentes*, 11). The council asserted as well that confirmation binds the baptized more closely to the Church (*Lumen gentium*, 11). Sensing the inadequacy of theological commentary on this ritual, however, Vatican II also called for a further clarification of its place within initiation (*Sacrosanctum Concilium*, 71); but it left the task of clarification to the Church's theologians.

A contemporary theology of confirmation needs, then, to answer the following questions: What does this ritual signify and effect? Is it a sacrament? If so, why? When was it instituted? Does it confer a character of its own? If so, how does the character conferred by confirmation differ from that conferred by baptism? We shall examine these questions also in the chapter that follows.

c. Controversies Concerning Eucharistic Communion. The Eucharist has occasioned three major controversies. Theologians disagree concerning Christ's real Eucharistic presence, they dispute the sacrificial character of Eucharistic worship, and they complain about theological neglect of the eschatological dimensions of Eucharistic worship. In this chapter, we shall consider only one of these controversies, disagreement about the real presence. We shall single out this particular dispute because it touches directly the significance of the third rite of initiation—first Holy Communion—for one's interpretation of Christ's real Eucharistic presence necessarily conditions one's understanding of the realities with which one communes in receiving the Body and Blood of Christ.

In the final chapter of this study we shall consider the other two controversies that have exercised Eucharistic theologians. Moreover, in that same chapter we shall return to the question of the real presence. At that point I shall argue that a sound understanding of the real presence of Christ in the Eucharist, one that extends the idea of presence to include not only Christ's real and efficacious presence to us within the Eucharist but also our presence in faith to him, provides the theological link between the sacrificial and eschatological dimensions of Eucharistic worship. For the moment, however, let us focus our attention on first Holy Communion and on the ways in which one's understanding of Christ's Eucharistic presence conditions one's understanding of communion itself.

Patristic Teaching About the Real Presence

The Fathers of the Church all affirmed the presence of Christ in the Eucharist, but they offered contrasting accounts of the precise moment when he becomes Eucharistically present. In the West, theological opinion tended to attribute the transformation of the bread and wine to the institution narrative. The Eastern Church found the transformative moment in the invocation of the Holy Breath that follows the institution narrative. As we shall see in the final chapter, both prayers consecrate the bread and wine and therefore play a decisive role in making Christ sacramentally present under the appearances of bread and wine.

The Origin of Medieval Perceptions of the Real Presence

During the Middle Ages theologians tried, not always successfully, to understand precisely how Christ becomes present in Eucharistic worship. In 1059 the Council of Rome condemned the Eucharistic theology of Berengar of Tours. In his philosophy, Berengar made no distinction between the reality of an entity and the way it appears. He equated reality with what we see, hear, taste, touch, and smell. He therefore concluded that the Eucharistic words of consecration do not really change the bread and wine into anything, since after consecration both continue to appear to the senses as bread and wine. He allowed that one might call the consecrated bread and wine tropically, or symbolically, bread and wine, in the same way that one could call Christ a lion or a lamb. By changing the bread and wine's significance, the words of consecration made them into symbols of his Body and Blood under the aspect of his passion. The Eucharistic ritual, therefore, brings the reality it symbolizes to mind, but it does not contain that reality.[3]

3. For a lucid and detailed exposition of Berengar's position, see Charles E. Sheedy, *The Eucharistic Controversy of the Eleventh Century Against the Background*

Lafranc, Berengar's principal adversary, insisted that in interpreting the change effected by the consecration of the bread and wine one must distinguish between what appears to the senses and the reality present in the Eucharistic worship. Moreover, Lafranc seems to have held that Christ becomes physically present in the Eucharist, even though we cannot see him there.[4]

The Council of Rome rejected Berengar's sharp distinction between the sacramental symbol and the reality it contains. It insisted that the consecrated bread and wine are "not just the sacrament" but truly the Body and Blood of Christ which the priest breaks and which the faithful consume (DS 690).

We stand here at the origins of medieval debate on Christ's real Eucharistic presence. Subsequent thinkers would discuss the issue with much more nuance than either Berengar or Lafranc. Nevertheless, their confrontation focused the attention of medieval discussion of this question rather narrowly on Christ's presence in the bread and wine. As we shall see, it took centuries before the terms of the discussion stretched to include other ways in which Christ becomes present in the Eucharist.

The Development of Medieval Perceptions
of the Real Presence

In 1341 Pope Benedict XII asserted that a transubstantial change occurs in the consecrated bread and wine and denied an opinion attributed to Armenian Christians that after the consecration the sacred elements constitute only an exemplar, likeness, or figure of the Body and Blood of Christ and not the reality itself (DS 1018).

Early in the thirteenth century, Hildebert of Tours had coined the term "transubstantiation" in order to describe the change that consecration makes in the Eucharistic bread and wine. Its coinage gives evidence of the ways in which Aristotelian philosophy was changing the medieval theological mind. Aristotle called realities that subsist in themselves "substances." He called their modifying attributes "accidents" and reduced them to eight generic kinds: quality, quantity, action, suffering, habit, position, place, and time. Medieval

of Pre-Scholastic Theology (Washington, D.C.: Catholic University of America Press, 1947).

4. For a careful historical reading of Lafranc's contribution to the development of Eucharistic theology, see Jean de Montclos, *Lafranc et Berengar: La controverse eucharistique du XIe siècle* (Louvain: Spicilegium Sacrum Louvaniense, 1971).

theologians found these categories helpful for nuancing Lafranc's distinction between the unchanging sensible attributes that persist after the consecration of the bread and wine and the deeper reality that changes. While the substances of the bread and wine change, their accidents remain.

Some medieval theologians defended a theory of consubstantiation. They held that after the consecration both the substance of the bread and wine, on the one hand, and the substantial reality of the glorified Christ exist side by side in the consecrated elements. By the thirteenth century, however, most theologians defended some version of transubstantiation. They taught that the consecration transforms the substance of the bread and wine into the Body and Blood of Christ, even though the accidents of bread and wine remain (Peter Lombard, *Book of Sentences,* IV, d.xi-xii; Hugh of St. Victor, *On the Sacraments,* II, ii, 7-11; Bonaventure, *Commentary on the Book of Sentences,* IV, d.xi, ar.un., qq.1-3; Albert the Great, *On the Sacraments,* V, i, q. 3, a.2-q.4, a.5; Thomas Aquinas, *Summa Theologiae,* III, q. lxxv, aa.1-8, q.lxxvi, aa.1-8, q.lxxvii, aa.1-6; John Duns Scotus, *Oxford Commentary on the Book of Sentences,* IV, d.xi, qq.1-d.xii, q.2).

In its condemnation of John Wycliff in 1418, the Council of Constance rejected the theory of consubstantiation, but it offered no positive explanation of Christ's real presence to replace Wycliff's condemned propositions (DS 1151–1153).

The Council of Florence advanced official thinking on the subject when it taught in 1439 that consecration changes the substance of the bread and wine into the Body of Christ and the substance of the wine into his Blood but in such a way that the whole Christ is present in both the bread and wine (DS 1321). Such an approach to Christ's Eucharistic presence set aside any naively literal interpretation of Eucharistic change that would assert that only the bread becomes the Body of Christ and only the wine becomes his Blood. Moreover, as in the teachings of the Council of Trent, one ought to read the term "substance" in the documents of Florence in a nontechnical sense. It meant roughly the same as "reality."

The Real Presence in Classical Protestant Theology

Ulrich Zwingli regarded the consecrated bread and wine as only bread and wine. In Eucharistic worship, which he regarded as simply a memorial service, Christians commune with the Body and Blood of Christ through faith only (Zwingli, *On True and False Religion,* 18). Martin Luther in *The Babylonian Captivity of the Church* avowed that the medieval doctrine of consubstantiation made more sense to him than did the idea of transubstantiation (Luther, *Works,* 14:34-35). In 1526 and 1527, however, he published two diatribes against the "fanatical" position assumed by Zwingli and those who followed him. In both works Luther insisted on the reality of Christ's presence in the Eucharist (Luther, *Works,* 36:335-361; 37:13-149). John Calvin held that Christ is really but only spiritually present in the Eucharist. He denied the substantial character of that presence even though he insisted on its reality (Calvin, *Institutes,* IV, 17; *Short Treatise on the Lord's Supper,* 2).

Trent on the Real Presence

The Council of Trent responded to these Protestant debates by reaffirming the legitimacy of using the term "transubstantiation" in order to describe the change that takes place in the bread and wine after consecration. In its own explanation of that change, however, Trent avoided the technical terminology of Aristotelian philosophy. Developing the position enunciated at the Council of Florence, Trent held that after consecration the whole Christ—body, blood, soul, and divinity—is truly (*vere*), really (*realiter*), and substantially (*substantialiter*) present in the consecrated bread and wine. The term "substantially," however, functions as a synonym of "truly," and "really."

Moreover, in explaining the reality of Christ's presence in the consecrated bread and wine, Trent opposed the "substance" of the bread and wine to the "appearances" of bread and wine (not to the "accidents" of bread and wine) that remain after consecration. In the following chapter we shall probe some of the implications of that distinction.

Finally, Trent also held that one should not understand the Eucharist as a mere sign or or as a metaphor for the presence of Christ. The council also denied that Christ becomes Eucharistically present only by his power (*virtute*) or only at the moment of Communion (DS 1651–1656).

Transignification and Trasfinalization

Contemporary theology has produced two other terms for describing Christ's Eucharistic presence. Certain forms of existential philosophy equate reality with meaning. In such a philosophical context, it makes sense to describe the real change that the consecration effects in the bread and wine as transignification, as the transforma-

tion of the meaning of the bread and wine and therefore of their reality. Theologians who equate reality with purpose describe the
change as transfinalization, because consecration changes the purpose of the sacred elements. Official church teaching allows both
positions as complements to a theory of transubstantiation (Pope Paul
VI, *Mysterium Fidei*).

Vatican II spoke of Christ's real presence in all the Church's liturgical celebrations, of his presence in the entire Eucharist, in its minister, and in a special way in the Eucharistic species (*Sacrosanctum Concilium,* 7). Its teachings echo those of Pope Pius XII who found Christ
Eucharistically present in the Eucharistic sacrifice in the person of
the minister, in the consecrated species, and in the prayer and praise
of the worshipping community (*Mediator Dei,* 19). More recent papal
and conciliar teachings attempt therefore to broaden our understanding of Christ's Eucharistic presence by insisting on other forms of
presence than his presence in the consecrated species.

The tangled debate over Christ's real Eucharistic presence raises,
then, two interrelated questions for anyone who tries to explain the
meaning of Holy Communion: (1) With what realities does one enter
into Communion when one receives the consecrated bread and wine?
(2) What effects this Communion and how? In order to reply to both
questions, however, one must first come to an understanding of the
meaning of Christ's Eucharistic presence.

In the chapter that follows we shall attempt to address the issue
of Christ's Eucharistic presence as well as the other issues that debate over the Christian rites of initiation has raised. Before dealing
with these controversies, however, we need to clarify the meaning
of the term "sacrament" and to reflect on the kind of faith commitment that the rites of adult initiation seal. Those reflections will, hopefully, create a context for addressing the unresolved questions that
surround these Christian rituals.

CHAPTER VII

Baptism, Confirmation, First Holy Communion

In the preceding chapter we considered biblical foundations for a theology of adult initiation, the historical development of the rites of initiation, and some of the major controversies that these rituals occasioned in the course of history. In the present chapter we shall reflect on the significance of the revised rites of initiation and attempt to respond to the controversial issues they have raised. Before we begin to ponder the sacramental rituals of the Church, however, we need to clarify the meaning of the term "sacrament" itself.

The present chapter, therefore, divides into four parts. The first part attempts to formulate a working definition of the term "sacrament" that hopefully any Christian can accept. The second section tries to understand the structure and significance of the rituals that incorporate adult converts into the Church. The third part meditates on some of the important consequences of Christian initiation. The fourth and final section of this chapter ponders the institution and sacramentality of the rites of initiation. As the argument advances, it will attempt to address the controverted issues surrounding these rites which we considered in the preceding chapter.

1. Toward an Ecumenical Definition of the Term "Sacrament." The catechism of the Council of Trent defined a sacrament as "an outward sign instituted by Christ to give grace." This definition has much to commend it: a strong Christological focus as well as an insistence both on the symbolic character of sacramental worship and on its saving purpose. Contemporary theology has, however, tended to grope for alternative definitions, not all of them equally adequate. Moreover, judged by contemporary standards the language of the Tridentine definition itself falls short of complete adequacy.

Criticisms of the Traditional Understanding of "Sacrament"

One could, for example, question the utility of insisting on the "outward" character of sacramental acts. The fact that we cannot directly observe the evaluative responses of others causes us at times to speak of them as "interior" rather than "exterior." A closer look at experience, however, suggests the futility of trying to distinguish too sharply between its inner and outer faces. Through our evaluative responses we become present to realities that stand within experience and give it its shape and texture. The sacraments too stand within the experience of worship, not outside it. They define its significance.

The Tridentine definition describes the sacraments as "instituted by Christ." That phrase, however, raises a host of questions. In what sense did Jesus Christ "institute" the rites of the Church? I shall try to show in the pages that follow that all the Christian rituals give us access to some facet of Jesus' ministry. Anyone, however, who imagines Jesus of Nazareth defining the canonical essence of the Church's official rituals indulges in an anachronistic fantasy. The rituals that the Church celebrates all evolved historically. One may, of course, legitimately interpret that evolution as the work of the risen Christ who acts in his Church through the divine Mother's illumination. If so, however, the phrase "instituted by Christ" requires considerable theological elaboration.

Existential theologians would, moreover, take exception to the way the Tridentine definition of a sacrament describes its saving effect. They would object that when we speak of a sacrament "giving grace," we objectify and misrepresent what actually transpires in sacramental worship. They would prefer to speak of the sacraments as gracious, interpersonal encounters with Christ rather than as signs that "give grace" as though they were handing over some thing.

The Number of the Sacraments

Moreover, ever since the Reformation the Christian Churches have quarreled over the meaning of the term "sacrament" and over the number of the sacraments. Luther agreed with the Tridentine definition in that he too regarded every sacrament as a visible sign of divine grace. He also agreed that Christ must have instituted every sacrament of the Church. He insisted, however, on the sacrament's inner, spiritual significance. Moreover, he believed that faith and faith alone endows the sacramental sign with the power to establish communion between worshippers and God (Luther, *Treatise on the Blessed Sacrament and the Brotherhood*). Calvin accepted the Tridentine definition verbatim but distinguished sharply between the external sign, which he regarded as incapable of causing grace, and the inner transformation of believers effected by God's direct saving action in each soul (Calvin, *Institutes,* IV, 14, 22). Zwingli too denied all efficacy to sacramental rituals. He regarded them as merely signs and expressions of faith (Zwingli, *On True and False Religion*). Catholic theology, by contrast has tended to regard the rituals of the Church as containing the grace they signify and cause. Theologians have, however, offered different explanations of how the sacraments cause grace. The majority speak of God as the primary efficient cause of the grace of the sacraments and of the minister and ritual as instrumental causes of grace. A primary cause uses an instrumental cause to produce an effect; for example, a writer uses a pencil to make a mark on a piece of paper. A second explanation of the way sacraments work portrays the rituals not as efficient, instrumental causes of grace, but as prayers that effect grace by the moral response they evoke in the sacramental worshipper. A third position regards the sacraments a mere occasions of grace that symbolize God's foreordained saving intentions toward us. Still a fourth position argues that the sacraments act efficaciously but by signifying the grace they confer.

These different approaches to the term "sacrament" express different perceptions of how they work. Moreover, classical Protestant theology tended to deny the sacramentality of any Church ritual not clearly instituted by Jesus in the New Testament. As a consequence, all the Christian Churches now agree on the sacramentality of only two rituals: adult baptism and the Eucharist.

Toward an Ecumenical Definition of Sacrament

That very fact, however, suggests a possible theological strategy for advancing beyond the past debates over the definition of the term "sacrament." Can we not derive from the two rituals whose sacramentality all the Churches acknowledge a working definition of the term "sacrament" to which any contemporary Christian can consent? Let me suggest such a definition.

Sacrament as Symbol

Adult baptism and the Eucharist resemble the rites performed in other religions in that they exemplify *symbolic acts.* At the close of chapter four I distinguished three kinds of symbols: expressive symbols, interpretative symbols, and communications. Sacraments qualify as communications. As human actions they signify shared beliefs. They employ concrete sensible realities, gestures, and words in order to express an evaluative perception of both divine and human realities. As communications they put those who employ them in communion with the triune God and with those who live in him through faith. They express that faith, and they embody a shared human response to the action of divine grace in the Christian community as a whole and in its members.

Sacrament as Ritual Act of New Covenant Worship

Sacraments also qualify as *ritual actions.* They advance in a traditional manner and are handed down from one generation of Christians to the next. Christian sacraments, however, differ from the rituals employed in other religions in that they yield access in faith to the definitive, historical self-revelation and self-communication of God accomplished in the incarnation of the Father's only-begotten Son and in the divine Mother's Pentecostal mission in and to the Church. Taken together these two historical events revealed God definitively and sealed a new covenant between humanity and the triune God. By a sacrament in the strict sense of that term we mean then, not just any religious rite, but a *symbolic, ritual act of new covenant worship.* Such an act either seals the new covenant of grace initially, as does adult baptism, or renews the Christian covenant, as does the Eucharist.

Sacrament as an Ecclesial Profession of Faith

These two rituals enjoy a public, ecclesial character in that they express the shared faith of the Christian community as such. As we have seen, shared faith consciousness differs from personal faith in a manner analogous to the way in which natural communal awareness differs from natural individual consciousness. Communal awareness results from the complex processes of historical self-interpretation in which communities engage and from their attempt to clarify and embody their shared hopes. Shared faith results from sharing the divine Mother's charismatic inspirations. Every Christian sacrament, therefore, *expresses the shared faith of the church universal.*

The Sacramental Minister

As public, ecclesial acts, the celebration of the sacraments requires public, ecclesial authorization. Sacraments, therefore, *must be
celebrated by a person officially authorized to conduct them in the name
of the Christian community and of the God it worships.* Authorization
can and has occurred in a variety of ways as sacramental discipline
has evolved.

Jesus' Ministry: The Source of the Sacraments

Adult baptism and the Eucharist *derive in some way from the
historical ministry of Jesus;* but as acts of new covenant worship, they
also *give access in faith to the paschal mystery of Jesus' death, glorification, and mission of the Holy Breath.* Contemporary theologians dispute whether or not the historical Jesus baptized his followers. As we
have seen, the Synoptic Gospels never describe Jesus baptizing, although the Gospel of John suggests that, while at one point Jesus did
administer a baptism like John the Baptizer, he subsequently abandoned the practice. Christian baptism, however, derives its saving
significance, not primarily from the baptismal ministry in which the
historical Jesus may or may not have engaged, but from Jesus' own
baptismal experience: from his baptism by John, from the fulfillment
of that baptism's significance in his passion and death, and from the
risen Christ's historical revelation as Breath-baptizer.

The Eucharist too derives it saving significance not simply from
the prophetic gesture that Jesus performed at the Last Supper, when
he gave his disciples bread and wine as his Body and Blood, but also
and especially from the historical events that that prophetic gesture
foreshadowed: His death, glorification, and sending the divine Mother
to inspire the shared life and worship of Christians.

Sacraments and the Paschal Mystery

We may, then, conclude that *because sacraments give worshippers access in faith to the paschal mystery, they challenge one prophetically to faith in the Lordship of Jesus, in the Father he proclaimed, and
in the life-giving Breath he sends.*

Sacramental Efficacy

Catholic theology has traditionally taught that the sacraments
contain the grace they signify, even though theologians have offered

different interpretations of how that occurs. Protestant theology has tended to insist on the primacy of faith in the communication of sacramental grace. These two positions do not differ as much as might at first appear. Catholic theology tends to assume that when Christians gather to worship they mean what they say, unless evidence points clearly to the contrary. Classical Protestant theology developed in protest to the decadence of late medieval sacramental worship. It tended, therefore, to approach the sacraments with a hermeneutics of suspicion and to insist on the personal commitment that genuine sacramental worship requires. In order to contain grace and communicate it effectively, however, a sacramental ritual must express faith and lead to faith. We may, then, include a final trait in our descriptive definition of a sacrament: *sacraments effect the graces they signify to the extent that they express and deepen faith.*

An Ecumenical Definition of Sacrament

Adult baptism and the Eucharist, then, justify the following description of any sacrament. When we use the term "sacrament" we mean (1) a symbolic, ritual act of new covenant worship (2) that expresses the shared faith of the Church universal, (3) that is therefore celebrated by a person authorized to speak in the name of the Christian community and of the God it worships, (4) that derives in some way from the ministry of Jesus, (5) that, by challenging one prophetically to faith in Jesus' Lordship, in the Father he proclaimed, and in the Holy Breath they send, gives access in faith to the paschal mystery of Jesus' death, glorification, and sending the Holy Breath, and (6) that effects the grace it signifies to the extent that it expresses faith and deepens faith.

We have clarified in a preliminary way the meaning of the term sacrament. As we shall see, our descriptive definition will apply analogously to each of the sacramental rituals since each fulfills the six conditions described above in a slightly different way. Let us, then, begin to reflect on the symbolic significance of the rites that incorporate adults into the Christian community.

2. The Significance of Christian Initiation. The revised rite of adult initiation contains nine ritual moments: (1) The celebrant greets the elect and explains to them and to the congregation the significance of the act they are about to perform. (2) The rite of initiation then begins with the litany of the saints. (3) After the litany the celebrant blesses the baptismal water. (4) The elect then renounce Satan. The celebrant anoints them with the oil of catechumens. (5) The elect profess their Christian faith. (6) The celebrant baptizes them. (7) Three explanatory rites then follow: (a) an anointing that symbolizes the participation of the newly baptized in the priestly, prophetic, and royal ministry of Jesus, (b) the clothing of the neophytes in a white garment, and (c) their presentation with a lighted candle. (8) The celebrant then confirms the newly baptized. (9) Initiation culminates in the elect receiving their first Holy Communion in the Eucharist that follows baptism and confirmation. Let us reflect on each of these rituals in turn.

a. The Celebrant's Greeting. The celebrant's greeting inaugurates the sacramental action. It sets the tone for the rituals that follow. The celebrant reminds the community that they are about to welcome new brothers and sisters into God's human family (RCIA, 220).

b. The Litany of the Saints. The rite of initiation itself begins with the litany of the saints. The litany reminds the candidates that they are joining not just the living Church but the communion of all of God's saints on whose patronage and intercession they can rely in their efforts to live a Christian life (RCIA, 221).

In praying the litany, the assembled Eucharistic community asks the Church triumphant to intercede for those who are about to enter God's human family. The litany seeks, then, to evoke a sense of the Church as a *matrix of divine grace* that the elect are about to enter and in which they will seek sanctification. The litany also evokes a sense of the Church as a *universal, historical reality* by naming patrons from every age and from different parts of the world. Finally, the litany also presents the Church as an *eschatological reality,* as a community destined to share in the glory of the risen Christ. It therefore reminds the elect that in joining God's human family, they simultaneously enter on a path that leads to endless life with Christ in God.

c. The Blessing of the Baptismal Water. After the litany has concluded, the celebrant blesses the water to be used in the rite of baptism (RCIA, 222). In a cascade of biblical images the prayer of blessing explains the symbolic significance of the water with which the celebrant will baptize the elect.

The Waters of Chaos

The prayer alludes to the waters of chaos that God's word subdued on the first day of creation, to the flood waters that purified the world of sin at the time of Noah, to the flood waters of the Red

Sea through which Israel marched from slavery to covenanted freedom, to the waters of the Jordan in which John baptized Jesus, and to the water of Christian baptism itself. Let us ponder briefly each of these images in the light of the conversion experience that they seek to illumine.

The prayer of blessing first recalls *the waters of chaos* on which God breathed at the dawn of creation in order to render them docile to his creative word (Gen 1:1-3). The prayer interprets the divine creative act as a foreshadowing of the Holy Breath's sanctification of baptized Christians. The prayer of blessing thus reminds the elect that through its sanctifying consequences baptism introduces them into the new creation that Jesus' resurrection begins and that the first creation foreshadowed. In what, then, does this new creation consist?

The New Creation

The image of a new creation derives from Jewish apocalyptic thinking; but it also appears in the New Testament which reinterprets it and endows it with new and specifically Christian connotations. In Jewish apocalyptic writings, the image of a new creation connoted disillusionment and religious pessimism. Suffused with a self-righteousness that it derived in part from its origins in pharisaical piety, Jewish apocalyptic as it developed came to look upon this world as corrupt even beyond redemption. Jewish apocalyptic writers therefore described an "end time," a final period of history, in which God would redeem his promises to the righteous members of his chosen people. Led by God's anointed leader, righteous Jews would conquer the world, despoil the nations, punish faithless Jews, and enjoy the fruits of their victory. Eventually, however, God would have to destroy this corrupt and unredeemable universe and replace it with something else, with a wholly new creation.

In the New Testament, however, the image of the new creation connotes very different attitudes and beliefs. Jesus repudiated both the self-righteousness and the secular messianism that typified Jewish apocalyptic piety. Moreover, his disciples looked upon his own ministry as beginning the end time and upon his incarnation and resurrection as the start of a new creation. For Christians, then, the image of a new creation in no way connotes despair over this world's capacity for redemption. On the contrary, the image asserts that the incarnation, death, and resurrection of Jesus effects the redemption of this sinful world so decisively and with such novelty that it begins the transformation of the world we know into the new creation. In the New Testament, then, the new creation does not replace the old with something else, as it does in Jewish apocalyptic piety. Instead, it transforms sinful human flesh redeemed by the blood of the Cross into the image of the sinless, risen Christ.

The Water of the Flood

The second image of water that the prayer of blessing invokes reinforces the first. The prayer recalls next *the waters of the flood* that purified the world from sin and foreshadowed God's covenant with Noah (Gen 7:1–8:19). This image too finds fulfillment in baptism, that washes away sin and seals the new covenant of grace in the hearts of the baptized. Taken together these two images yield an appreciative insight into the experience of conversion that baptism seals. Not only does the transvaluation of one's heart, mind, conscience, and social involvement that repentance begins re-create one's personality and, indeed, one's very self; but that re-creation begins the purification of every aspect of one's person from sin and reconsecrates one for the rest of one's life to the service of God and of humanity in the image of Jesus. Since God holds the initiative in both initial and ongoing conversion, the response of faith that baptism seals embodies a covenant, a mutual, binding, interpersonal commitment with specific moral conditions, conditions defined by the life and ministry of Jesus.

The Waters of the Red Sea

Appropriately, then, the prayer of blessing next alludes to the *waters of the Red Sea* through which the Israelites marched from slavery to freedom and to covenanted faith in their liberating God. The image points to the new freedom that conversion to Christ brings, a freedom that heals, perfects, and elevates elementary human freedom. As we have seen, as Christian conversion transvalues affective, intellectual, and moral conversion, it transforms elementary human freedom into responsible personal freedom. As it transvalues sociopolitical conversion, it commits the baptized to the responsible, liberating search for a social order that embodies the justice of God.

The Waters of the Jordan

Having celebrated both the transcendent destiny of the baptized, their purification from sin through converted commitment to Christ, and the graced liberation that the new covenant effects, the prayer of blessing appropriately assimilates the waters of Christian baptism to the *waters of the Jordan* in which John baptized Jesus (Mark 1:9-11; Matt 3:13-17; Luke 3:21-22). The prayer of blessing thus reminds the elect of the most fundamental purpose of Christian baptism: it draws Jesus' followers through conversion into his own baptismal experience. Christian baptism commits one to lifelong docility to the divine Mother in putting on the mind of Christ. It will demand that the baptized allow his vision of the kingdom to give practical meaning to Christian hope, faith, love, and longing for justice. Moreover, Jesus' own baptism culminated ultimately in Calvary. In the same way, Christian baptism commits believers to stand unyielding against the same dark forces that crucified their Lord: violence of heart, a hypocritical conscience, and the unjust and coercive uses of power. They too, like Jesus, must resist them even to the death.

Water from the Side of Christ

Appropriately, then, the prayer of blessing next alludes to the *water that flowed from the pierced side of the crucified Christ* as he hung dead upon the cross (John 20:34-37). In John's Gospel, the water from Christ's side recalls the vision of Ezekiel in which living water flowed from the Temple of God to give life to the land (Ezek 47:1-12). In John's Gospel the water flowing from the Temple of Jesus' body also foreshadowed the Holy Breath whom, as the risen Christ, he would send to effect the forgiveness of sins and to slake human thirst for eternal life (John 20:22-23). This fourth image, therefore, summons the elect to trust in the baptismal Breath to effect the lifelong forgiveness of their sins and to well up within them as a stream of endless life.

The Baptismal Waters

Finally, the prayer of blessing alludes to the *waters of baptism* themselves by recalling the risen Christ's command to his followers that they make disciples of all creatures by baptizing them in the triune name (Matt 28:16-20). In Matthew's Gospel this commissioning of the disciples to baptize all people fulfills John the Baptizer's prophecy that another mightier than himself would come after him and would baptize with a Holy Breath and fire. With this final scriptural allusion, therefore, the prayer of blessing reminds the elect that the baptism they are about to receive will plunge them into the paschal mystery. That mystery consists in this: that when in our sinfulness we betrayed God's Son and killed him cruelly by hanging him on a tree, not only did the Father raise him in glory, but together Father and Son also breathed into weak and sinful human hearts the Holy Breath of forgiveness, purification, and peace. Passage through the waters of baptism will draw the elect into that saving mystery of divine redemptive love.

The prayer of blessing illustrates well the way in which intuitive thinking functions within Christian prayer. The prayer piles one biblical image on top of another in a rapid recapitulation of the whole of salvation history. Instead of explaining the images, it allows the rich connotations of each to illumine the others. At the same time, each allusion casts light on a different facet of the paschal mystery coming to actualization in the lives of the elect.

d. The Renunciation of Satan. The elect's conversion to Christ first gave them conscious access to the paschal mystery. During the years of catechumenal preparation the elect have been allowing the divine Mother to teach them the meaning of the hope, faith, love, and longing for justice that all true Christians share. The rite of initiation now publicly seals that experience of conversion by inviting the elect to renounce Satan (RCIA, 224).

Satan in the Old Testament

In order to understand the significance of this ritual we shall first reflect on the figure of Satan as it develops in the Old and New Testaments. We shall conclude that the renunciation of Satan expresses not only repentance from personal sin but also the rejection of original sin. We shall in the process ponder the scope of original sin and two traditional ways of understanding it theologically.

The figure of Satan emerges from Hebrew angelology. He appears initially in the book of Job (Job 1:6-12; 2:1-8) and in an obscure prophecy of Zecharaiah (Zech 3:1-5). When he first steps onto the stage of Hebrew myth, Satan does not yet wear the devil's robes. He appears instead as one of the "sons of Elohim," as an angel in the court of the Lord. Where did these angels come from, and what role did Satan play in the court of God?

When the Hebrews conquered the promised land, they fought adversaries who worshipped other gods than theirs. Hebrew monotheism deplored idolatry. At the same time, the Hebrews felt reluctant to deny all reality to the gods of their adversaries. These gods symbolized powerful natural forces as well as the nations who worshipped them. The fact that those who adored idols sometimes prevailed in battle against the forces of Israel gave the Hebrews proof enough that they needed to take the gods of the nations very seriously, but their monotheistic faith told them not to take pagan deities too seriously. The Hebrew mythic imagination therefore reduced the gods of the nations to the status of angels in the court of the Lord. In so doing, Hebrew theology accomplished two things: (1) It affirmed the Lord's dominion over the natural forces these gods symbolized, and (2) it asserted his sovereign sway over the nations as well.

The figure of Satan changed his character as Hebrew angelology evolved. He appeared initially as the angelic prosecuting attorney in the heavenly court of the Lord. He had the responsibility of ferreting out the least iota of religious hypocrisy by putting apparently pious people to the test. This he accomplished by causing them sufferings that popular Hebrew piety regarded as the wages of sin. Accordingly, in the story of Job Satan killed off Job's family, destroyed his possessions, inflicted him with a loathsome disease, and finally caused him to sin by calling God to account.

Satan in the New Testament

One strain of New Testament thought linked the fall of Satan to the mission of Jesus and of his disciples. Their proclamation of *Abba's* merciful reign cast Satan out of heaven's court (Luke 10:17-20). The forgiving Father whom Jesus proclaimed had no need in his court for a sinister angelic prosecuting attorney.

Moreover, the Christian imagination attributed to Satan the temptations and sufferings that beset the innocent Son of God. In the process of doing so, it transformed Satan into a symbol of the antichrist, of the forces of sin that Jesus came to conquer. In the Synoptic Gospels Jesus' confrontation with Satan in the desert immediately after his own baptism began his testing and foreshadowed his passion and death on the cross (Mark 1:12-13; Matt 4:1-11; Luke 4:1-13). Satan, then, personifies all those forces that oppose God's reign, that conspired to murder the Son of God, and that continue to persecute Christians.

For the first Christians, then, the figure of Satan symbolized many different things: the unforgiving rigors of the Law; its power to coerce, convict, and to condemn, especially unjustly. He symbolized the malicious principalities and powers of this world that oppose the kingdom proclaimed by Jesus. Satan personified everything that contradicts the reign of God and the obedience of faith. Satan stood for sin itself.

In renouncing Satan, therefore, the elect repent publicly of their own personal sins. Satan, however, symbolizes more than one's own personal sins. He personifies everything in the world that contradicts the mission of Jesus. He stands therefore for situational sin as well.

Personal and Original Sin

The term "personal sin" designates any evil acts that I myself have performed before God. "Situational sin" includes not only the personal sins that others have committed but institutionalized sinfulness as well. Christian theology calls the sinful situation of the unbaptized "original sin."

As we have seen, the human mind grasps any reality whatever either imaginatively and intuitively, on the one hand, or rationally and inferentially, on the other. We also perceive situational sin in both of these ways. When we understand the sinfulness of the human condition imaginatively, we describe ourselves as the children of Adam and Eve living in bondage to Satan. When we percieve that same sinful reality abstractly and rationally, we say that we are born in a state of original sin.

Let us reflect on the scope of each of these ways of perceiving situational sin, for they throw light on the scope of the commitment embodied in adult baptism. Each mode of perception contains unexpected nuances. An intuitive perception of situational sin engages the free interplay of biblical images, as we saw in analyzing the prayer that blesses the baptismal waters. A rational theory of original sin engages inferential and prudential reasoning. A sound theology of original sin needs, then, to distinguish and coordinate these two ways of thinking about the sinfulness of the human condition.

The Sin of Our First Parents

When Christians describe themselves imaginatively and intuitively as the children of Adam and Eve, they invoke the story of the first human couple narrated in Genesis. That story asserts that God created a good world but that human deviation from God's will has marred creation's goodness. The serpent in the story symbolizes mysterious, earthly forces different from us humans that tempt us to sin. The story of the first couple's sin also names human rebellion against God as the source of social oppression (Gen 2:4–3:19).

The Book of Genesis does not identify the serpent with Satan. Since, however, the serpent tests the first couple in the same way that Satan tests the protagonist of the Book of Job, it comes as no surprise that the Christian mythic imagination eventually blended the two figures.

An intuitive Christian perception of the sinfulness of the human condition invokes much more, however, than the second and third chapters of Genesis. It derives more immediately from belief and hope in the risen Jesus as the new Adam.

The New Adam

The new Adam reverses the sin of the first human couple. The old Adam sprang from the earth and fathered an unredeemed, earth-bound race; the new Adam comes from heaven and recreates humanity by sharing with it his own divine glory. Through his death, resurrection, and mission of the divine Mother, he redeems humankind and offers it eternal life in God. The first Adam fell from grace and suffused the human condition with salvific ambiguity; the second Adam dispels that ambiguity by sealing a new covenant between God and his creatures and by revealing God's universal, saving will. The new Adam also replaces the hypocrisy of the old with a summons to repentance and to the obedience of faith. Finally, the serpent conquered the first Adam with the connivance of Eve. The new Adam, however, triumphs over sin and Satan and frees the human conscience from bondage to the law by replacing it with the liberating law of his Holy Breath.

The new Adam also reverses the consequence of the first Adam's sin. He redeems human labor from oppression by endowing it with a new purpose: His followers must work not only to sustain their own lives but also and especially to have something to share with those in greatest need. He redeems human sexual oppression by teaching husbands and wives the meaning of mutual, atoning love. Through hope, faith, love, and the Christian search for justice, the new Adam triumphs over the sinful chaos that distorts human hearts and human social relationships. Through the divine Mother's charismatic inspirations he builds up the Church into his body and effects the graced transformation of human society. The sin of the first Adam transformed death into a meaningless return to dust; the new Adam conquers death by his resurrection and by sending his life-giving Breath. He thus teaches us to perceive death in hope as the gateway to new life in God. He overcomes the hostility of nature by beginning the new creation.

The Christian, then, measures the sinfulness of the human condition by the extent to which it contradicts the will of God revealed to us in Jesus and in the divine Mother who imparts to us his mind. Appropriately, then, the Christian imagination interprets the repentant passage from sinful living to the obedience of faith as putting off the old Adam and putting on the new. That graced re-clothing transforms every facet of human life and of every human social relationship.

Original Sin Understood Perspectively

Understood intuitively, then, the renunciation of Satan not only expresses repentance of one's own past personal sins but it also pits the elect against all those sinful forces in their experience prior to baptism that contradict the saving will of God revealed to us in Jesus, the new Adam. When Christians attempt to understand those same sinful forces rationally and prudentially, they elaborate a doctrine of original sin.

The Christian conscience measures both personal and original sin by the will of God; and it discovers the divine will normatively revealed to us in Jesus, in the perfection of his obedience to the Father and in the ethics of discipleship he lived and proclaimed.

When I use a Christian ethics of discipleship to measure the guilt or innocence of my choices, I understand in concrete ways the meaning of personal sin. I sin personally whenever I prefer egotistical self-reliance to trust in God's providential care for me, whenever I choose self-indulgence rather than love, whenever I prefer greed to generosity, whenever I despair of God's promises, whenever I refuse to love in the name and image of Jesus, whenever I consent to human bondage and oppression.

When we Christians use the same ethics of discipleship in order to understand the sinfulness of the world into which we are born, we explore the meaning of original sin. The term ''original sin'' describes the sinful situation of the unbaptized rather than their personal sinfulness. In the concrete, then, original sin means different things to different people; for each individual experiences the world's sinfulness from a different angle of vision. My personal sinfulness contributes to the experience that others have of original sin, for it augments the collective sinfulness of their situation. Similarly, before one's own baptism the personal sins of others contributed to one's experience of original sin because those sins augmented the total sinfulness of the world into which one has been born. Moreover, the sum total of personal sin that infects one's world corrupts one in both conscious and unconscious ways.

As a situational concept, however, "original sin" embraces more than the personal sins of others. It includes institutionalized sin as well: racism, sexism, classism, anti-Semitism, unjust discrimination of any sort, nationalistic chauvinism, militarism, economic exploitation, aggressive war, the arms race, national and economic colonialism. A theory of original sin designates as sinful any structure of human society incompatible with gospel living. Original sin includes ideologies of isolation, exploitation, and domination that confuse human minds and poison human consciences. It includes consumerism and overconsumption,[1] political venality and irresponsibility, capitalistic greed and communistic totalitarianism. Parents do not transmit original sin by sexual intercourse, as Augustine mistakenly thought. Original sin does, however, include the sexual depravity and perversity of the societies into which we are born: promiscuity, rape, prostitution, incest, abortion, marital infidelity.

We have been trying to understand the meaning of the renunciation of Satan demanded of the elect in the rite of adult initiation. Properly understood in the light of a theology of Christian conversion, this ritual brings to completion the process of personal purification through which the elect have passed during the catechumenate and in the course of the scrutinies that preceded baptism. The renunciation of Satan expresses an unqualified repudiation of anything that would separate the elect from Christ or cause them to abandon the way of discipleship on which they have embarked. In renouncing Satan the elect repent publicly of their own personal sin. They also commit themselves to oppose the forces of original sin. Those forces include not only the personally sinful acts performed by others but also the corruptions of institutional sin. The figure of Satan personifies all these evils. In rejecting him, the elect reject them.

e. Profession of Faith. The renunciation of sin and of Satan gives public, ritual sanction to the first fundamental movement within Christian conversion: the movement away from sin and evil. The profession of faith that follows the anointing gives public, ritual expression to the second movement within Christian conversion: com-

---

1. By "consumerism" I mean an economy that fosters, often manipulatively, the purchase and use of goods whether one needs them or not. By "overconsumption" I mean the effect of consumerism.

mitment in faith to the triune God and to the community of those who believe in him.

The elect profess publicly their faith in the articles of the creed in response to questions put them by the celebrant. By that act they appropriate personally and in the presence of the worshipping community the shared faith of the Church (RCIA, 225). When understood in the light of the dynamics of conversion, this rite also commits the elect to the lifelong process of ongoing conversion, to the transvaluation in faith of their hearts, minds, consciences, and social involvements.

f. Baptism. Having approved and sealed the repentance and faith of the elect, the rite of initiation now incorporates them into the Christian community by baptism in the triune name. The washing takes place either through immersion or infusion (RCIA, 226).

The blessing of the baptismal waters has already prepared the elect and the assembled community to understand the meaning of the baptismal ritual. Most fundamentally, the rite of baptism recalls Jesus' own baptism by John and symbolizes that through incorporation into the Christian community. The divine Mother draws the neophytes to share in that experience. In his own baptism Jesus experienced himself as Son of God, as the beginning of a new Israel, and as Messiah in the image of the suffering servant. Through baptism Christian neophytes experience themselves as children of God consecrated to live in Jesus' image, as commissioned by the divine Mother to prolong his mission, as prophetically empowered to confront and confound the forces of sin and evil over which he triumphed, as committed to live in the worship of atoning love. Baptism commits the neophytes not only to live lives that embody gospel values but also, if need be, to die for the faith. Those empowered by the divine Mother to make such a commitment experience it as a personal re-creation, as a purification, as a liberation, and as a covenant with God.

A theology of Christian conversion throws light on the practical consequences of such a commitment. The divine Mother comes to the baptized to teach them to live the morality of discipleship that Jesus himself lived and proclaimed. She comes to teach them the meaning of hope, faith, love, and the Christian search for justice. She comes to inspire them to bear witness for the rest of their lives to the kingdom by the quality of the lives they lead. She consecrates them to the task of building up the Church by sharing their possessions and themselves with others on the basis of need and not of merit only. She comes to form them into a Church whose mutual forgiveness authenticates its worship. She comes to transform them into Christian missionaries who proclaim repentance and the immanence of God's reign to unbelievers, including those who shape the policies of large, oppressive, institutions. She comes to strengthen her children to set their lives at risk, if need be, that God's just kingdom be established on earth as in heaven.

g. Three Explanatory Rituals. Three explanatory rituals follow the rite of baptism. They symbolize the difference that membership in the Church makes in the life of the baptized and thus consecrate them to the task of sanctification through ongoing conversion. First, the celebrant anoints the neophytes with oil in order to remind them that through baptism they now share in the royal, the priestly, and the prophetic mission of Jesus. They have entered the reign of God, they have joined God's priestly people, and they have been commissioned to bear witness to Christ by living sinless lives in his image (RCIA, 228).

Next the neophytes are clothed with a white garment. The clothes we wear symbolize the way we relate to other people. Casual dress befits informal occasions; we dress formally at official functions. Clothes symbolize class and social status. Religious habits symbolize membership in a particular order or congregation. Costumes transform us symbolically into other people.

The clothing of the neophytes in a white garment symbolizes their total transformation in Christ: the innocence of life to which they now stand committed and the transformation of all their social relationships that incorporation into the body of Christ effects (RCIA, 229).

Finally, the celebrant hands the neophytes a lighted candle. The flame symbolizes their faith in Christ that they must now guard, tend, and hold up before the world. Their acceptance of the candle symbolizes their willingness to do precisely that (RCIA, 230).

h. Confirmation. As we have seen, contemporary theologians tend to espouse four different theological approaches to the rite of confirmation. Some push for the restoration of the "ritual integrity" to Christian initiation even in the case of the baptism of infants. Still others urge a pastoral approach to the confirmation of those baptized as infants rather than a return to fourth-century practices, but they lack a clear theological justification for the pastoral strategies they espouse. A third group of theologians denies that confirmation means anything more than the reaffirmation of one's baptism. Others insist that confirmation does mean something different from baptism but cannot agree about the ritual's concrete significance. How ought one to respond to this doctrinal confusion?

The Origins of the Sacrament of Confirmation

If, as contemporary scholarship suggests, confirmation began as a rite of dismissal that concluded the first (baptismal) stage of initiation and ushered the baptized into the second (Eucharistic) stage in the course of adult initiation, then, once the rite of confirmation as such took shape in the fifth century and afterwards, confirmation ceased to function liturgically as a mere rite of dismissal. As a solemn invocation of the Holy Breath reserved to the bishop, the rite of confirmation acquired new liturgical prominence and significance. In that case, one must face the question: had this liturgical transformation of the rite of initiation any theological justification?

Toward a Sound Theology of Confirmation

As theologians have wrestled with this vexing question, they have at times run up against a number of speculative dead ends. Some, for example, have needlessly objectified the graces of initiation at the same time that they have arbitrarily and erroneously confined the efficacy of the rites of initiation to the moment of their administration. Theologians of this mindset tend to ask: if the rite of baptism gives the Holy Breath to the baptized, then how can the rite of confirmation give them something they already possess? They have found this question understandably unanswerable, like every bad question.

Baptism, however, does not give the Holy Breath to the baptized the way one might give a pencil to someone, or a box, or a screwdriver. Sacraments do not give things, objects, to people. Instead, the sacraments set them in different kinds of saving, life-giving relationships with the triune God. In baptism, the neophyte begins to relate to the Breath of Christ in a new way: as one accepted into the Christian community of grace.

Moreover, the graces of baptism span a lifetime. They do not happen once and for all at the moment the celebrant pours the water and pronounces the baptismal formula. Baptism does not fill the soul with grace in the way that one would fill a milk bottle.

In my opinion, the rite of confirmation would qualify as a legitimate development of the rite of water baptism if it asserts something about the baptized Christian's relationship to the Breath of Christ that the rite of water baptism as it was originally administered asserted only implicitly and unthematically.

In that case, confirmation both would and would not say something more than baptism. It would say more in the sense that the explicitation of something only implicitly asserted says more than its mere tacit assertion. How often have we not said to someone who clarified a tacit assertion, "Why didn't you say so?" Moreover, as we shall see, confirmation, once it evolved into a distinct moment in the rite of initiation, would begin to say more than baptism because in explicitating something only implicitly asserted in baptism as it had been originally ministered confirmation would thereby circumscribe the meaning of baptism in comparison with the meaning baptism had prior to the emergence of the rite of confirmation as a distinct ritual. Nevertheless, the new rite of confirmation would indeed assert something that water baptism prior to the liturgical emergence of baptism had itself asserted, albeit only tacitly and implicitly. The meaning of these assertions will become clearer as we explore their implications.

Inadequate Approaches to Confirmation

Here we need to acknowledge candidly the scandal that results from the failure of theologians to reach anything like a consensus concerning the meaning of confirmation. We can, however, identify in advance some of the reasons why they have failed to reach such a consensus.

Some theologians have employed inadequate methodological strategies for discerning the meaning of confirmation. Among the methodologically inadequate strategies that they have invoked, I would include historicism, ritualism and formalism.

Historicism looks to history to provide the norms for liturgical reform. History itself, however, yields no normative insights into liturgical worship. It can tell us how worship evolved, how people in times and circumstances other than our own approached their God. History alone, however, cannot tell contemporary Christians how they ought to worship here and now. The history of confirmation poses special problems in this regard. Its origins remain shrouded in some obscurity, it evolved in ways that raise serious liturgical problems about the way in which it ought to be administered, and those who practice the ritual cannot agree on what it means.

Ritual formalism offers another inadequate methodological strategy for resolving the debate about confirmation or about any other sacrament. Ritual formalism ignores the functional character of ritual. By the functional character of ritual I mean that sacraments exist for people, not people for the sacraments. Ritual formalism values elegance and symmetry in liturgical structure, but without ever asking whether abstract elegance and symmetry best serve the pastoral needs of living Christians. Jesus left his followers no code of canon law; but he did make his own attitude toward religious rituals clear: rituals must serve the needs of people (Mark 2:27-28). No theological resolution of the confirmation debate ought to violate that principle.

Both historicism and ritual formalism tacitly invoke a third methodological presupposition that leads nowhere in sacramental theology. They fall into the fallacy of abstractionism. By that I mean that they study Christian ritual in abstraction from the religious experiences that give sacramental worship its significance.

Besides methodological inadequacies other theological motives have fed the centuries-old confusion that surrounds confirmation. The rite of confirmation developed into a distinct sacrament during the early Middle Ages. With rare exceptions, however, from the Middle Ages to the present, Western theologians have paid scant attention to the Holy Breath and to the ways in which she functions in Christian conversion. Until only recently, Western theologians commonly taught that the divine Breath's charisms had ceased after the first generation of Christians and that to covet them amounted to spiritual pride. Indeed, until relatively recently the theological community as a whole has manifested scant interest in the forms and dynamics of conversion. Small wonder, then, that in their attempt to give an account of what the Council of Florence described as the Pentecostal moment in Christian initiation (DS 1317), theologians have lapsed into confusing and sometimes contradictory abstractions.

A Foundational Interpretaton of Confirmation

The work of Bernard Lonergan may, however, provide the key to resolving the debate about confirmation. He has suggested that the work of theological reconstruction should begin with a foundational analysis of the forms and dynamics of conversion. He has also suggested that a sound insight into the conversion process offers norms for distinguishing sound from unsound theological doctrine. Let us apply his suggestion to the debate about confirmation.

As we have seen, within the experience of Christian conversion the divine Mother confers two distinct kinds of graces on converts:

graces of sanctification common to all Christians and empowering charisms of service specific to individual believers. In other words, the adult convert must relate to the divine Breath in two distinct but interrelated ways: as the one who teaches converts to grow in holiness by putting on the mind of Christ and as the one who empowers converts by her charisms to serve others in the name and image of Jesus. The charisms differ from the grace of sanctification in their personal particularity; for, while the Divine Mother calls all Christians to some form of charismatic service, she calls different individuals to serve in different ways: as prophets, administrators, teachers, healers, helpers, pastoral leaders, discerners, etc.

As far as we can tell, in the first centuries of Christian worship, the rite of initiation advanced in two stages: water baptism followed by the Eucharist. The rite of water baptism sealed the neophyte's experience of adult conversion to Christ and committed converts to living the rest of their lives in openness to the divine Mother's twofold call to sanctification and charismatic ministry.

Scholars debate when the rite of initiation acquired a triadic structure. We have some evidence, which not all liturgical historians accept, of the development of something like a rite of confirmation in the African Church during the third century. The decision to create a second, Breath-centered moment in the rite of initiation and to reserve to the bishop her solemn invocation upon the newly baptized seems, however, to have entered the Roman Rite at the beginning of the fifth century through the initiative of Pope Innocent I. What, then, did the ritual signify to the Pope who inaugurated it?

What Pope Innocent Did

When we peer back through the mists of history to the beginning of the fifth century, we can discern only vague shapes; but some patterns do emerge. In a letter to Decentius, the bishop of Gubbio, Innocent appealed to Acts 8:14-17 in order to justify reserving to the bishop alone the solemn invocation of the divine Breath upon the newly baptized. Acts 8:14-17 narrates how Peter and John came from Jerusalem to Samaria in order to lay hands on the Samaritans whom the deacon Philip had baptized in order that they might receive the Holy Breath (DS 215). Innocent erroneously interpreted this incident in Acts as a first-century celebration of the rite of confirmation. Why and how did the good Pope err in his reading of Acts?

In Acts 8:14-17 Peter and John come to invoke the Pentecostal Breath upon the Samaritans because, despite their baptism by Philip, they fail to exhibit any visible, charismatic signs of her presence in their lives. The passage describes the "Pentecost" of the Samaritans, recalls implicitly the Pentecost of the Jews (Acts 2:1-42), and anticipates the "Pentecost" of the Gentiles (Acts 10:1-48). At the beginning of Acts, the risen Christ had predicted all three "Pentecosts" (Acts 1:8).

Innocent chose to cite the "Pentecost" of the Samaritans rather than the Pentecost of the Jews or Gentiles in order to justify the transformation of the post-baptismal chrismation of neophytes into a solemn invocation of the Holy Breath reserved to the bishop alone because the Pope incorrectly interpreted that event as providing a first-century precedent for what he was doing to the Christian liturgy in the fifth. He was suggesting that in the apostolic Church the baptismal invocation of the Holy Breath had been reserved to the apostles in the same way that he was reserving it to the bishop. While such a reading of Acts gives contemporary historical-critical exegetes the willies, it probably lay within the scope of the allegorical reading of the Bible so dear to the hearts of the Fathers of the Church.

Assessing What Pope Innocent Did

In my opinion, Pope Innocent both did and did not have justification for his citation of Acts 8:14-17 in order to justify his reform of the rite of Christian baptism. He had justification in the sense that he was indeed introducing a distinct Pentecostal, Breath-centered ritual into the rite of Christian baptism. He did not have justification for the citation because Acts 8:14-17 does not describe standard liturgical practice in the apostolic Church, which almost certainly did not regularly invoke the Holy Breath in a distinct, solemn ritual upon those who had just been baptized. Peter and John pray over the Samaritans because for some inexplicable reason Philip's baptism had not "taken." It had not borne fruit in the charismatic manifestations of the Pentecostal Breath which ordinarily followed upon the ritual in the apostolic Church. Acts 8:14-17 does not, then, describe the ordinary ritual practice of the apostolic Church. It describes an anomaly of worship that Philip does not know how to handle. He therefore turns to the apostles as the leaders of the community so that they can remedy the situation.

Innocent I may well have misinterpreted Acts 8:14-17 in yet another way. As we have seen, Jerome described the rite which Innocent created as a prayer that the Holy Breath would bestow upon the newly baptized her seven gifts of wisdom, understanding, council, fortitude, knowledge, piety, and fear of the Lord. Jerome described accurately the Roman ritual he observed because the solemn episcopal invocation of the Holy Breath prayed for precisely that: the coming of the Breath with her sevenfold gifts. The prayer made no mention of the Pauline charisms that Peter and John invoked upon the Samaritans. In creating the rite that eventually evolved into the sacrament of confirmation, Pope Innocent certainly misinterpreted Acts 8:14-17 as a celebration in the first century of a ritual he was creating in the fifth. He may, however, also have misread the prayer of the apostles described in Acts as an invocation of the sevenfold Breath of God on the Samaritans rather than as an invocation of Pauline charisms described by Luke.

In other words, Pope Innocent may well have perceived quite correctly that his liturgical innovations were providing the Roman Rite of Christian initiation with a distinct, Pentecostal moment; but the faulty exegesis he employed to justify his transformation of Christian baptism continued well into the twentieth century to dog the sacrament which resulted from his actions. Until the Catholic biblical renewal in the twentieth century, Catholic sacramental theologians commonly and erroneously cited Acts 8:14-17 as an instance of the celebration of the rite of confirmation in the apostolic Church. Moreover, as we shall see, even the revised rite of confirmation fails to extricate itself fully from the exegetical confusions that lie at its origins.

Confirmation in the Latin Church

The action of Pope Innocent did, however, transform the rite of Christian initiation in significant ways. Once confirmation entered Christian initiation in the Roman Rite as a distinct, solmen invocation of the Pentecostal Breath upon the newly baptized, it took two rituals (water baptism and confirmation) in order to assert what water baptism alone had asserted in the first centuries of Christian worship. Let us reflect on the implications of the preceding assertion.

The addition of confirmation to adult initiation had two effects upon the rite of Christian initiation: (1) It clarified liturgically the fact that through adult conversion one stands in a twofold relationship to the Breath of Christ who calls one not only to sanctification in the image of Jesus but also to service through the empowering charisms she imparts. (2) The addition of a distinct ritual invocation of the Pentecostal Breath on those already baptized also circumscribed somewhat the original significance of water baptism. On Pentecost the Holy Breath created the Church by a communal outpouring of her charisms. If confirmation invokes the charism-dispensing Breath on the newly baptized, then baptism must signify something else: lifelong receptivity to the divine Breath's sanctifying inspirations as graces distinct from the charisms of the Pentecostal Breath dispensed by confirmation.

The emergence of the rite of confirmation thus gave Christian baptism two distinct foci: the first baptismal and Christological and the second pneumatic and Pentecostal. After the emergence of confirmation as a distict rite of initiation baptism in the Roman Rite signified and sealed the converts' commitment to put on the sanctifying mind of Christ by allowing his Breath to draw them into Jesus' own baptismal experience. Confirmation, as the Council of Florence saw (DS 1317), now signified their willingness to live in lifelong openness to the Breath's charismatic inspirations whose outpouring once created the Church on the first Pentecost and continues to create it as Pentecost evolves historically. Before the emergence of the rite of confirmation, the rite of water baptism alone had committed the baptized to both forms of openness to the Breath of Christ. With the emergence of confirmation, it took two rituals instead of one to say the same thing.

When Innocent I set in motion the historical processes that thus transformed the liturgical significance of Christian baptism he certainly did not foresee all the consequences of his decision. Political events both in the Church and in civil society probably motivated his actions to a significant extent. He very probably wanted to vindicate the superiority of episcopal to presbyteral authority in the face of the growing liturgical activism of priests. The fourth century, as we shall see in a later chapter, began the transformation of presbyters, who until that time had functioned as elders of a local Church, into Eucharistic celebrants in their own right and eventually into parish priests. The conquest of the Western empire by the first wave of barbarian invaders imposed new responsiblities on the Latin episcopacy to bring order into a situation of increasing chaos. An enhancement of the liturgical authority of the Latin-rite bishop enhanced his ecclesial authority and social standing as well.

Did God write straight with crooked political lines when he allowed Innocent to transform the Christian rite of initiation for political reasons? In order to answer that question we need to reflect more deeply on the relationship between myth and ritual.

The Meaning of Myth

First of all, we need to distinguish between a myth and a fairy tale. When we tell fairy tales we do something playful. When we recount myths we do something of utmost human seriousness. By a "fairy tale" I mean a fanciful story that one could tell as a gift of love to a small child. By a "myth" I mean a story that creates a world. Religious myths create religious worlds. They narrate the origin and end of all things in order to communicate a realistic, intuitive insight into the human condition and into humankind's ultimate purpose and destiny. For example, the story of the creation of the world and of the sin of Adam and Eve creates the religious world of Hebrew faith. Similarly, the faith-inspired story of Jesus, his birth, life, ministry, death, and resurrection creates the religious world in which Christians live.

Because myths create the worlds in which religious people live and take the choices that either make or mar their religious destinies, myths have a necessary relationship to religious rituals. Rituals give shared symbolic expression to the religious world in which a community of believers lives and prays. In other words, they symbolize the religious myths that create a community's shared faith consciousness.

The Gospels: Narrating the Christian Myth

The story of Jesus—his life, ministry, death, and glorification—provides Christianity with its fundamental myth. It teaches Christians the religious and moral terms on which to perceive reality: the reality of God, of themselves, of the world, of other people.

The Gospels tell the story of Jesus, but they do so in different ways, with different narrative and theological emphases that seek to highlight different aspects of his person and ministry.

The paschal mystery—the death and glorification of Jesus—lies at the heart of each of the Gospels; for these events endow the life and ministry of Jesus with its ultimate religious significance. The Gospels, however, for different theological reasons narrate the events of the paschal mystery differently. The Gospel of John, for example, insists on the religious unity of those events. John insists that not only the passion of Jesus but also his sending of the Spirit contribute something essential to the total event of Easter (John 3:14-15; 6:50-59; 12:23-33; 13:31-2; 17:1-26; 19:31–20:30).

Matthew's Gospel too links the resurrection of Jesus closely with his sending the divine Breath. Matthew ends his Gospel with the command of the risen Christ:

All authority in heaven and on earth has been given me. Go therefore and make disciples of all nations, baptizing them in the name of the Father and of the Son and of the Holy Breath, teaching them to observe all that I have commanded you; and lo, I am with you always, even to the close of the age (Matt 28:18-20).

This commission of the risen Christ fulfills the prophecy of John the Baptizer made at the beginning of Matthew's account of Jesus' public ministry. The Baptizer had prophesied that another would come after him who would baptize "with a Holy Breath and with fire" (Matt 3:11-12). The risen Christ's sending of his disciples to baptize in the triune name fulfills that prophecy. In other words, water baptism in the triune name and the Breath baptism foretold by John not only coincide but both also proceed directly from the crucified and risen Christ.

The Mythic Sanction of Two-Stage Initiation

The two-stage rite of Christian initiation practiced in the early centuries of Christian worship derives its mythic and theological warranty from John's and from Matthew's account of the paschal mystery; for in the two-stage rite of Christian initiation the single rite of water baptism effects the neophyte's incorporation into the Eucharistic community that first Communion seals. The fact that baptism does it all—conforms one to the crucified and risen Christ and communicates to the baptized the charism-dispensing Breath that proceeds from him—has important symbolic significance. It symbolizes, as the Gospels of John and of Matthew narrate, that the events of the paschal mystery enjoy a tight unity that demands that we see in the death of Jesus, in his resurrection, and in his sending the Breath a single saving act of God; for no part of the paschal mystery has full or ultimate intelligibility separated from the others.

The Mythic Sanction of Three-Stage Initiation

Luke's Gospel, however, narrates the events of the paschal mystery differently from John and from Matthew. While Luke narrates the death and resurrection of Jesus as a single event, he postpones the sending of the Holy Breath until after Jesus' ascension. When she arrives, she proceeds, of course, from the risen Christ. Still, Luke's theological concern to link the story of the Church to that of Jesus leads him to endow the event of Pentecost with a special narrative significance in its own right that sets it apart from the death and resurrection of Jesus (Luke 24:48-9; Acts 1:1-5; 2:1-21). None of the other Gospels narrate the paschal mystery in the way that Luke does.

Luke's account of the paschal mystery gives theological and mythic foundation for a three-stage rite of initiation. In a three-stage initiation, water baptism focuses on the first two events of the paschal mystery: the death and resurrection of Jesus. It invokes the divine Breath on the baptized to conform them to their crucified and risen Lord through the forgiveness of their sins and sanctification of their lives. The rite of confirmation focuses on the event of Pentecost and endows it with enhanced ritual significance just as Luke's Gospel endows it with enhanced narrative significance.

Both a two-stage and a three-stage initiation have, then, theological and mythic justification in New Testament theology. Both rituals accomplish the same thing but with different symbolic emphasis.

Did Pope Innocent realize when he reserved the solemn invocation of the Pentecostal Breath to bishops that he was shifting the mythic warranty for initiation in the Roman Rite from John and Matthew to Luke/Acts? Did some vague sense of the mythic implications of his action lead him to seek warranty for it in the Lukan tradition? We will almost certainly never know the answers to those questions in this life. By the same token we cannot assert with certitude that they deserve a negative answer. In all of this, of course, we are attempting to construct not a purely historical argument, but a foundational one: an argument that reads the historical evolution of Christian worship in the light of a strictly normative insight into the demands of Christian conversion. We are concerned, therefore, not primarily with what any given ritual meant but with what it ought to mean.

The Imposition of Hands

In this context, we should observe that contemporary exegesis offers considerable resources for avoiding the blunders in scriptural interpretation that lie at the origins of the rite of confirmation. The New Testament consistently associates the imposition of hands with the Holy Breath's charismatic activity: with healing (Mark 16:18; Acts 9:12; 28:8), with public commissioning for charismatic leadership

(Acts 13:3; 1 Tim 5:22; 2 Tim 1:6-7), or with a general outpouring of charismatic gifts (Acts 8:17; 19:6). In the rite of confirmation, therefore, the celebrant prays that the divine Breath strengthen the neophytes with an abundance of charismatic graces (RCIA, 233).

Invoking the Spirit

The celebrant next imposes hands and invokes the sevenfold gift of the Breath on the newly baptized. The inclusion of this ancient prayer in the revised rite of confirmation bears witness to the structural inertia of ritual. Following as it does upon the prayer for openness to the Pauline charisms the prayer for the seven gifts of the Breath could serve as a reminder to the newly baptized not to restrict the number of the charisms to the Pauline lists. Since, moreover, in a traditional Catholic theology of grace the seven gifts sanctify those who receive them, prayer should also remind the baptized that authentic charismatic service must embody and express personal holiness (RCIA, 234).

The Anointing

The oil used in the rite of confirmation has rich biblical connotations. In the Old Testament perfumed oil, because of its use on festive occasions, symbolized joy (Prov 27:9; Qoh 9:8; Amos 6:6). The prophet Isaiah foretold that those who would participate in the joy of the messianic banquet would be anointed with scented oil (Isa 25:6-7, LXX). Because of its use in the medicinal treatment of wounds and the purification of lepers, oil also symbolized healing (Lev 14:10-32; Luke 10:34; Mark 6:13; Jas 5:15).

The Hebrews also used oil in the consecration of both persons and things. They consecrated altars by pouring oil over them (Gen 28:18; 31:13; 35:14). An anointing with oil consecrated the kings and high priests of Israel (1 Sam 16:13; Lev 8:12). Prophets received no such anointing, but Isaiah compared prophetic illumination to a divine anointing (Isa 61:1), since it consecrated one to the ministry of the word. Jewish messianic hope looked for the coming of national leaders "anointed" by the Breath of God, and the New Testament proclaims Jesus as Messiah (the anointed one) and Breath-baptizer.

In a sense, the oil used in confirmation connotes all these biblical images. Through their joyful and mutual charismatic ministry, the confirmed neophytes share in Jesus' own baptismal anointing and prolong his prophetic ministry in space and time. The divine

Mother's empowering Pentecostal illumination consecrates them to serve as actively ministering members of the priestly people of God and anoints them to proclaim the good news prophetically in acts of healing and of service (RCIA, 235).

Confirmation, the Charisms, and the Lay Apostolate

The distinction between sanctifying grace and the charisms that we discovered in our examination of the dynamics of Christian conversion grounds, then, both the legitimacy and the importance of the rite of confirmation. Indeed, the emergence of the rite of confirmation may have helped motivate that distinction in medieval theology. The existence of confirmation as a second moment within adult initiation distinct from baptism gives explicit ritual expression to an important dimension of Christian conversion. Baptism commits Christian converts to grow in sanctity as the divine Mother teaches them to put on the mind of Jesus by living in his image. Confirmation, as Vatican II suggested, consecrates Christian converts to the work of the lay apostolate by committing them to lifelong openness to the divine Mother's charismatic call to service.

By commissioning the baptized as lay apostles charismatically guided by the Breath of Jesus, the rite of confirmation dedicates them to use their gifts both to build up the body of Christ and to Christianize secular society (*Apostolicam actuositatem*, 5-7, 9-14). Church, family, youth ministry, social work of all sorts, and the search for justice in national and international affairs constitute some of the principal contemporary fields of the lay apostolate (*Apostolicam actuositatem*, 9-14). Confirmation dedicates Christians not only to personal apostolic work but also to every kind of group apostolate whose efforts their personal charisms can further (*Apostolicam actuositatem*, 15-20). Moreover, in publicly and officially commissioning the newly baptized as lay apostles, the Christian community commits itself to providing them with the spiritual training, support, and resources they need in order to minister effectively (*Apostolicam actuositatem*, 28-32).

In their recent pastoral letters the North American bishops have also challenged the American Church as a whole, but lay apostles in particular, to recognize the forces of antichrist abroad in our culture: the arms race, racism, sexism, the scandal of domestic poverty, the even greater scandal of world hunger that attends the economic colonialism in which the nations of the First World hold those of the Third World enthralled. In a very real sense both baptism and confirmation set Christians in opposition to these and to other forces of sin and oppression in society. Baptism does so by separating believers from this sinful world and by consecrating them to the task of personal transformation in Jesus' just image. Confirmation commits the baptized collectively and personally to active, prophetic opposition to sin and injustice. It dedicates one to live in charismatic docility to the divine Mother in actively spreading the reign of God.

The preceding foundational account of the purpose of confirmation allows us, as Lonergan suggested it would, to begin to distinguish between sound and unsound interpretations of the ritual and to validate the truth surfacing in apparently conflicting accounts of its significance. We have discovered two broad areas of theological disagreement about this sacrament. Theologians disagree about this rite's significance and about the pastoral handling of the confirmation of those baptized as infants. In the present chapter we can deal only with the first of these two areas of disagreement. We must postpone consideration of the place of confirmation in the sacramental initiation of those baptized as infants until we have established an adequate theological context for dealing with the issues raised by infant baptism. In order to establish such a context, however, we need to ponder the significance of Christian matrimony, for the theology of infant baptism requires a sound insight into the responsibilities of Christian spouses to nuture their children in the faith. Hence, until we have analyzed the foundations of Christian marriage we lack the resources needed to resolve contemporary disputes about the confirmation of those baptized as infants.

Resolving the Issues Concerning Confirmation

We are, however, in a position to resolve the issues that divide those who deny that confirmation adds any significance to water baptism and those who affirm that it does add something to baptism but cannot agree on what confirmation symbolizes that baptism does not.

Paradoxically, the preceding analysis finds a truth struggling imperfectly to expression in both of the above positions. The two groups that espouse them disagree because they have failed to appreciate adequately how the emergence of the rite of confirmation changed the significance of adult initiation. The historical evidence seems to indicate that Christian initiation originally advanced in two major stages—first baptism, then first Eucharistic Communion. The emergence of the rite of confirmation divided the first stage of the original rite of initiation into two symbolic stages. Thereafter the first two stages of initiation symbolized quite explicitly the two distinct but interrelated ways in which Christian converts relate to the Breath of Christ: as the one who sanctifies them and as the one who empowers their charismatic ministry. Prior to the emergence of confirmation baptism alone had symbolized both relationships. In this sense, therefore, confirmation does indeed affirm something that water baptism already symbolizes when adult baptism advances in only two, not three, stages.

Nevertheless, once the rite of confirmation endowed Christian initiation with a Pentecostal moment that called attention to the distinction between the Breath's call to sanctification and her call to service, the emergence of confirmation circumscribed the ritual significance of the original rite of baptism, transforming it into a rite that consecrates the Christian neophyte to lifelong docility to the Breath of Jesus in putting on the mind of Christ and thus growing in holiness. Confirmation by contrast ritualizes the Christian neophyte's commitment to life in lifelong openness to the divine Mother's charismatic inspirations. In a three-stage rite of adult initiation, therefore, confirmation signifies more than baptism because it takes both confirmation and baptism to signify ritually what in a two-stage ritual baptism alone expressed.

The preceding account of the rite of confirmation also allows us to bring some order into the conflicting accounts of this sacrament's significance. First of all, it allows us to exclude two interpretations of confirmation as false and misleading. Secondly, it allows us to recognize other seemingly contradictory accounts of the meaning of confirmation as complementary rather than contradictory.

We may exclude the following interpretations of confirmation as false and incorrect: (1) For Christians confirmation functions as an adolescent rite of passage into adulthood. (2) Confirmation provides the Christian equivalent of a bar- or batmitzvah. Confirmation does not qualify as an adolescent rite of passage because it can be administered to people of any age. Confirmation, therefore, also signifies something different from the bar- or batmitzvah, which functions as a Jewish rite of passage in which the young Jew freely assumes as an adult the burdens of the Law. Confirmation does not signify submission to the Torah but openness to the Pentecostal Breath of Christ who empowers one to serve others in his name and image.

Other theological interpretations of the significance of confirmation have a certain legitimacy and call attention to different aspects of the ritual while unfortunately abstracting from the principal graces it confers. The grace of confirmation does change the baptized Christian and deepen the foundation laid by Christian baptism. It does so by empowering the baptized to grow in holiness through the performance of specific acts of service. It does strengthen the faith of the baptized and bring it to new maturity, because a fully mature faith finds expression in charismatically inspired deeds of service. Confirmation does commission one ecclesially because it sanctions the ecclesial exercise of the charisms that create the shared faith of the Church and build up the body of Christ. Confirmation does endow the faith witness of Christians with a secular orientation because the charisms empower Christians to mediate Christ to the world. As charismatically empowered witnesses to Christ, the confirmed do exercise an apostolate of peacemaking and reconciliation. Indeed, the attempts of theologians to describe the graces of confirmation fail principally through abstraction. Those explanations call legitimate attention to different aspects and consequences of the ritual, but they do so while prescinding from the very graces that give such abstractions concrete meaning: the charismatic inspirations of the Breath of Christ.

i. First Holy Communion. The rite of adult initiation culminates in first Holy Communion (RCIA, 241-243). As we have seen, the significance one attaches to this ritual depends in part on the way in which one understands Christ's Eucharistic presence. Medieval and Reformation debates over the real presence often focused too narrowly on Christ's presence in the consecrated bread and wine. Those debates often advanced in an inadequate, dualistic philosophical frame of reference that made it difficult to conceive the presence of Christ both in heaven and in the consecrated elements. In addition, Reformation debates often assumed an indefensible, dualistic sundering of the inner world of spirit and the outer world of the senses.

Toward a Foundational Interpretation of the Real Presence

If the Christian Churches ever hope to reach agreement on the meaning of the Eucharist, they need to find ways of talking and thinking about the reality of Christ's Eucharistic presence that avoid the pitfalls and snares of these ancient controversies. Contemporary Eucharistic theology has produced two new words for talking about Christ's Eucharistic presence: "transignification" and "transfinalization";[2] but neither term sheds much light on how Christ becomes

2. The reader will recall that the doctrine of transignification holds that the reality of the sacred elements changes because their meaning changes with their

Eucharistically present. The term "transignification" in particular would seem to presuppose an illegitimate equation of reality and meaning that ignores the difference between meaning and significance. Events signify; our evaluative responses to events endow them with meaning. Moreover, like "transubstantiation" these new terms focus too narrowly on the moment of consecration and in contrast to Vatican II, abstract Christ's presence in the consecrated elements from his presence in the Eucharistic action as a whole.

Instead of employing new technical terms, the position I will suggest uses ordinary language and builds on insights imperfectly and inadequately articulated in the documents of the Council of Trent. Trent asserted the real presence of the whole reality of the risen Christ—body, blood, soul, and divinity—under the appearances of bread and wine. In other words, the council's Eucharistic doctrine rests, not on a distinction between substance and accidents, as did the Eucharistic doctrine of late medieval scholastic theologians, but on a distinction between reality and appearance. One can, I believe, draw upon ordinary language in order to clarify that distinction in ways that go beyond and amplify the teachings of Trent.

The Eucharist celebrates the presence of the risen Christ in the Christian community as a whole. Christ becomes present in the Church wherever the divine Mother transforms it in sanctification and in mutual charismatic service. The Christian community's shared hope, faith, love, and labor for justice manifest sacramentally, therefore, the presence of the risen Christ within it. So too does the sharing of all the charisms, which, as we have seen, creates the Church's shared faith consciousness. Where the divine Mother acts, the risen Christ acts because the identity of life that the divine persons share ensures that whenever they act on the world they act as one.

Eucharistic Anamnesis

In the Eucharist the Christian community gathers to remember through the divine Mother's anointing those very events of salvation history that brought it into existence. Moreover, their recall creates its shared sense of identity as a community of faith. Eucharistic worship also embodies the shared, eschatological hope of the community and renews its commitment to live as faith in Christ demands. For all these reasons, we may legitimately speak of a special presence

consecration, while the doctrine of transfinalization teaches that the reality of the sacred elements changes because their purpose changes with their consecration.

of Christ within Eucharistic worship. Let us probe the implications of this last statement.

All the Christian Churches agree that in the Eucharist we remember the passion, death, and glorification of Jesus. In every act of remembering we become present to some past reality and it to us. A Eucharistic act of recall involves, however, much more than mere factual recollection of a past occurrence (1) because it engages the Eucharistic worshipper in ways that mere factual recall does not and (2) because Eucharistic recall makes the worshipping community present to the God who redeemed it in the death and resurrection of Jesus Christ and who confronts the community as the future toward which they are moving.

Moreover, in every Eucharistic celebration the Christian community repeats the only repeatable part of the rite of initiation: Eucharistic Communion. Through its Eucharistic worship, therefore, the Christian community renews its commitment to Christ both collectively and individually. It does so in a solemn, public act of covenant renewal that responds to God's prior saving action in the worshippers' own lives. Every time it gathers to worship Eucharistically, then, the Christian community renews corporately its covenant of initiation.

The *anamnesis,* the remembering, that occurs in every Eucharist accomplishes all these things to the extent that it expresses integral conversion before God. In every act of Eucharistic worship, therefore, the risen Christ becomes sacramentally present in a special way by actively conforming those who participate in such worship to his image.

In virtue of his presence in the entire act of worship, the risen Christ also becomes present in a special way in the consecrated bread and wine used symbolically to recall his own prophetic interpretation of his passion to his disciples, an interpretation that the paschal mystery fulfills. Through their symbolic use within Eucharistic worship, therefore, the consecrated elements make the reality of Jesus' passion and of the paschal mystery present to the worshippers. The risen Christ, in his divinity and glorified humanity, accomplishes this as he actively transforms those who partake in the Eucharist into his image.

Three Senses of "Appearance" and "Reality"

In order to understand how the risen Christ becomes present in the consecrated elements we need to distinguish three different senses of reality and appearance.

In the first use we commonly make of these terms, the reality itself appears. The leaves appear on the trees; the speaker appears on the podium. In other words, some reality appears by becoming immediately conspicuous and by being actually perceived as such.

In the second common use of the terms "reality" and "appearance," a reality also appears but not immediately and conspicuously. Instead, one perceives one reality that lacks immediate conspicuousness through a process of inference from another reality that does appear immediately and conspicuously. For example, we say that in a court trial the guilt or innocence of the accused appears, i.e., is correctly inferred, from the testimony of the witnesses. To someone instructed in astronomy, the workings of the solar system appear every morning in the rising of the sun. This second sense of "reality" and "appearance" invokes the first but goes beyond it, for it describes a process by which some hidden reality becomes apparent to us through inferences that we make on the basis of other realities that "appear" to us in the first sense of that term.

In the third sense of "reality" and "appearance," we distinguish them sharply. Here we speak of the "mere appearance." We say that something only appeared real but in fact was not. When we speak in this way, we replace a false perception of reality (the mere appearance) with a true one (the reality itself correctly perceived). For example, we say that a stick thrust into water only appeared to be bent, because on withdrawing it from the water we found it straight, not bent. In other words, we acknowledge that the water refracted the light rays emanating from the stick in a way that caused us to infer erroneously that it had in fact been bent. On withdrawing the stick from the water, we acknowledge our error; but, instead of taking responsibility for it, we scapegoat the stick. We say it deceived us by only appearing bent.

Reality and Appearance in Eucharistic Worship

The doctrine of Christ's real Eucharistic presence invokes all three senses of the terms "reality" and "appearance." It asserts that before their symbolic use in an act of Eucharistic worship, the bread and wine appear to be ordinary bread and wine. Here we invoke the first sense of "reality" and "appearance." Before their actual use in a Eucharistic *anamnesis* the bread and wine are as they appear: bread and wine, nothing else.

Next, the doctrine invokes the idea of the "mere appearance." It asserts that after their symbolic use in an act of Eucharistic *anamne-*

sis, the bread and wine only appear to be bread and wine. In other words, one would err were one to interpret the consecrated elements as only bread and wine; because, when used in an act of Eucharistic *anamnesis,* the consecrated bread and wine undergo a real and profound change. I have suggested that one can legitimately equate reality and experience. If one does so one also equates reality and process, since "experience" means a process made up of relational elements called feelings. If one accepts such a philosophical understanding of reality, then history defines the being of any entity, not some fixed and unchanging substantial essence. Indeed, in a world of experiences essences function only as fallible modes of sensation and perception. It would follow, therefore, that bread and wine used in Eucharistic worship in virtue of their use (*ex opere operato*) cease to be what they were.

In order to understand how they change, we must invoke the second sense of "reality" and "appearance." In the use of the consecrated bread and wine as the focal sacramental symbols within an act of Eucharistic *anamnesis,* a deep reality appears within the act of worship. Faith acknowledges that deep reality through inference as the risen Christ actively conforming the assembled community to his image in a Breath-filled act of covenant renewal that makes the paschal mystery living and really present in the lives of the assembled, worshipping community.

As we have seen, all reality, all experience, enjoys a symbolic structure, including sacramental realities. Sacramental rituals qualify as communications. Unlike other more pedestrian forms of communication, however, they communicate divine, transcendent realities. The bread and wine used in Eucharistic worship are, then, really changed because they are symbolically transformed in such a way as to communicate to us the living reality of the risen Christ—body, blood, soul, and divinity—actively present in the Breath-filled worship of his people.

When do the bread and wine undergo such a change in the course of worship? They change whenever within a given ritual tradition that action occurs which posits the symbol that puts the worshippers in communication with the risen Christ. Those ritual conditions may within limits vary from one liturgical tradition to another, as indeed they have in the Western and Oriental liturgies.

For how long does the change in the consecrated elements last? It lasts as long as they can be recognized in faith as sacramental symbols that communicate divine realities.

The Meaning of First Holy Communion

With what realities, then, do Christian neophytes commune when they first partake of the Body and Blood of Christ? Most obviously, they communicate in the Christian community's solemn covenant renewal. First Holy Communion completes the rite of adult initiation. Nevertheless, athough one can communicate for the first time in Eucharistic worship only once, one may participate again and again in Eucharistic worship thereafter. Hence, in every subsequent Eucharist in which baptized Christians participate, they renew their original covenant of initiation.

By participating in the worship of a local Eucharistic community, Christian neophytes also commune for the first time in the Eucharistic worship of the Church as a whole; for each local church makes the universal Church present in a particular place and time.

Moreover, Eucharistic worship expresses the Church's eschatological longing. It foreshadows the messianic banquet of the Lamb. It recalls the death of the Lord until he comes. It celebrates the worshippers themselves as the first fruits of redemption. It advances Christians on the path toward final resurrection with Christ. Through their first Holy Communion, therefore, Christian neophytes enter into communion with the world to come: with all those saints who have gone before them in faith and who worship at the throne of the Lamb, with the God who is already becoming their future.

Through their first Communion, neophytes enter as well into communion with Jesus' own sacrificial self-immolation on the cross. They accept their share in the divine forgiveness that his atoning sacrifice reveals and dedicate themselves like Jesus to suffering the consequences of sin without sinning. The Eucharist expresses, therefore, the worship of God's priestly people and reconsecrates them to the service of atonement.

Finally, in receiving the Body and Blood of Christ for the first time, the newly baptized enter into full sacramental communion with the God Christians worship. In these focal symbols of Eucharistic worship, through the divine Mother's empowering inspiration, they receive sacramentally the risen Lord who by this covenant renewal conforms them to his own image and consecrates them to the Father's service.

3. Consequences of Adult Initiation. We have reflected on the significance of the rites of Christian initiation. In the course of doing so, we have responded to some of the questions that the history of these rituals raises.

In the present section of this chapter we shall consider four consequences of adult initiation. First, we shall reflect on the way in which it takes away original sin. In the course of doing so, we shall have occasion to clarify the relationship between original sin and concupiscence. Second, we shall reflect on how Christian initiation takes away the punishment due to sin. Third, we shall try to make practical sense of the new birth that Christian initiation effects. Finally, we shall try to understand the meaning of the "character" conferred by baptism and by confirmation. In the course of pondering these four consequences of adult initiation, we shall try to respond to all but four of the other questions that the history of Christian initiation raises. (As I have already indicated, we shall postpone consideration of infant baptism for another chapter.)

a. Original Sin and Concupiscence. Christian baptism takes away original sin. It does so by transforming it into concupiscence. Let us try to understand how this occurs.

As we have seen, official Church teaching endorsed neither Augustine's pessimistic interpretation of human nature nor his sexually colored understanding of original sin and concupiscence. The Council of Trent defined concupiscence in situational terms. Its decree on original sin contrasted the notion of "concupiscence" with that of "sin." Trent defined "concupiscence" not as sin in the true and proper sense of that term but as whatever in the experience of the baptized comes *from* sin and leads *to* sin (DS 1515). By that I take the council to mean that concupiscence differs both from one's own personal sins and from original sin.

As we have seen, we best understand original sin not as one's own personal sins but as situational sin. Christian initiation takes away original sin by changing the situation of the baptized. It takes them from a situation of natural vulnerability to corruption by the sins of others and by institutionalized sinfulness, and it introduces them into the realm of grace we call the Church. It does so by sealing a process of conversion in a covenant commitment in which the baptized recognize and reject the sin in their own lives, in the lives of others, and in human institutions. The experience of adult conversion and of the sacraments that seal it transform, therefore, the convert's perceptions of the sinfulness of the world in which they live. The converted recognize both personal sin and situational sin as sin and abhor it. Christian initiation also changes the way the baptized relate practically to sin: after baptism they resist it as the members of a community of grace and with the resources that membership in that community affords.

How Baptism Changes Original Sin into Concupiscence

Christian initiation does not, however, abolish all the world's evils. The same forces that prior to baptism one experienced as original sin continue to function in the experience of the baptized. After baptism, however, neophytes experience those same forces as "concupiscence," as coming from sin and leading to sin. Take, for example, the case of a businessman who prior to conversion to Christianity regularly defrauded his customers under pressure to keep up with the competition. After conversion and baptism, he will continue to experience the pressures that had caused him to sin before he embraced Christ. Prior to baptism he experienced those as original sin because they actually disorted his conscience and caused him to sin against justice. After conversion and initiation transform his perceptions of reality, however, that same businessman will recognize the economic pressures that led him in the past to act unjustly as temptations to sin, as forces in his environment that proceed from greed and tempt one to injustice. In other words he will experience them consciously as coming from sin and leading to sin, that is, as concupiscence.

In other words, after baptism Christian neophytes no longer live in a state of original sin because membership in a realm of saving grace fortifies them against situational evil. They recognize temptations to sin as corrupting and confront them in the power of the Breath of the victorious Christ. By changing the way one perceives and relates to situational evil, conversion and the baptism that seals it transform the experience of original sin into an experience of concupiscence in Trent's sense of that term.

b. The Punishment Due to Sin. Christian initiation also takes away the punishment due to sin. Here, however, we need to interpret this traditional Christian belief with caution. Humans display a perennial tendency to project their own vindictiveness onto God. They falsely imagine that God takes pleasure in the suffering of the guilty. The passion, death, and resurrection of Jesus give the lie to such deceptions. The triune God reacts to human sins by suffering their consequences in atoning love.

Christian initiation seals repentance of one's personal sins, but it cannot undo the fact that one committed such acts. A conversion sealed by the rites of initiation can, however, teach neophytes to deal with the present consequences of past sinfulness with the atoning love of Christ.

Breath-baptism, as we have seen, draws one into the incarnate Word's service of atonement. Christian initiation and the experience of conversion that it seals take away the harmful consequences of one's own personal sins by teaching neophytes to suffer their consequences in self-forgiveness and without committing further sins. In teaching converts to react to the consequences of their sins as God does, Christian initiation and the conversion it seals transform those consequences from a punishment into a source of grace and divine life.

c. Christian Rebirth. Through the rites of Christian initiation, neophytes experience a second birth. A theology of conversion gives practical meaning to this traditional Christian image. Converts come alive in new ways. They experience new affective freedom, new ways of understanding themselves, reality, and God, a new and enhanced moral selflessness, a new courage to oppose human oppression. They do so, not all at once, but in the course of a lifetime, for the graces of initiation span an entire human life. Through the ongoing conversion that it inaugurates, Christian initiation begins, then, the life-long transvaluation of the other forms of conversion, their transformation into supernatural hope, faith, love, and dedication to the establishment of God's just kingdom on earth as in heaven. Christians experience such ongoing transformation as coming alive, as rebirth in God. The divine Mother enlivens us by empowering us to grow in holiness and in charismatic ministry to the Church and to humanity.

Moreover, the baptized come alive in other ways as well; for in being possessed by the Breath of Christ they possess a "down payment" on their own resurrection. They already share in the life of the glorified Jesus, who in his resurrection became "a life-giving Breath." This new risen life the divine Mother conceives in them through the ongoing conversion.

d. The Meaning of the Character. The unrepeatable rites of baptism and confirmation supposedly confer a sacramental character. In what does this character consist? As we have seen, when Augustine of Hippo described the permanence of baptism as an indelible tattoo, or brand, he introduced the term "character" into theological discourse. Medieval sacramentalists reified the character, describing it as a mysterious mark that the unrepeatable sacraments leave on the soul, a mark that conforms it to Christ the high priest of the new covenant. The conciliar tradition affirms the existence of the sacramental character but offers no clear explanation of its reality. How, then, should a contemporary theology of conversion interpret these traditional doctrines?

A theology of conversion validates traditional theological beliefs by grounding them or invalidates them by demonstrating their incompatibility with an experience of integral, fivefold conversion. When closely analyzed, however, the experience of conversion suggests that if we continue to speak of a sacramental character, we need to purify the idea of needless metaphysical mystification.

The Character as a "Mark on the Soul"

Every action, including acts like baptism and confirmation, "makes a mark on the soul" in the sense that they give incremental definition to the emerging human self. They further define us as persons either by creating new habits within us or by reinforcing old ones. Each choice we take also marks us permanently, for we cannot undo a decision once we make it. If every choice marks us, so does the choice to become a Christian. Does the choice to convert sealed by the rites of initiation, however, mark us in some special way? When we administer unrepeatable sacramental rites, both the rite's minister, who acts in the name of the Church, and the one who receives the sacrament take a joint, official, public decision. That decision changes the one who receives the sacraments decisively and permanently. Like every decision, this unrepeatable one, once done, cannot be undone. In addition, however, the decisions taken in baptism and confirmation change one publicly and socially. They do so by initiating one into a community of faith. Initiation into the Church brings with it permanent ecclesial rights and responsibilities, especially the right to ongoing instruction in the faith and the right of access to the means of sanctification, including the right of access to all of the sacraments. These rights imply the responsiblity of Church leaders to provide and of believers to take advantage of them.

Christian matrimony initiates baptized Christians into the ranks of the married, but Catholic theology does not traditionally speak of marriage as conferring a character. Why not? Because sacramental theology traditionally reserves such talk for rites of initiation whose readministration Church discipline forbids. After the death of one's spouse, however, Church discipline permits Christians to remarry.

The repeatability of the marriage ritual has, then, traditionally disqualified it from inclusion among the rites that confer a character, even though the rite of marriage, like initiation, gives incremental definition to the emerging Christian's life and reality and in addition entails specific ecclesial rights and responsibilities.

When in the course of the Donatist controversy the Christian community finally decided that one need not rebaptize heretical and schismatic believers, it transformed initiation into an unrepeatable act. At that moment, the Church decided that the rite of reconciliation provides the appropriate sacramental method for dealing with such persons. That decision fixed a fundamental point in Church discipline: heretics, schismatics, and other serious sinners whose baptism the Church recognizes have in principle access to full Church membership as soon as they fulfill through repentance and reconversion the moral conditions that membership requires.

The Character and the Priesthood of the Faithful

These insights help clarify what it might mean to say that the rites of Christian initiation "conform one to the priesthood of Christ," provided, with the Letter to the Hebrews, we do not interpret Christ's priesthood in narrowly cultic terms. Here we need to distinguish carefully two ways in which initiation effects such conformity. The baptized exercise their priesthood in part by participation in the public worship of the Church but also by any act they do that mediates Christ to the world. Once initiated sacramentally, they enjoy thereafter in virtue of their initiation a morally conditioned right to share as members in the life of the Church, its sacramental life included. They enjoy only a morally conditioned right, for responsible adult participation in the life of the Christian community presupposes the kind of conversion that the rites of initiation seal.

As a consequence, personal transformation through sanctification and mutual service conforms one to Christ the high priest more profoundly than does a permanent, morally conditioned right to share in the life of a sacramental community. The eternal Son of God became our high priest by "emptying himself": by taking flesh and by entering into perfect solidarity with sinful humans, even to the point of dying the death of a sinner and an outcast. As Christians grow in the same kind of selfless love for one another as Jesus showed in dying, rising, and sending the divine Mother, they participate profoundly and sacramentally in the priesthood of Jesus. Such participation in the priesthood of Jesus flows from the graces of sanctification and service that the rites of initiation bestow, graces that span a lifetime. They actually fulfill the moral conditions for Church membership.

By serious sin the baptized can fall from grace and forfeit profound moral conformity to Christ the high priest. At that point, serious sin reduces their share in his priesthood to a mere disciplinary reality, to the fact that in virtue of their baptism they still enjoy a permanent, morally conditioned right to participate in the life of the sacramental Church provided through repentance, conversion, and reconciliation they fulfill the moral conditions necessary for doing so.

Traditionally, the character conferred by a sacrament differs from the graces that sacrament gives; for one can lose the latter but not the former. One cannot lose the character because one cannot undo the decision to enter the Church on the terms it sets once one has taken that official, public step; nor can one change the conditioned, public right to share in sacramental worship that that decision, in virtue of Church discipline, creates and creates permanently. Nevertheless, in and of itself, the baptismal character alone conforms one to Christ only virtually, for it endows one with only a morally conditioned right to share in the Church's shared life and worship. As a consequence, actual holiness conforms one more profoundly to Christ than does the character conferred by baptism. The baptismal character infuses, then, no fictive essence of priesthood into the souls of the baptized. The only conformity to the priesthood it confers consists in this: that those who take the decision to enter the Church sacramentally enjoy thereafter by Church discipline a permanent, though morally conditioned, right to share in the life of God's priestly people.

The Character of Confirmation

Does confirmation confer a character of its own? It seems unlikely that theologians would have ever claimed a special character for confirmation had it not evolved into a separate sacrament in the Latin Church. Once that occurred, theologians assumed that confirmation as an integral part of the rite of initiation also conferred its own proper character, distinct from that conferred by baptism.

In baptism converts commit themselves as members of the Church to lifelong openness to the divine Mother who teaches them to put on the mind and heart of Christ by growth in hope, faith, love, and dedication to the Christian search for justice. In the second moment of adult initiation, one makes a different kind of commitment.

One commits oneself to lifelong openness to whatever charisms of service the divine Mother chooses to give one. The distinction between the commitment embodied in these two rituals roots itself, therefore, in the distinction between sanctifying grace, on the one hand, and the Pauline gifts, on the other.

As we have seen, all Christians share the same call to holiness; but, while the divine Mother calls all to some form of charismatic service, not all are called to the same kind of service. The particularity of charismatic grace distinguishes it from the call to sanctification common to all Christians. By the same token, because the call to sanctification and the call to service differ, they can legitimately find embodiment in two distinct rituals.

Like every human decision, the commitment one makes in confirmation, therefore, changes one definitively and permanently. Moreover, confirmation enjoys official, ecclesial consequences analogous to those that flow from baptism. Baptism incorporates one into the Church and bestows a morally conditioned right to share in its life, especially the right to instruction in the faith and the right to access to all the other means of sanctification, including all the sacraments. Confirmation consecrates the newly baptized to the lay apostolate and confers upon them the morally conditioned right and duty to exercise their charisms for the service of others and for building up the body of Christ (*Apostolicam actuositatem,* 3).

Like the rights conferred by baptism, the right to exercise lay ministry rests on specific moral conditions; for authentic charismatic ministry must embody the mind of Christ and must acknowledge the divine Mother's action in other gifted members of the Church, including its official leaders. Authentic charismatic ministry respects legitimate Church order and promotes the unity of Christ's body, not its fragmentation through sin.

As in the case of baptism, one celebrates the ritual which confers the right and duty to exercise public charismatic ministry in the Church only once in one's lifetime. It therefore confers permanent, morally conditioned rights and responsibilities. Christians who fall from grace need not, then, be reconfirmed sacramentally in order to function as lay apostles within the Christian community. They need only through repentance, reconversion, and reconciliation fulfill the moral conditions required for exercising such ecclesial rights and responsibilities.

Because it confers different morally conditioned ecclesial rights and duties from baptism, confirmation confers its own special "character." As in the case of baptism, however, mere possession of morally conditioned rights and duties (as opposed to their exercise) conforms one only virtually to Christ. The actual exercise of those rights in ways that sanctify oneself and serve others conforms one more profoundly to Jesus. Moreover, since the service of others in Jesus' name and image mediates Christ to the world, it constitutes an exercise of the priesthood of the faithful and in this sense actually conforms one to Christ the high priest, while the character that grounds the right to serve as a lay apostle does so only virtually. For example, an excommunicated Christian who retains the right to minister charismatically in the Church after repentance and reconciliation remains to that extent conformed to Christ in virtue of the character conferred by confirmation. A fully committed Christian in good standing, however, who actually exercises a charismatic ministry informed by hope, faith, and love exhibits a much stronger conformity to Christ than that conferred by the character of confirmation alone.

In the course of the preceding reflections, we have answered all but three of the questions raised in our survey of the controversies occasioned by Christian initiation. In the section which follows we shall attempt to respond to two of these remaining questions but shall reserve discussion of infant baptism to a later chapter.

4. The Institution and Sacramentality of the Rites of Adult Initiation. Catholics and Protestants both agree that Jesus instituted the sacrament of baptism, and both include it in the canon of the sacraments. When, however, did Jesus institute this ritual?

The New Testament Witness to the Institution of Baptism

Matthew discovers the origins of ritual baptism in a commissioning command of the risen Christ (Matt 28:19). John the evangelist seems to agree (John 3:5; 20:22-23), although, as we have seen, John does portray Jesus as having baptized some people during his ministry and as having later abandoned the practice. If Jesus did abandon the practice of baptizing his disciples, his earlier actions would have provided at best a half-hearted "institution" of this Christian ritual. Luke portrays ritual baptism as flowing spontaneously from the Christian community's collective inclusion in Jesus' baptismal experience through the arrival of the gift-giving Breath on Pentecost (Acts 2:38). Other New Testament documents speak of the significance of Christian initiation but say nothing about its ritual institution. In other words, we find in the New Testament different traditions and some vagueness concerning the historical origins of this central Christian ritual.

On one point, however, all the evangelists agree: Christian initiation draws converts into Jesus' own baptismal experience by giving them access in faith to the same divine Breath as inspired his ministry and whom he in risen glory sends into his Church. Jesus' own baptism, therefore, provides the historical prototype of Christian baptism. Jesus, therefore, "instituted" Christian baptism by submitting to John's baptism, by proclaiming God's reign in the power of the Holy Breath, by undergoing a baptism of suffering on the cross, and by baptizing his Church in his Holy Breath after he rose from the dead.

Toward an Ecumenical Consensus About Confirmation

Jesus clearly instituted the Eucharist at the Last Supper, as both Protestants and Catholics agree. Most Protestants, however, deny that Jesus ever instituted the rite of confirmation, while Catholics persist in defending its sacramentality and divine institution. In my own opinion both groups find themselves in a position to make a certain number of theological concessions that might eventually lead to ecumenical agreement on this debated point. The Catholic community would do well to learn from the history of Christian initiation and cease describing confirmation as an independent sacrament. Rather, the ritual invocation of the Pentecostal Breath constitutes a distinguishable moment within the total process of sacramental initiation, a moment which evolved in the course of history and which made ritually explicit a commitment already implicitly present in the original rite of baptism.

Protestants, for their part, might well concede that the experience of conversion which adult initiation seals demands a twofold openness to the third person of the Trinity: an openness, on the one hand, to her sanctifying activity and an openness, on the other, to her charismatic call to service.

If Catholics and Protestants could then agree that the rites of Christian initiation ought to seal both forms of committed openness in some ritual manner, they could then begin to deal with the disciplinary question of how to do so in the course of Christian initiation. Since the Church for centuries sanctioned a two-stage rite of initiation, Catholics need not insist that Churches that practice such a form of initiation necessarily adopt a three-stage ritual, provided those Churches also agree that in the rite of baptism their members commit themselves to the same realities as Catholics do by the two rites of baptism and confirmation. One would also hope that Churches which practice a two-stage ritual of initiation would have the openness of mind to allow Catholics to maintain their more symbolically explicit three-stage rite of initiation.

When viewed, not as an independent sacrament, but as a moment within the rite of sacramental initiation, confirmation, however, enjoys all the traits which belong to a sacrament. It seals the new covenant in a public act of worship by committing the baptized to lifelong charismatic ministry within the Church. It expresses the universal Church's faith in the divine Mother's charismatic anointing. The Christian community must authorize the celebrant of confirmation to perform the ritual in its own name and that of the triune God. The rite gives one access in faith to an important aspect of Jesus' ministry: his own lifelong openness to the divine Breath's charismatic inspirations and his sending her on Pentecost to create the Church by an outpouring of her charisms. Confirmation draws one into the paschal mystery by committing one to minister actively and selflessly to others in response to the divine Mother's charismatic anointing. In the course of that ministry one proclaims the Lordship of Jesus, the Fatherhood of God, and the abiding presence of their Breath. Finally, confirmation effects graced openness to the gift-giving Breath to the extent that it expresses faith and deepens faith.

The Institution of Confirmation

How, then, should one explain the institution of this ritual? The rite of confirmation has a foundation in the ministry of the historical Jesus in that it gives Christian converts access in faith to the divine Breath who revealed him by her charismatic inspirations as Messiah, as the Breath-filled beginning of a new Israel. He enjoyed her charismatic inspirations in personal plentitude. Indeed, one could argue that Jesus, as the Gospels describe him, possessed all of the Pauline charisms. The Church, however, has access to those same inspirations only collectively, as a community, and must share the gifts in order to reach a communal insight into the person and mission of Jesus.

Jesus, then, may be said to have "instituted" confirmation in sense similar to the one in which he may be said to have instituted water baptism: by possessing the gift-giving Breath in eschatological abundance and by sending her on Pentecost to create the Church as she empowers converted Christians to engage in mutual charismatic ministry.

The dynamics of initial Christian conversion, when properly understood, require, then, that ritual initiation into the Church embody a twofold openness to the Breath of Christ: openness to her sanctifying activity through the process of ongoing conversion and lifelong openness to her charismatic call to service. The rite of confirmation makes that second commitment ritually explicit within the total process of initiation.

5. Conclusion. In the course of this chapter we have attempted to understand the significance of the rites of adult initiation. We have interpreted them in the light of the conversion experience they seal. The rites of initiation seal an experience of initial conversion and inaugurate an life-long experience of ongoing conversion. In the remaining sections of this study, we shall attempt to explore the ways in which the public cult of the Church supports and fosters the process of ongoing conversion in the lives of Christians.